4/05

D0857355

Paranoia & Contentment

Paranoia & Contentment

A Personal

Essay on

Western

Thought

_____

John C. Hampsey

UNIVERSITY OF VIRGINIA PRESS

CHARLOTTESVILLE & LONDON

University of Virginia Press

© 2004 by the Rector and Visitors of the University of Virginia

All rights reserved

Printed in the United States of America on acid-free paper

First published 2004

9 8 7 6 5 4 3 2 1

Library of Congress Cataloging-in-Publication Data

Hampsey, John C., 1954–

   Paranoia and contentment : a personal essay on Western thought /
John C. Hampsey.

     p.   cm.

   Includes bibliographical references and index.

   ISBN 0-8139-2294-1 (cloth : alk. paper)

   1. Contentment.   2. Creative thinking.   I. Title.

   BJ1533.C7H35   2004

   190—dc22   2004006719

To my mother & my father

Contents

Acknowledgments

The writing of this work, which began back in 1993, drew, unconsciously at first, on one of the key tenets I had yet to realize—paranoic vision means no elision. This is why I found myself composing, almost by necessity, in a paranoic manner—hybrid and meditative, with all the unconventional challenges that would entail, so that I would thus be enabled to express and herald the importance of paranoic thinking in the Western tradition.

I would not have been able to maintain my belief in this endeavor without the much appreciated support from many individuals, including my old friend Rose Pass, who has faithfully read and commented upon most everything I have written; my colleagues at Cal Poly, especially Dean Harry Hellenbrand, whose reinforcing spirit was essential at key points along the way, and Doug Keesey and Steve Marx for their feedback and opinions; the College of Liberal Arts and the university itself for support grants and a sabbatical, especially during the early phases of the manuscript; the staff in the English Department for their tireless patience and assistance; Melanie Reese, for her research help during the final revision stage; Susan Brady, my wonderfully accomplished copy editor; the humanities editor at University of Virginia Press, Cathie Brettschneider, who believed in this project from the beginning and who championed my cause; also Ellen Satrom, managing editor, and Emily Grandstaff, publicist, at the University of Virginia Press; my wife, Patricia Ponce, who never doubted the importance of the project or my ability to complete it; and finally my four-year-old daughter, Maya, who somehow understands.

I would also like to express my gratitude to the editors of the following publications, in which portions of this work previously appeared:

Acknowledgments

portions of chapter 5 appeared in the *Gettysburg Review* as "On Fragmentation" (vol. 1, no. 3 [1988]: 445–50), in the *Antioch Review* as "Houses of the Mind: The Architecture of Childhood" (vol. 51, no. 2 [1993]: 251–63), in the *Colby Quarterly* as "Trapped in Sibyl's Jar: Hopkins's Dialectic of Self in 'Spelt from Sibyl's Leaves'" (vol. 26, no. 4 [1990]: 226–31), and in the *McNeese Review* as "The Queen of the Air: Consistency in Ruskin's Moral Aesthetics" (vol. 32 [1989]: 49–58); portions of chapter 6 appeared in the *Gettysburg Review* as "'So the Cap Fits!': Strange Truths in Kafka's America" (vol. 3, no. 2 [1990]: 400–406), and in the *Alaska Quarterly Review* as "What Self?: Notes on Modern First-Person Narrative" (vol. 9, nos. 1 & 2 [1990]: 153–64); and portions of chapter 3 appeared in the *Midwest Quarterly* as "Doom, Providence, Accident: An Essay" (vol. 42, no. 2 [2001]: 133–49). "Sappho No. 2," from *Greek Lyrics,* translated and copyright © 1960 by Richard Lattimore, is used by permission of the University of Chicago Press.

Paranoia & Contentment

Introduction

The idea for this book began quite whimsically, with an inquiry into the root meaning of "paranoia." The word comes from the Greek and originally meant beside (*para*) the mind (*noia*). In the spirit of the Greeks, crude curiosity took me over then (for the Greeks, curiosity is the root of knowledge, as in Odysseus's desire to visit the Cyclops for no useful reason other than to "see them"), and I wanted to know how we had drifted from a seemingly value-free concept—beside-the-mind thinking—into the modern notion of paranoia as a sickness based on fears and delusions.

My first plan, then, was to see if anyone had written a book on the evolution of the paranoia concept in the West (no one had). However, my intentions altered substantially when I realized how quickly the original paranoia concept had transmogrified into the notion of "off-track" thinking that is destructive, such as Plato's use of the word to describe Orestes' distracted consciousness when he kills his mother in Aeschylus's *Oresteia*. Plato's negative concept of off-track thinking is in direct contrast with his lifelong dedication to the ascent of the soul through the practice of pure reason, or on-track thinking. In fact, after Plato, the notion of beside-the-mind thinking leading to something positive vanishes almost entirely, and instead paranoia becomes a designated danger, accompanied by the dread of the loss of contentment.

Confronting this fundamental paranoia/contentment condition in the West urged me back to the original concept: beside-the-mind thinking potentially leading to imaginative expansiveness. I termed this the "paranoic," and it became my new chief interest. And the post-Platonic notion of paranoia as dis-tracted fears and delusions, upon which nearly every book on the subject of paranoia had focused, I termed the "paranoidic." From the paranoidic, the clinical tradition evolved; for example, paranoid schizophrenia as an acute mental disorder. Overall, the paranoidic condition—in a wider social sense and as a common everyday neurosis—became a serious liability within the modern culture of contentment.

In recent decades, paranoia has joined the jargon of political scientists and historians, such as Richard Hofstadter in his landmark work *The Paranoid Style in American Politics,* and of literary critics who feast on such postmodern writers as Thomas Pynchon or Don DeLillo. Meanwhile, as the notion of paranoia has been nudged into the therapist's office and the scholar's study, most of modern culture has taken to the playroom to focus on methods for securing the contrived dialectical opposite of the paranoidic: contentment.

The aim of my book, then, became predicated on this profound shift in the classical Greek world from the paranoic to the paranoidic. In the process, the idea of paranoia itself acted as a cultural lens though which I could reexamine the evolution of Western thought in a way that hadn't been done before.

The following study, then, focuses on key paranoic thinkers and key paranoic moments when Western being seems to journey into the mystical blue. My hope is that this will interest not only scholars but also students of the Western tradition and anyone with a curiosity about intellectual and cultural history.

Furthermore, as a work championing the salient moments of the paranoic in Western history, the study itself is written in a somewhat paranoic way, which is why the book's narrator intermixes, into his analysis and argument, brief pieces of fiction and memoir.

Ultimately, the goal is to provide a new understanding for the vicissitudes of Western thought and for the sufferings that have often resulted from the paranoidic displacing the paranoic. Moreover, the very questioning of the Western predilection for the paranoidic means questioning the mental power behind the indefatigable quest for contentment—namely, the Western hierophant, rationalism.

The book's call for renewing the paranoic may seem like no match for the weighty centuries of paranoidic and rationalistic culture. Indeed, all I can offer is a rowboat out into the mystical blue, into the expansive and dangerous contingency. However, one never knows when embracing the paranoic may actually lead to moral and cultural regeneration, to the mind envisioning new models of the world and the self, to re-imagining the experience of others so that we may act for a good beyond the self.

In a 1994 speech at Independence Hall, Philadelphia, Václav Havel, the great Czech playwright and former president, thought along these lines when he declared that Enlightenment culture was dead and that "the modern age has ended." He was talking about the era of rationalism, which began in the Renaissance and came to fruition in the eighteenth century, and which had failed to explain the meaning of life— "Experts can explain anything in the objective world to us, yet we understand our own lives less and less."

The results of this failure are quite serious, for even though rationalism managed to create a global civilization, people still "behind its back as it were, cling to the ancient certainties of their tribe," which is perhaps why cultural conflicts across the globe seem to be increasing. The truly reliable path, therefore, must "be rooted in self-transcendence . . . the only real alternative to extinction."

As much as I admire Havel's call for the self to move beyond "selfhood consciousness," he may be only partially correct when he talks about cultural conflicts arising because rationalism has failed as a transcendent thought. Romanticism—Western culture's oppositional response to rationalism—has failed for us as well, due to our elision from the paranoic.

In the modern world, this joint failure causes people to oscillate between an Enlightenment/Romanticism polarity. Dostoyevsky was the first to highlight this maddening condition in his prophetic *Notes from Underground* (1864), which makes a scathing indictment of Enlightenment culture in part 1, wherein two plus two can never equal five, as grandly paranoic as that would be; and a brutal satirization of Romantic culture in part 2, wherein the book's antihero, in his ultra-self-conscious moments of elevation and debasement, can manage only to "sound like a book."

In the final pages, the Man from Underground retreats to his mouse hole under the floor, claiming that he is actually better than us since he has heroically accepted more reality than we are willing to admit to, carrying "to the limit what [we] haven't dared to push even halfway—taking [our] cowardice for reasonableness." Thus, Dostoyevsky's antihero trades the Enlightenment/Romantic world for "Realism" and claims to be "more alive than [us] in the end."

The Man from Underground's retreat into existential exile after trying to partake of the societal world is also, for Dostoyevsky, the failure of philosophy in dealing with the Western world's fundamental ethical dilemma: how to mediate the competing "goods" of self and community. From Socrates' "turn to the self first," to Plato's "turn toward the State first," to Hegel's trusting of the Absolute Idea, to Nietzsche and Heidegger depending on will and creativity to overcome nihilism, to Sartre's naïve theory of intersubjectivity whereby in choosing for our self we simultaneously choose for all, Western philosophy has failed at the quest to mediate between public and private needs, and our modern legacy has been a split between ideas of social utopias wherein people give up freedoms and self-expression for security and so-called happiness (the legacy of the Enlightenment), and the free existential underworld of self-expression and consciousness (the legacy of Romanticism), which often results in suffering and anomie.

This intractable dilemma became part of the legal and ethical structure of the medieval world with the movement toward law and jurisprudence (based on the rights and security of the community over the tyranny of sovereign individualism). In the seventeenth century, Hobbes brought to light the modern complexity of this dilemma with his argument for the right of the "individual" to survive, which could only be realized, paradoxically, through the individual's surrender of all natural rights to the absolute authority of a sovereign.

For Rousseau, a century later, the product of this dilemma was what he termed the "bourgeois," or those who have been taught to live for themselves in the midst of people for whom they do not care but for whom they are nonetheless obliged to feign interest. Rousseau lamented that there is no longer a "good" in which all can share and bond, that people are attached only by bonds of self-interest. "We have physicists, chemists, astronomers, poets, musicians, painters; we no longer have citizens."

Rousseau's answer was "general will," or people acting and voting for what is best for all, rather than for what benefits their self-interest. Unfortunately, Rousseau didn't really offer a way to convince the individual to act for the general will, especially if the intended good didn't seem to benefit that individual (which led to Kant devising his bloodless "moral imperative").

Václav Havel's answer to this Western ethical dilemma—his call for "self-transcendence"—is predicated on self-fulfillment and a simultaneous connection to the "Gaia principle," the notion that life on earth is part of a larger universal purpose. In Havel's words, "we are an integral part of higher, mysterious entities against whom it is not advisable to blaspheme." Such a notion may sound inspiring, but it still displays the dread resulting from paranoidic thinking ("it is not advisable to blaspheme"), rather than the more liberating and expansive experience of paranoic thinking. For the only way to contemplate self-fulfillment, and at the same time connect to some larger Oneness, is through the paranoic.

And we have already heard the call of the paranoic, from inside the culture of contentment, where the call is hard to understand because paranoidic consciousness keeps eliding us away. But the paranoic heroes are still there, to beckon and inspire us to listen again—Abraham and Socrates and Jesus and Hypatia and Joan and Blake and Kierkegaard and Schreber . . .

Row out into the middle of the lake sometime; stay inside after work until the space-out begins; etch something into a rock or tree and go back to find it later—"with time quick as the weaver's shuttle," as Job said; until after a while, inside the paranoic, even Creation itself can seem a mistake, as the Gnostics and William Blake believed—a supremely paranoic notion, with the billions of galaxies with billions of stars too much.

Rather than be weighed down by the cosmos and the gods (by influence of the paranoidic), the paranoic soul can struggle beyond, which is a much grander vision than Havel's transcendence of the self. Because the paranoic is fuel.

1

Damning the Dialectic

Paranoia

I had been fooled by the paranoidic a thousand times before, like at New York's Grand Central one time when I paced around waiting to meet a friend and found myself trying to discern the looks of all the rushing travelers just in case there was someone I might have known in an accidental way, all the while hearing only the voices flowing overhead from the balcony—so distinct from the drone below, and a dog barking somewhere, like there always is, even though dogs aren't allowed inside Grand Central Station.

When I started looking for the dog I finally saw my friend leaning over the balcony intently staring down at me, as if he had been there all along and I just hadn't seen.

Such a train-station scenario, as paranoidic tale, may not seem that startling, but it helps, nevertheless, in getting one thinking about the origins of consciousness. For paranoia has been a part of consciousness since the beginning; we just seldom think of it that way.

I'm not concerned here with clinical definitions of "paranoid psychosis" or "paranoid delusions," which you'll find in other books where you will read of "mental derangement," "chronic mental unsoundness," or "hallucinations of grandeur and persecution." Rather, I'm concerned with paranoia as cultural truth, as a way of understanding the history of human thought, and perhaps as the best way to describe Being itself.

Undoubtedly, most people will balk at such a notion since they have been trained, from an early age, to view paranoia as something one is supposed to avoid in order to be happy. And perhaps they are right, because philosophers have spent centuries screening paranoia away.

And thus we enter the third millennium still denying ourselves access to "paranoic consciousness" (beside-the-mind thinking that is creative and expansive), practicing instead "paranoidic consciousness" (beside-the-mind thinking based on fears and delusions in the face of a projected loss of contentment). This lamentable loss of the paranoic, and the reigning of the paranoidic, is why modern beings still don't grasp their essential selves. Herded into the "satisfaction realm" by booby-prize notions of contentment, they have all but forgotten the splendid seas of free, nonpsychotic, expansive consciousness. Imagine, for instance, if the fruitless paranoidic consciousness in my train-station scenario were translated into paranoic vision. Then what might I have seen? A vision of Jacob's Ladder slanting beyond Grand Central's baroque balcony?

And this is why I find myself returning to the primal Western signpost and staring, as if for the first time, at the word "Paranoia," which points in two directions: out to the illimitable sea, the blue contingency of the paranoic; and inland toward the paranoidic firma of the culture of contentment.

Like the sublime prophet Jeremiah, who wailed poetically in his Old Testament Lamentations over the destruction of Jerusalem, I want to lament the loss of the paranoic in Western consciousness. Jeremiah, called by God to see and feel what "real" tragedy was; Jeremiah, a poet so gentle that many believe Jesus to be his incarnation; Jeremiah, the prophet of hope, too, if he really did believe in God's mercy and restoration.

But, positioned at the foot of the Paranoia/Contentment signpost, I am no Jeremiah, nor much of a Rousseau either, who cried violently at the foot of a signpost he happened to pass in 1749 on his way to see his friend Diderot, who was jailed at the time in Vincennes.

Rousseau's sign advertised a prize from the Dijon Academy for the best essay on how human manners had been improved by the arts and sciences. And there, suddenly, Rousseau suffered an emotional and inspirational fit. As he described it in a letter, "I felt myself dazzled by a thousand sparkling lights . . . my head whirling in a giddiness like that of intoxication." When Rousseau collected himself, he found that his waistcoat was soaked from tears he had shed over a vision of the terrible sufferings of humankind. This epiphany led to Rousseau's lifelong complaint against social injustice: "men are born free, but everywhere are in chains" (an interesting variation of Euripides' lines in *Hecuba:* "no man on earth is truly free, all are slaves of money or necessity").

And it is fitting that Jeremiah's (and Rousseau's) grand lamentation carries with it a certain sense of the absurd; for in the classical tradition "to lament" means to "bark nonsense," in my case over the missed cultural opportunities for paranoic consciousness. ("Lament" comes from the Greek "*leros*," meaning "nonsense," and the Latin "*latrare*," meaning "to bark.")

And so, by virtue of the absurd, I can't necessarily believe that an epiphany will follow my lament (as it did for Rousseau), which is all right since epiphany-expectation may lead to increased stress inside the paranoidic, perhaps destroying one's paranoic plans before they are even conceived. All of which implies that paranoia about writing a book on paranoia may actually help one to recognize the paranoidic way in which the truth of paranoic consciousness has been kept from our lives. Like navy pilots who train on the mantra "sky is good, ground is bad" in case of flight dizziness or disorientation, I want to proclaim that "paranoia is good, contentment is bad" in the case of cultural dizziness.

For paranoia can at least make us conscious of the very lies that have been told about paranoia for centuries, and help to remind us of how some of history's greatest figures shared some sense of paranoic consciousness that many investigative critics later labeled "paranoid delusions." I'm thinking here of figures such as Abraham, Socrates, Jesus, Hypatia, Joan of Arc, William Blake, Daniel Paul Schreber . . .

Contentment

Our paranoidic misapprehension began with Hippocrates, the fifth-century BC Greek physician who was the first to talk of psychic disorder and mental illnesses such as epilepsy, mania, and melancholy, and who conceived of paranoia as "dis-tracted thinking" that eliminated contentment. Hippocrates' actual terms were "*parakruein*," "*paraphron*," and "*paraphrosyne.*" However, an earlier record of the "paranoia" term can be found in Aeschylus' *Seven Against Thebes* (467 BC), where the chorus, speaking of the tragic union of Oedipus with his mother, announces: "Madness was the coupler of this *distracted* pair."

And ever since, we have been convinced that paranoia is an issue of disease avoidance and have been warned against displaying paranoia-like tendencies. In reality, our situation is one of dis-ease. For by making the collective choice to order life's priorities upon contentment, our culture has given up thinking that there could be something more. Even then we risk only a calculated answer: "Of course there is more. We want fulfillment; we want a meaningful life. We want to accomplish something before we die."

But isn't this contentment as well? The minute one takes "meaning" and turns it into something to feel accomplished about, that's contentment, only in a higher caloric form.

The larger question is, of course, more difficult: Is contentment really worth the dedication of our lives? Or have we merely accepted the gambit because everyone else before us has? And what is it we really fear by placing such a premium upon contentment? Not death or pain, because they are not fair antonyms to contentment. The desire for contentment stems not from the fear of suffering and loss, but from the fear of acknowledging universal contingency (the notion that anything can happen anytime), which is the very food of paranoia and the central truth of existence.

Contingency is the reason Thomas Jefferson revised his Declaration from "life, liberty, and happiness" to "life, liberty, and the *pursuit* of happiness." By the time of Jefferson, however, the idea of happiness in the West had already been transmogrified. Meanwhile, happiness in a natural sense—feeling at peace within one's environs and without want—no doubt diminished with the growth of civilization, which continually offered more to want and more to worry about losing in an increasingly complicated setting.

Natural happiness, if it ever did exist, would have occurred unconsciously and therefore would not be in dialectical opposition to the debilitating paranoidic. In fact, the moment one could actually say, "Ah, now I am happy . . . in this moment," the fear of contingency would set in and trap the individual in a self-patronizing paranoidic situation.

And even though "natural happiness" probably never existed, Western writers have obsessed over the idea and expressed an urgent need to protect the illusion. Natural happiness is what the French writer and philosopher Jean-Jacques Rousseau so blithely imagines in his ahistorical vision of "nascent society" in *A Discourse on the Origin of Inequality* (1754). And Diderot, the famous encyclopedist, elaborated further in his dialogue "Supplement au voyage de Bougainville" (1770), when he contrasts the generous and natural joy of the Tahitians, who are free from all possessiveness, to the jealous and stifled impulses of the visiting Westerners. Diderot, however, shrewdly avoids any naïve dichotomy (to which Rousseau sometimes subscribes) between natural impulse and the artificial restraints of Western civilization.

Two hundred years earlier, Michel de Montaigne, the great French thinker and creator of the personal essay, in his brilliant essay "Of Can-

nibals" (1580), refers to lost natural happiness when he speaks of the so-
called New World Savages:

> I am sorry that Lycurgus and Plato did not know of them; for it seems
> to me that what we actually see in these nations surpasses not only
> all the pictures in which poets have idealized the golden age and all
> their inventions in imagining a happy state of man, but also the con-
> ceptions and the very desire of philosophy. They could not imagine a
> naturalness so pure and simple as we see by experience; nor could
> they believe that our society could be maintained with so little arti-
> fice and human solder. This is a nation, I should say to Plato, in which
> there is no sort of traffic, no knowledge of letters, no science of num-
> bers, no name for a magistrate or for political superiority; no custom
> of servitude, no riches or poverty, no contracts, no successions, no
> partitions, no occupations but leisure ones, no care for any but com-
> mon kinship, no clothes, no agriculture, no metal, no use of wine or
> wheat. The very words that signify lying, treachery, dissimulation,
> avarice, envy, belittling, pardon—unheard of. How far from this per-
> fection would he find the republic that he imagined. (153)

Perhaps Rousseau and Diderot and Montaigne are only offering the
escapist fantasies of overcivilized dreamy Western males. Yet, for others,
if such happiness on a cultural scale can be imagined, then it might indeed be possible. (Similarly, theists argue that if one can imagine God,
then God must exist.)

One thing is certain: natural fulfillment can certainly not be attained
by trying to go back in time, by trying to be Tahitian. Rather, it must
begin in the mind, as most paranoic visionaries have believed (William
Blake, for example).

Nevertheless, it is hard to commit to the paranoic gamble. Perhaps
we are too fastened down by the banal bolts of contentment. For even
our visions of heaven are only rarified versions of earthly contentment,
which is why most Western religions simply extract the most stable images of contentment on earth and then eternalize them into visions of
everlasting bliss. It's all there: your favorite food, your favorite music,
your favorite pasture, ad infinitum. But it's the same every time. As rock
musician David Byrne says, in Heaven "they're always playing your favorite song."

Mark Twain offers an ironic insight on this when he notes how Christians managed to fill heaven with all the activities they honestly hated—

nonstop singing of hymns and praying and other cherubic activities—while all the things they really enjoyed were excluded.

Kenneth Patchen's *Memoirs of a Shy Pornographer* (1945) provides a related cautionary tale. At the end of the book, the hero, Budd, explains what the Other World is like. Ironically, it isn't any different from the world he left behind, principally because he didn't know what he had really wanted by the time he left. So in the end, he is stuck with what he already had.

Our inability to envision paranoically, then, will only lead to a forever declaration inside the culture of contentment. And in this way our daily lives become ineluctably embroiled in the paranoidic—fear of losing jobs, family, faith, money, reputations, houses, lovers—which is the declared enemy of the culture of contentment. Meanwhile, the positive paranoic, which can invest in contingency and liberate the mind, which can lead human consciousness into the blue unknown, elides away. (I use "elide" not in the conventional sense of "to omit," but in a hybrid sense of quicksilvering away.)

Maybe our paranoic therapy should begin in small antiparanoidic ways, just to see if we can imagine unbound consciousness free from the dread of contentment loss—all of which makes one giddy, because it isn't easy convincing people they are mistaken in avoiding the dreaded grandeur of paranoia in order to build their nests of contentment.

As in a *New Yorker* cartoon I saw one time where an overweight middle-aged man sits comfortably in his bourgeois living room reading the newspaper while his wife fusses with a flower vase behind him. Suddenly the man looks up and proclaims: "What the hell was that? Something just swept over me, like contentment or something!"

And so perhaps contentment does arrive every now and then, willy-nilly, for a moment or two, and departs before you know it. But it's piecemeal; it teases and vanishes. Contemptfully serendipitous, contentment seems to say, "See, you can't machinate me."

But paranoia as the paranoic—now there's something you can really sink into. And I expect it gets more thrilling the deeper you go. Because Hippocrates and all of his followers may have been wrong. Maybe it's all right to let consciousness go "beside itself," to get away from our strangling expectations of contentment, to think what few minds (for fear of madness or ostracism) have dared to think before, to feel the pure hyperconscious tide of Being itself.

For some, the tide floods in unbidden. And I'm not just talking here of paranoid psychotics. Because the jetties of illusion—which we have built trying to convince ourselves that we are content, that we are safe from the seas of contingency—could wash out, and the paranoia/contentment dialectic finally crumble. Sheer dread would set in then, followed by the dangerous beckoning of the paranoic.

But the dialectic is hard to kill, and theme parks of contentment have been erected on top of us for so long that we can hardly breathe. And all I am offering for escape is a tiny rowboat and the belief in the value of free-oaring into the blue mysteries of Being.

Fyodor Dostoyevsky, the great mystical and fleshy Russian novelist, brilliantly attacked the absurd human desire for happiness in his little dystopian book *Notes from Underground* (1864). Yet Dostoyevsky was mistaken when he asserted that the result of increased consciousness was necessarily suffering. Rather, the result of increased consciousness is paranoia, and one cannot necessarily assume that paranoia will lead, every time, to suffering.

The hyperconscious Man from Underground is radically paranoid, of course, but his paranoia only adds to the suffering he already experiences. Creating such a narrator and using him as a test case, therefore, may lead to flawed conclusions. I am not so sure that increased consciousness leads first to loss of contentment and then to suffering. Why can't increased consciousness lead to loss of contentment, then to paranoia, then to paranoic vision? Could that not be the case instead?

However, Dostoyevsky is dazzlingly correct when he argues that humans are capable of acting against their interests; that they will time and again reject any rational process toward happiness that is offered to them; that they will throw their birthday cake on the ground and ruin the party for the sake of "whim." Because doing what one wants, at least every now and then, is a lot more seductive than any piecemeal promise of contentment. To prove this, Dostoyevsky argues, humans will even inflict pain upon themselves. And is that the mark of a rational creature lovingly embracing the contentment-logic of "two plus two"? Humans will reject being turned into an "organ stop" (Dostoyevsky's metaphor) even if it means toppling their theme parks of contentment.

But try to explain such an anti-utopian notion to people, and they will laugh in your face and calmly assert that they never act against their interests, never take pleasure in inflicting pain upon themselves.

Perhaps this is why we should begin with merely emphasizing the virtue of deliberately thinking about the fact that one is "thinking," since such preliminary paranoic consciousness may lead to modest realms of uncharted existence. At the least, such paranoic contemplation will complicate things nicely and allow for some interesting causalities.

If you don't believe me, just turn to history. People in the Middle Ages invented fascinating stories of demons and spirits in conscious and unconscious response to their misery. Such fantastic paranoic imagining seemed better than simply acquiescing into nonexistence like some vacuous reptile, which is why I'll take superstition any day, even though my neurosis for logic fights against it, because superstition always leaves such a colorful imprint upon human history.

With the steely Renaissance, however, stories of demons were often judged fallacious, and science and rational thought replaced Old World paranoia, and thus the march toward "real" (i.e., scientific) truth began. Yet no one considers that maybe Renaissance thinkers were guilty of paranoia as well, perhaps even a more dangerous form of it. Because the Renaissance belief in the ability of the rational mind to explain all mysteries was nothing less than a humanistic delusion of grandeur (clinical paranoia). Indeed, the Renaissance notion that "Man is the measure of all things" (borrowed from the Greek sophist Protagoras) is as superstitious as any notion the Middle Ages might have causally formulated.

Renaissance thinkers, likening themselves to Greeks, had great disdain for the Middle Ages. The Greeks and Romans, they maintained, understood that rational human beings were happy human beings. And once again, happiness was dragged into it.

The classical emphasis on happiness was the result of Aristotle's pragmatic ethics. For it was Aristotle, Plato's star student, who brought the question of virtue down from Plato's ethereal sky by offering the Golden Mean—or a moderate and secure method for achieving contentment. Aristotle's Golden Mean was a rational but relative means for avoiding excess on any continuum; for example, plotting the point of happy moderation between pride and humility.

Aristotle connected happiness to virtue (*Âreté*), which he defined as the "excellence of a thing," and virtue to "entelechy," or the ability for all things to achieve their potential. Human potential would be realized through a life of reason since the practice of "reason" is what made human beings "excellent." And for more than two thousand years we've been stuck with an undisputed connection between reason, contentment, and potentiality. The more contentment we think we have, the more we believe in our own potential for contentment, and the more we become rationally paranoid over losing what we've gained or could gain.

In this manner, from our Greek beginnings, the paranoidic necessitated our drive for contentment until, after the late Middle Ages, the splendor of paranoic expansiveness had been almost entirely snatched away. Even the medieval predilection for ghosts would eventually be misappropriated, by the postmodernists for instance, who would view ghosts as a mere projection of the naturally paranoidic mind reacting to an existence rooted in fear of the unknown. Fear, yes, but the very projection of ghosts proves that medievalists were capable of diving into their fear, swimming into the mysterious blue, and coming up with something visionary.

The alternative—shunting human contingency into a comfort zone (based on what the German philosopher Heidegger called "inauthentic being towards death")—means living without thinking about finality. Self-help books may make this scenario sound appealing, but life without fear of contingency equates to very little life at all.

Freud articulated a universal disappointment with "contentment" when he acknowledged the basic unreality of happiness and maintained that the point of psychoanalytic therapy was to go from neurotic suffering to normal unhappiness.

The mention of Freud gets me thinking about Daniel Paul Schreber, the most frequently quoted patient in psychoanalytic literature. But I don't want to talk about Schreber yet.

The Paranoic versus the Paranoidic

Rather, let's think about how paranoic consciousness took a prophetic step forward with the publication in 1760 of Laurence Sterne's novel *Tristram Shandy.* Indeed, the book has the most ingenious beginning, wherein the narrator, Tristram, "reports" on the very night he was conceived. Critics are fond of saying how Sterne was centuries ahead of his time in creating such a self-reflexive narrator who indulges in digressions and self-analysis. And certainly, amidst the book's eighteenth-century setting, it is possible to see Tristram as one of the great paranoic individuals in literary history, in company with the characters of Dostoyevsky and Beckett. For only a work concerned with paranoic consciousness would posit a connection between the circumstances of biological conception and one's fate in life.

> I wish either my father or my mother . . . had minded what they were
> about when they begot me; had they duly consider'd how much

depended upon what they were then doing;—that not only the pro-
duction of a rational Being was concern'd in it, but that possibly the
happy formation and temperature of his body, perhaps his genius
and the very class of his mind; . . . Had they duly weighed and considered all this, and proceeded accordingly,—I am verily persuaded I
should have made quite a different figure in the world, from that, in
which the reader is likely to see me. Believe me, good folks, this is not
so inconsiderable a thing as many of you may think it. (3)

A few pages later the narrator proclaims to the reader, "SHUT THE DOOR!"
before any more of his story-consciousness can be told.

Not only does the rest of the novel demonstrate a consistent distrust
of the insidious forces of contentment (products of the new capitalism)
because they blunt the individual's subjective value, but the hero's
"opinions" offer striking examples of eighteenth-century paranoic
thought. And the fact that Tristram is trapped in eighteenth-century circumstances, yet still maintains a liberated consciousness, proves that
the book's "paranoia" is visionary.

The French writer Denis Diderot, a contemporary of Sterne, also saw
individuals as trapped by circumstances that seemed artificially imposed. Diderot believed that if people attained harmony within their
circumstantial world, between their own consciousness and the "facts"
surrounding them, then happiness would follow. The problem is the
world itself, which, Diderot believed, had become so artificial that individuals became "affected" and out of touch with their natural impulses (one of Dostoyevsky's key complaints a century later).

Agreeing with Montaigne's idea that human beings are constantly in
flux, Diderot viewed the individual's endeavor to avoid pain as an agi-
tation to an already turbulent condition. Long before the nineteenth
century would find the idea fashionable, Diderot understood that a
human being was a shifting mix of conflicts and contradictions. His famous metaphor for depicting this was a "swarm of bees." The "swarm"
image allows human identity to be preserved, but only through a wild
multiplicity.

The fact that it took until Diderot and Sterne and Rousseau to dis-
lodge the notion of humans as fixed entities with a prescribed essential self has made it all the more difficult for people to accept their paranoic insights. Diderot's reply to the absurd notion of fixed Being was,
"Ah, but Marble does not laugh!"

This explains why most readers have a tough time with the character Rousseau presents in his *Confessions*. One minute the autobiographical character is proud, the next humble; one minute fleshy, the next spiritual; one minute vain, the next self-deprecating; one minute idealistic, the next sleazy.

Other great Romantic writers met similar resentment when they clanged the bell of human paradox. Goethe's Werther, in *The Sorrows of Young Werther* (1774), with his contradictory, manic-depressive behavior, causes the reader great frustration. Werther is capable of ecstatically loving both nature and himself, and yet wishing for the destruction of both. In one scene he castigates himself for loving a betrothed woman, followed by the curious statement, "How I worship myself, since she loves me."

Then there is Blake, whose *Songs of Innocence and Experience* (1794) depict "contrary states of the human soul" that are simultaneously present, unlike the mainstream Romantic belief in a "chronological" condition wherein the individual passes into Experience after Innocence.

Most portentous, however, is Blake's hero, Jesus—a hero not for any religiously dogmatic reason but because Jesus, as a man, rebelled against the tyrant God-the-Father and achieved his own godliness. For Jesus was a man who suffered the torturous flux of consciousness. Yet most Christians will defensively argue otherwise—that Jesus always knew he was God. But if Jesus knew he was God, then Jesus was marble, and if he was marble, then he could not laugh and wasn't a man.

If Jesus knew he was God, then the entire Christian myth can be interpreted cynically. If Jesus knew he was God, then there was no real sacrifice, no real suffering, no real battle with the devil. It was all one ironic excursion—the leaving of the holy house, the human birth and growth, the preaching, the miracles, the thorns and tortured death—all just play acting. If Jesus knew he was God, then the tale is empty, a charade by a poseur who made dupes of everyone: the Christians who believe and the non-Christians who fight against believing.

Rather, Jesus could only believe he was God, like Abraham in Kierkegaard's *Fear and Trembling* (1843), who could only believe with dread and by virtue of the absurd, in his God. Jesus could only *believe* he would be saved and live again, that he would return to the ever-expansive drawing rooms of his father.

If Jesus never had to deal with the notion of his own nonbeing, never had to deal with Abraham's sense of human dread, then how could he be human? If he never had to deal with contingency-paranoia, then he never really knew terror, and he never mentally or spiritually suffered. Moreover, if he didn't doubt his godliness, because doubt is wherein faith lives, then he never considered his own madness, and he was no prophet. For prophets know paranoia. It is their ever-arching sea; it engulfs them and sets them free—like Abraham, like Jeremiah, like Kierkegaard, who believed that our ability to deal with the anxiety of nonbeing is proof of the existence of God.

Thus Jesus as a man had to channel his "being" through his anxiety of nonbeing. And it is only in this way that we have a mystical story; only then do we have something compelling; only then do we have the penultimate paranoic tale. Jesus, the most influential figure in history, as a paranoic, as a swarm of bees, as a man who suffered terrible mental anguish because of his paranoic illusion, yet who never dropped out for the sake of contentment but rather followed his paranoic vision through to the end, reprised in resurrection, by virtue of the absurd.

Remember, he could have done otherwise: he could have remained a carpenter; he could have enjoyed family life with Mary Magdalene and maybe even started a little storefront church. But instead he followed his mind's liberating impulse. Despite the doubt, paranoia, and persecution, he believed in his eschatological vision. He came, he grew paranoic, he sacrificed, he transpired.

Only with Jesus as believer can I imagine, for a moment, what it was like receiving those first intimations of divinity—perhaps when he was four years old, the age most children first come to grips with their mortality and deny it; or at age seven, when he may have first condemned his intimations as fantasy; or at age thirteen, when, after his triumph in the Temple against the high priests, he may have actually fallen into doubt and questioned his sanity; or at fifteen and sixteen, when late adolescence brought on full-bloom paranoia. Imagine his trepidations about speaking of his premonitions, his fear of being misunderstood, or of being accused of madness and blasphemy.

Then consider Jesus' greatest paranoic moment of all, and one of the greatest paranoic moments of all time: Gethsemane. (No, his greatest moment was not his act of forgiveness on the cross, which makes for great "story," or his sensationalized rising from the dead, which is certainly eschatologically triumphant.)

The story goes that Jesus sweated blood in the garden at Gethsemane because he feared for his life and dreaded his imminent torture and crucifixion. ("My Father, if this cannot pass . . . Thy will be done," according to Matthew.) But the "blood-sweat" had to result from much more than fear of physical pain. Soldiers going into battle experience similar fear, and they don't sweat blood. No, in order for Jesus' mind, emotions, and body to be mixed into one (the only way one could sweat blood), he had to be experiencing terrible doubt and anguish over his paranoic visions. His greatest fear had to be over what was happening internally, not externally. "What if I am really not God?" he had to be thinking. And, "haven't I carried this thing far enough?"

One must not forget that Jesus wasn't alone in his madness (although most people don't want to think about this; they want to consider Jesus as the only pariah, as *solus ipse*). During the first century in Judea and Samaria there were dozens of fanatics and prophets claiming to be well-connected with God, claiming authority for religious reform and attacking Roman law and Jewish dogma. These prophetic colleagues were also accused of madness and excessive religiosity; some were tortured and killed.

In fact, since Plato (four centuries earlier), people in the Eastern Mediterranean world had recognized the specific condition of "religious madness." Of course, Plato was talking about severe pagan religiosity, but the idea is the same. And, until the early nineteenth century, "fanaticism," "exaltation," and "prophesying" were maintained in specific diagnostic notches. But when the modern clinical concept of paranoia was established, "radical religiosity" fell under the general "paranoid" rubric within the subcategory of "grandiosity," one of the principal components of clinically diagnosed paranoidic illnesses, along with "suspiciousness" and "delusions of persecution." Thus, if Jesus were alive today, he would probably be considered a paranoid psychotic. (Abraham, undoubtedly, would be the star specimen in some psychiatric ward.)

The key problem in defining the identity of Jesus is that the four gospels offer various portraits: Jesus as man, as prophet, as priest, and as son of God. The church eventually canonized the four gospels but never did agree on a unified image of the man himself, crucified outside Jerusalem in roughly 30 AD.

At the Council at Constantinople in 451, the church proclaimed that Christians should believe that Jesus was truly human and truly divine, and that neither identity altered the other. This imprimatur upon the notion of dual essence was aimed at eliminating the idea, popular at the time, that Jesus was half-and-half. After Constantinople, the doctrine would be that Jesus was 100 percent human and 100 percent divine (never mind the later schizophrenic implications of this). Soon, the "double 100 percent" notion became orthodox in churches in the West and in most churches in the East.

Unfortunately, the notion served to undermine paranoic Christian thought, since Christians would henceforth read the gospels as a way to fulfill a doctrine already deemed true, and the image of Jesus as a historical being elided away, as did the notion of Jesus as an astounding paranoic visionary.

Nevertheless, Jesus' voice outlasted time and history to become, perhaps, the Western world's greatest cultural and moral force, and all because he followed his paranoic consciousness: he sweated blood at Gethsemane; he dove into the deep blue.

Ironically, one of the symptomatic claims of the clinically paranoid is that they are Jesus, or are receiving information directly from the Father himself. The connection between clinical paranoia and delusions of divinity, most psychologists agree, is due to the irrational component inherent in all religious experience. And psychologists have had a lot to say about the differences between excessive religiosity and paranoia, between the fanatic and the prophet.

Theorists such as Freud and Fromm have considered religion a defense mechanism and a collective neurosis. Freud connected religious neurosis to his libidinal theory, especially the infantile fixation on a strong father figure (oedipal complex). Fromm conceived of religious neurosis as a private form of mysticism.

William James's *The Varieties of Religious Experience* (1902) argues that valid religious experience can occur in the psychologically normal person as well as in the hysterical and clinically paranoid. He concludes that religiosity in a paranoid person may or may not be valid religious experience, and that it would certainly be impossible to determine this by purely psychological criteria. Nevertheless, one possible test he offers is based on positive/negative criteria: the true religious mystic is basically optimistic; the religious but clinically paranoid is pathological and pessimistic and usually speaks of prophecies that are dreadful.

Jesus, as one might have guessed, has been psychologically reviewed, and the results have been mixed. Some say he is clinically paranoid because of his claim to be supernatural, and because he had delusions and hallucinatory experiences, such as his grandiose behavior in the Temple at age twelve, his communication in the wilderness with Satan, his claims of miraculous cures, and especially his description in front of the Jewish High Council of himself sitting at the right hand of God.

Albert Schweitzer, in *The Psychiatric Study of Jesus* (1958), found the case of clinical paranoia unsound because it was based on the Bible, which is ahistorical, and because researchers were not sufficiently familiar with the culture of Jesus' time. Schweitzer viewed the historical Jesus as an apocalyptic visionary who incorrectly expected the Kingdom of God to arrive in his own lifetime. From this, Schweitzer concluded that the "historical Jesus" is a mostly useless concept in modern Christianity. Nevertheless, the spirit of Jesus ineluctably showered down through the ages.

Doctrine getting in the way of text is why most Christians today still don't want to acknowledge that, based on the gospels, Jesus was a prophet who believed in the imminent arrival of the kingdom of God. And, of course, when this "imminent arrival" did not happen, Jesus' disciples believed, instead, that God had raised Jesus from the dead, which resulted in a new Jewish movement based on the expectation of Jesus' return—an ideal that, under the paranoic teachings of Paul, would eventually spread to the Gentiles.

In my opinion, Jesus had to be paranoidic because he expressed grandiose opinions of himself, but also paranoic because, in Kierkegaardian terms, he believed himself to be in "absolute relation to the Absolute." As a paranoic, Jesus becomes the visionary man who mythically remakes the world.

Nevertheless, it is only as a "paranoidic" that I am comfortable with him as role model, that I can draw some kind of parallel between him and me, when I am standing before the dresser in my bedroom stooping to empty out my pockets at the end of the day . . .

I stand there, checking each pocket several times. At first it is because I'm afraid that I may have left something behind. But soon that worry dissipates, and I know I'm checking purely out of a mindless compulsion. I get caught up so easily, so predictably, in the ceremony of precaution.

Soon I am plunging hands to pockets in a pattern I cannot alter. Time, space, and causation are left behind, and it is only me and my movements. Like Sisyphus, I am caught in absurd repetitive gestures, only in a more quotidian way. I think—this will be the last time. OK, one more . . . two, and . . .

Until it seems I will never be able to stop, that I will die this way, or they will drag me away—"That's it, you're out of here." And the skipping needle moves off the record.

And then, for no specific reason, except maybe whim or perhaps fatigue, or after a wave of disgust, it stops, and I am back in the room again, back to the whole again. Until the next day.

Such an absurd compulsion could, of course, be eliminated in a snap of fingers, which is the sad actuality of the paranoidic, spiraling so easily into inanity, so dis-tractedly estranged from the paranoic. For the paranoic is Dasein-esque, to borrow Heidegger's word. (*Dasein,* according to Heidegger, is the self's consciousness of existing in time.)

Thinking paranoic leads into an inundating blue; thinking paranoic is our terrible window into authentic Being, but it is a dangerous wayfaring, as Nietzsche would say.

The Austrian-born psychologist Bruno Bettelheim claimed that people who suffer paranoia seem to function well in concentration camps because the terrible reality of the camps barely outstrips their deepest, wildest fantasies. Kierkegaard supports this notion in his essay "Dread as a Saving Experience by Means of Faith" when he states that true dread is located inside man rather than out in the world.

And I guess that's why Meriwether Lewis, the heroic American explorer, could miraculously endure a two-thousand-mile journey across unknown rivers and mountains, surviving Indian attacks as well as near starvation and frozen flesh; but he could not, after returning East, endure his own anxiety and dread as he worked on editing his journals. He tried to tame his dread with pills and drunkenness, but the expected terrors of the first Northwest Passage paled before his unexpected inner paranoia.

At an inn outside of Nashville, in October 1809, Lewis shot himself twice. Failing to kill himself—according to Stephen Ambrose's recent biography—he then took out his razor and, after finishing with that, still begged his servants to shoot him. He was thirty-five.

And Daniel Paul Schreber, the presiding judge for the Court of Appeals in Dresden, Germany, waking up one morning in 1894 and realizing that he was being transformed against his will into a woman, and that God was responsible for it.

2

Classicism
Blues

Neoplatonism and the Hypatia Blues

In 415 AD, during the twilight years of the Roman Empire, the female Greek mathematician and philosopher Hypatia was gruesomely murdered by Christian mobs in Alexandria. One winces at the irony of Christians doing to the pagans what the pagans had done to the Christians. But history is filled with such remarkable reversals, ad nauseam.

Little is known about Hypatia's writings; her fame is largely due to her barbarous murder. (Ironically, again, it is the Vatican Library that conserves a portion of Hypatia's *On the Astronomical Canon of Diophantus.*)

More astounding, however, is the transmogrification during the Middle Ages in which Hypatia of Alexandria became Saint Catherine of Alexandria, a Catholic virgin martyr. According to the church's mythical spin, Catherine was a fourth-century Christian murdered by pagans because she discredited the pagan scholars with her spiritual wisdom and Christian faith. Condemned to die upon the wheel, she was temporarily saved by a miracle, only to be beheaded later.

Portions of this sham story were finally exposed in the sixteenth century, and, in 1969, the church dropped Catherine's name from the liturgical calendar.

In recent years, Hypatia has become a hot item—historical novels have been written about her and a feminist journal named after her. These tributes seem to reverse E. M. Forster's rather disparaging judgment in *Alexandria: A History and a Guide*: "The achievements of Hypatia, like her youthfulness, have been exaggerated; she was a middle-aged lady who taught mathematics. . . . She is not a great figure" (55–56).

A recent book by Maria Dzielska carefully attempts to set the record straight and even argues that Hypatia may have been closer to sixty when she died, rather than thirty-five. But for me, Hypatia's age is neither here nor there; I am mostly interested in her Neoplatonism and fascinated by her paranoic courage.

She was born in 370(?) in Alexandria, the Hellenic capital of Egypt and home to a million people. Her father was Theon, a respected mathematician and a member of the literary academy called the Museum. Theon obsessed over Hypatia's education, giving her lessons in poetry, rhetoric, and art. Physical training was included as well: Hypatia learned calisthenics, chariot-driving, swimming, and rowing. In 394, she was purportedly sent to Athens (Dzielska doubts Hypatia ever made this journey) to study with Plutarch the Younger, head of the Neoplatonist Academy.

She supposedly returned from Greece six years later, across the Mediterranean blue, to northern Egypt . . . to Alexandria, Canopic city of the Nile, founded in 313 BC by Alexander the Great on virgin soil (there was a small village there, but it was vanquished). Historical rumor has it that Alexander himself drew out the main points of the city—the agora and temples—with the food his soldiers were carrying, a fortuitous sign for this prospective city on the barren west coast of the silt-producing mouth of the Nile. Alexander himself would later be entombed there in a magnificent gold coffin.

Believing that the creation of new cities was a sign of power, Alexander established over seventy cities in his empire, which stretched from India to the Italian peninsula. Alexandria replaced the old Pharaonic city of Memphis as the seat of Egyptian power, and Alexander's General Ptolemy swiftly established his authority there. Alexandria thus became the "first city" of the Hellenistic world, a center of commerce, but most important, it became the home of the Greek copyists and the center of literature in the Hellenistic world.

No one knows exactly where the ancient libraries, which may have held up to one million volumes, were located, since they were later destroyed by fire, sand, and sea. (The new, recently completed library of Alexandria, which will eventually contain over eight million books, is built on what is purported to be the site of the ancient libraries.)

Alexandria also boasted multistory apartment buildings and a 400–foot lighthouse with an elevator. The gymnasium, however, was the most beautiful building and a sign of the pervasiveness of Greek culture. As in Athens, the gymnasium was a center not only for exercise but also for reading, discussion, and socializing. (The Greeks exercised naked, of course, which particularly bothered the non-Greeks in Alexandria. In fact, stripping oneself naked was considered a public sign of assimilation into the dominant [Greek] culture.)

More so than Athens in the fifth century BC, Alexandria was an amazingly pluralistic city. Egyptian culture, for instance, was allowed to prosper on its own. There were different court systems and legal codes (Egyptian and Greek). However, Greek culture was the pathway to genuine power, and, for the Greeks, superior culture always justified political control (a notion that has echoed throughout the Western world during the last twenty-five centuries).

Alexandria was divided into specific quarters: the southwest for the Egyptians, the northeast for the Jews, the north and west for the Greeks. By the time of Christ, Alexandria was the largest city in the world, only later to be surpassed by Rome. Intermarriage between Greeks and Egyptians eventually created a mixed population, and a marginal democracy lasted until Augustus declared the city to be under imperial Roman rule (30 BC).

By the time Hypatia arrived, many of the books and pagan temples had already been razed by Roman emperor Theodosius I. In 391, he officially abolished the worship of pagan gods and declared belief in the Trinity to be the required orthodoxy. (Theodosius II would bring the Olympics to a halt in 425.) Thus, in Hypatia's century, the curtain was coming down on the classical world, and Christianity was on the hegemonic rise.

Books had always been a cherished commodity in Alexandria. The city's librarians had collected and copied the wealth of Greek learning, especially the great dramatic works and the writings of Aristotle (saving them from certain destruction, especially at the hands of the Visigoths who invaded Athens in 395). In fact, all ships landing in Alexandria were searched for books; if any were found, they were quickly copied and then returned.

For a philosopher and Neoplatonist such as Hypatia, the literary destruction carried out by desperate fiat from Theodosius I (in 395) was a devastating blow. Nevertheless, when the head of the Museum offered Hypatia a teaching position in mathematics, she eagerly accepted and was soon head of the Neoplatonist school of Alexandria. (Here, again, Dzielska disagrees, maintaining that Hypatia never had a formal position, but taught only to private groups.) In any case, she earned a broad reputation among the Greek, Christian, Roman, Jewish, and Egyptian inhabitants of the city.

A female philosopher teaching in the fifth century was certainly a novelty. Hypatia attracted students from all over Africa and Asia Minor, and even included bishops such as Synesius of Cyrene. Socrates (380–450), a church historian from Constantinople, said that Hypatia "surpassed all contemporary philosophers," and that "she was not ashamed to spend time in the society of men who esteemed her highly." Although there are few records of Hypatia's writings, we know that she wrote on algebra, quadratic equations, Euclid's geometry, and the astronomical works of Ptolemaeus. She invented a hydroscope to determine the gravity of liquids, and an astrolabe to measure the altitude of planets.

From these achievements, many scholars conclude that Hypatia leaned toward the logical, rather than the mystical, side of Neoplatonism. I have my doubts, however. For even though Hypatia may have believed that "teaching superstition as truth is a most terrible thing," it does not necessarily follow that she wasn't highly involved in the mystical and esoteric. After all, she was the Alexandrine mistress of Neoplatonism, the dominant philosophy of the pagan world from the time of Plotinus (mid-third century AD) until the closing of the pagan schools in Athens by the Christian emperor Justinian in 529.

Neoplatonism was much more than simply a revival of Platonic thought. Neoplatonists aimed at a comprehensive philosophy, one that incorporated into Platonism the best of Aristotle, Pythagoras, and the Stoics. But it was also a religion, concerned with how the individual soul might reach God. Neoplatonism combined traditional Greek rationalism with Christian mysticism and the desire for salvation (even though Plotinus made few specific references to Christianity).

Plotinus (205?–270 AD), the greatest Greek philosopher of late antiquity, may not have actually been the founder of Neoplatonism. Some believe that it was his teacher Ammonius Saccus, a self-taught laborer from Alexandria, who may have been the actual founder. Unfortunately, Saccus, like Hypatia, left few writings behind.

Nevertheless, it was Plotinus, born in Lycopolis (Egypt), who rejected the Manichean dialectic of good and evil, transcendent and material, universal and particular. At the center of his paranoic antidialectical vision was the "One," an incomprehensible, all-sufficient unity.

Plotinus knew that it was the desire for contentment that drew the individual into nasty dualisms, such as pretending to know the ways toward damnation and true happiness. He and the later Neoplatonists instead practiced free visionary (paranoic) thought; they envisioned the process of "Emanation," by which the One gives rise to the Logos (or Divine Mind), which thrives on free intuitive thought and which contains the essences of all individuals. Below the Logos is the World Soul (Psyche), which links the intellectual and material worlds. Together, these three visionary and transcendent entities (the One, the Logos, and the World Soul) support the visible world, which includes human beings and corporeal matter.

To appreciate the virtue of Plotinus's hybrid paranoic seeing, one must appreciate a life in which the soul can rise through contemplation to the level of intelligence (Logos), and then, through mystical union, be absorbed finally into the One itself. The faculty that enables the soul to make such a journey is none other than the power of expansive consciousness. In Plotinus's thinking, what a human being becomes depends on the level to which he directs his consciousness, and this consciousness is intuitive, free, and therefore highly paranoic.

With sufficient mental courage and concentration, it is possible, according to Plotinus, to be identified through "ecstasy" with the supreme unity of the One, an experience that Plotinus claimed happened to him four times. Thus there are two pervasive movements in Neoplatonic thought: the metaphysical emanation from the One, and the mystical return to the One through reflection and paranoic contemplation.

However, Plotinus was no extreme mystic, and this is no Eastern religion we're talking about (even though he did travel to Mesopotamia with the emperor in order to learn something of the East). The Neoplatonists in Athens, and later in Alexandria, did absorb certain mystical influences from the East, such as divination, demonology, and astrology. But at the same time, Plotinus's thinking is based heavily on the tradition of Greek rationalism, and his theory of the One comes from Plato's later writings, especially the *Timaeus,* as well as from the Stoics who had identified the World Soul with the power of universal reason. What is most distinctive about Plotinus, however, is his notion of Emanation, which certainly resulted from his own practice of "dis-tracted thinking."

Thus, it is Alexandria that holds an important role in the development and demise of classical paranoic thought; Alexandria, whose greatest heroine might very well be the late Neoplatonist Hypatia. As a mystic, her philosophy was her religion. She argued for a wisdom that ultimately rejected the world of material good in order to understand "higher things"; she believed in "bending the mind to the divine."

Hypatia lectured on "apatheia," or being free from the tyranny of emotions. For her, being in harmony with the self meant a strong degree of indifference to things of the world. She wanted her students to aim for a higher union with the (pagan) divine, to "delight in intellect."

Hypatia's Neoplatonism, however, was never supported with theurgy and magic; there was no "service to the gods." Pagan cult practices were merely adornments of philosophic spiritualism for Hypatia. She loved spiritual philosophy for itself, not for the sake of gods.

Her famous student Synesius is an important source on this. In his Epistles, he claims she taught on ethical and religious topics by "dialogues," and that she never resorted to magic or cult practices. Rather than religious theurgy, Hypatia called for philosophic theurgy ("anagoge").

Many of Hypatia's followers became Christians; and Neoplatonism, of course, had a huge influence on early Christian philosophy, especially on St. Augustine (the Western world's first theologian), who was a Neoplatonist before he was a Christian. Augustine's Neoplatonic background enabled him to conceive of spirit as immaterial, and evil as "unreal substance" (in contrast to Manichean doctrine). Down the historical line, Neoplatonism would influence Aquinas (who thought of the Divine Mind dispersed into angels), Hegel, the German Romantics, and the British Romantic William Blake.

What makes Hypatia particularly provocative is the "oneness" her own life expressed: she was fleshy and spiritual, logical and mystical, beautiful and mathematical. With so much contained in one being, it is easy to see why she attracted a following, and why there were many proposals for marriage. Some think she turned them down because of her stoical dedication to philosophy—"I am wedded to the truth," she purportedly said. This same historical faction wants to portray her as a virginal goddess martyred by the dark hands of fifth-century Christians. But such a scenario may not be completely accurate.

Nevertheless, it is difficult for most to imagine a spiritual female mathematician who was also capable of experiencing physical love. This is why most accounts of Alexandria fail to discuss the beautiful prostitutes who charmed the streets. These worldly women had access to spices, perfumes, and soaps from the East (makeup and eye shadow had been in vogue there since the first century). The comic poet Machon wrote witty verses on the activities of the wealthy men and prostitutes in Alexandria.

Although Hypatia herself was purportedly quite beautiful, she maintained that true beauty could not be found in concrete objects. Eros, to her, was ultimately platonic, and physical beauty just a shadow or trace. After all, it was Plotinus who claimed that going after the body would only sink one into the dark where intellect cannot function.

Many of Hypatia's young students wanted to have affairs with her, and she had to repeatedly put them off. Based on the fragments of Damascius, Dzielska reports a particularly shocking account wherein Hypatia punished one student's professions of love by showing him her sanitary napkin and admonishing—"See, this is what you really love, my young man . . . you do not love beauty for its own sake" (50).

Some historians admit that Hypatia did have "affairs," but that no sex was involved; they cite the writings of her contemporaries to confirm this. But couldn't the case be otherwise: that her "contemporaries" found it necessary to elevate her reputation as a "pure woman" because the hegemonic Christian culture would only deify a single woman if she had practiced chastity?

This is why I believe Hypatia did have lovers, and one of them was the Egyptian prefect of Alexandria named Orestes. Such an affair, in combination with her Neoplatonic philosophy, was enough to make the prefect's political enemy Cyril—the archbishop of Alexandria (later canonized a saint)—encourage his band of monks to destroy her. In fact, Cyril's reputation results mostly from his attacks on church leaders, and his methods were brutal.

It might be possible to understand Cyril's personal animosity toward Hypatia, but for him to fear her Neoplatonism enough to incite murder? No, his motives had to be political; he wanted Hypatia out of the way in order to weaken Orestes' support. The English historian Edward Gibbon claims that Cyril had Hypatia murdered precisely because she had the political ear of Orestes, who opposed Cyril's wish to expel all non-Christians from Alexandria. Gibbon also argues that Cyril was jealous of Hypatia because scholars from all over the world attended her lectures.

But the point of my meditation upon Hypatia is not to rant about the nasty vicissitudes of history, or to indict bad monks and Christians, or to voice Bertrand Russell's fatalistic view of Hypatia as a sad end to the great classical world.

Rather, I simply want to make clear that Hypatia's murderers were deprived of high paranoic consciousness, and instead ingested low paranoid fears, making them incapable of imagining the terror of their actions or the suffering of Hypatia. For most assuredly, the loss of the paranoic can lead to a loss of consciousness, which can lead to a loss of self. And if one can't imagine the self, it is difficult to imagine the suffering of others.

Which is why one has to love Hypatia and her futile battle against the modus operandi of her emerging world. Paranoic thinking means bringing an end to dualisms, just as Neoplatonism meant to eradicate Manichaeistic thought. Unfortunately, by 400 AD, the paranoidic dice had already been cast within the classical mindset, and the paranoic ability to imagine oneself right into the charismatic blue was seriously threatened. Consequently, Neoplatonism itself, perhaps the most beautifully paranoic philosophy the West has produced—a philosophy that lives through infinite intuition, through system-building without relying upon systems, through mind expansion unlimited by debilitating infrastructures—suffered a mortal blow.

St. Augustine (354–430), erstwhile Father of the Church, would abandon Neoplatonism altogether. He had no idea, of course, what he would be getting us into with his City of God and City of the World scenarios. And even though St. Augustine always maintained a strong mystical nature—enough to neutralize, at times, his neurotic need to system-build—it is still indeed sad that Hypatia's paranoic promise would eventually be stamped out by Augustine's hegemonic Christian dualisms.

Ultimately, Neoplatonism was never a doctrine but rather a way of thinking. And, in this sense, it is truly antinomian. Neoplatonism, Alexandrine-style, was the most potent of all, precisely because it contained the most expansive parts of Greek, Hebraic, Egyptian, and Christian thought. This expansive philosophy, one of the last best chances for mental liberation in the West, haunts us with Hypatia as final tragic anecdote. In the end, she was killed because her thinking was judged to be "dis-tracted" and a political affront to paranoidic Roman-Christian culture.

It was late mid-day, the still hot air weighed heavily upon Hypatia as she stepped through the violent sunshine and into her waiting chariot. She was wearing a thin robe of blue with gold adornment, perhaps a bit sullied from the thick dust which permeated the air and which seemed to choke her during her afternoon lecture at the Museum.

She knew that her teachings were being judged heretical by the church, and that the church would continue to target her because she was a sci-

entist, an intellectual, and a woman (all three deemed dangerous). She knew that Cyril, the bishop of Alexandria, desired absolute power and unlimited jurisdiction. (A year before her death, Cyril had driven all the Jews, who had lived there since the time of Alexander, out of Alexandria.) Hypatia also knew that Cyril had been fomenting paranoidic hatred among his monks by spreading rumors of her sorcery and witchcraft.

Despite all of this, Hypatia was still on her way to see the Egyptian prefect, Orestes, her lover and friend. The day was March 10, the year 415. The square was mostly empty, the Christian students already off preparing for the spring festival of their resurrected god. In the late afternoon light, witnesses remember seeing Hypatia flying down the broad avenue (eight lanes wide) in her gleaming chariot.

As she made a slow turn past the Christian church called the Caesarium, Hypatia noticed a large crowd up ahead. Someone yelled, "There's the pagan woman!" And other voices began to taunt and scream insults at her. Soon Hypatia was trapped and could not easily turn her golden vehicle around.

The crowd wanted to drag the pagan woman down from her high chariot. Hypatia felt her body freeze as hundreds of sweaty hands reached for her. Two of her horses tumbled in anguish, the other two broke free. Christian fingers ground her into the dirt, then hauled her before the church and stripped her naked. They carried her inside, where, amidst the over-rich smell of incense (an odor never to be forgotten), Hypatia's body was cut to pieces with pottery shards cuffed in the hands of gleamy-eyed monks. Witnesses claimed later that they could hear, between Hypatia's screams, the horrible scraping of bone echoing throughout the church.

In a final frenzy, the monks dismembered her and lit her body fragments on fire, carrying them into the plaza where the dusk was just descending.

Afraid for his life and also beaten by the monks, Orestes (the Egyptian prefect) fled Alexandria two days later. An investigation was called for by the Roman authorities but never carried out. Saint Cyril issued a statement saying that the rumor of Hypatia's murder was nothing more than hysterical lies, and that Hypatia had, in fact, left for Athens days earlier.

One Christian historian, Scholasticus, did manage to proclaim the murder a "terrible offense against an innocent woman," but Alexandrians hardly listened. They were too busy with their resurrection celebrations.

Democracy Blues

The life and fate of Hypatia of Alexandria raises the question of other moments of paranoic achievement amidst the classical world's paranoidic history; how the idea of democracy, for example, paranoic in conception, eventually turned paranoidic.

The first mention of a democratic gathering in Western culture is Telemakhos calling for the Assembly of noblemen in Ithaca at the beginning of Homer's *Odyssey*. Telemakhos's purpose was to gain the noblemen's imprimatur for his journey to search for information about his father, Odysseus, who had not been heard of since he left nineteen years earlier for the Trojan War (which was also the last time the Assembly had been called together).

The Ithacan Assembly, purportedly occurring around 1180 BC, narrated by Homer around 780 BC, was a crude version of a "town meeting," especially when compared to the much more developed form of democracy established by Cleisthenes in Athens in 508, which would last until the conquering of Athens by Macedon in 322 BC. In democratic Athens, all political decisions were made by the majority vote of a direct nonrepresentational assembly of five hundred citizens; decisions were executed by a council whose members were chosen by lot. This democracy became even more radicalized under Pericles (c. 462 BC) to ensure that all decisions were kept in the hands of the people.

Two millennia later, the reappearance of democracy in the West would draw heavily on the rational arguments of Locke and Rousseau (*The Social Contract*, 1762), as well as on the fervor of the American and French revolutions and the Romantic movement's call for brotherhood and social justice based on seeing human beings as "feeling bipeds" rather than "reasoning bipeds." Beyond empathy, however, this modern democracy would also be based on the imaginative projection of "otherness," which also has its roots in Homer, specifically the call to duty, as represented by Hector in the *Iliad*.

Having the power to imagine the condition of others, rather than the expression of emotional sympathy, is certainly the force behind Hector's penultimate moment in book 22 of the *Iliad* when he tries to consider the right course of action as he stands alone outside the city gates in full view of his parents and countrymen as Achilles rushes toward him with immortal spear in hand. Hector's supremely paranoic, and seemingly mad, notion—that maybe he should lay his battle gear aside and instead ask Achilles for peace, return Helen, and share out all of Troy's wealth—results not from "feeling" for his family and Trojan countrymen but rather from his paranoic projection of their expected suffering if he dies at the hands of Achilles. In this sense, Hector's high paranoic moment is similar to the Romantic visionary William Blake's conception of Jesus as hero because of his achievement in moral imagination. That is, Jesus self-annihilates not because he feels for the world, but because he successfully imagines the world's suffering and acts out of supreme duty.

Even today, perhaps the best way to elicit care for others is not necessarily through emotional appeal but through imaginative projection. For if one can imagine the case of "others," one may begin to act for the "general will." The idea of imaginative projection would be central to many of the Romantic writers, especially Percy Shelley and William Blake.

The key question, of course, is why didn't the Greek paranoic notion of imaginative projection triumph in Western democracy? And the answer seems to be because the paranoic concept of "otherness" got lost amidst Western democracy's focus on the political will of the majority (what Rousseau termed "the will of all"), whose chief goal was to secure contentment rather than to strive for the greatest justice. Athenians, in particular, felt the pressure to think on the "same track" rather than "off track" in order to maintain their power and security. And this is still the case in modern democracies, wherein politicians seduce the voters into acting for the sake of continued contentment and security in the face of paranoidic fears, rather than encouraging them to project imaginatively (paranoically) and act for a wider visionary good.

Thus Western democracy may have been inherently flawed from the outset since it never focused on transcending the paranoidic, which is undoubtedly why political paranoia still overwhelms societies that are glibly offered a dream of contentment. Moreover, under Western orthodox thinking, most believe that the greater the democracy, the less the people's paranoia and the greater the chances of acquiring contentment. If one follows such thinking to its conclusion, modern America should ostensibly offer a less paranoid society than that of ancient Athens.

Eli Sagan, in his book *The Honey and the Hemlock: Democracy and Paranoia in Ancient Athens and Modern America* (1991), argues just such a case. "Greek democracy represents the first appearance on the earth of the most moral, most just, most mature, most humane form of society ever invented" (3). He argues further that a healthy individual must pass beyond the "paranoid state" in order to possess full adulthood; and that similarly, a healthy society must pass beyond its "paranoid state" in order to achieve full democracy. Classical Greece, according to Sagan, was less paranoid than Archaic Greece; and, in general, "democratic society . . . represents the least paranoid of any form of society yet seen" (15).

There are, however, several problems with Sagan's assertions. First, he mostly considers only the political aspects of paranoia, ignoring the cultural and intellectual implications. His idea of "paranoia," therefore, does not include any sense of the paranoic, and is limited instead to what I have defined as "paranoidic." This leads to Sagan's second problem: his assumption that complete health means the elimination of paranoia. Of course one would like to eliminate paranoidic consciousness and the paranoidic state, but such elimination is not possible while living amidst the devilish dream of contentment, as the demise of classical Athens proves.

In my mind, a healthy adult condition, whether for the individual or the state, means outgrowing paranoidic thinking and expanding into paranoic thinking; otherwise human consciousness will never gain the ability to imaginatively project. Eli Sagan partially senses this situation when he states that the relationship of the psyche to the world is one of paranoia. Yet when he argues that such a condition necessarily leads to a "paranoid position," he neglects to mention that such a result occurs only if the individual invests in the bargain of contentment.

Moreover, I don't believe "we are all born paranoid" (14), as Sagan asserts. Rather, we are all born naturally paranoic, and then shortly thereafter the expansive and dreamy consciousness of early childhood is replaced by paranoidic consciousness and its consequential fantasy of contentment. Sagan is correct, however, when he states that the mission of life should be to overcome the paranoid condition. Yet, claiming that "all nonpsychotic adults have succeeded more or less in going beyond the paranoid position" (14) simply isn't true. Because going beyond the paranoidic will never happen without embracing the paranoic.

Buying into the ruse of contentment only necessitates the manufacture of certain external and internal enemies to be feared through what Sagan calls a "paranoid positioning," leading human beings to believe in something that will decrease their paranoia and ensure their contentment. That something, in Sagan's mind, is liberal democracy, which convinces its constituents that it alone can eliminate their fears.

But democracy has not eliminated the fear of enemies at home and abroad, and this is the greatest failing in Sagan's thinking. Are Americans, for instance, less paranoid now than in 1945, or 1965? Or 1980, or 2003? Indeed, in the post-9/11 world, Americans believe they have more enemies to fear, and the push toward imperialism and aggression abroad and infringement of rights at home has only served to increase those fears.

Thus it is not necessarily true that the greater the democracy, the less the paranoia. Strong democracy does result, most assuredly, in a greater amount of available information, but greater information, on top of an already "paranoid positioning," may create a greater assortment of fears. As Sagan points out, Cato the Elder, a second-century Roman statesman, once asked, "what is to become of Rome when it has no more enemies to fear?" (25). The answer, of course, is that Rome tore itself apart in civil war.

Western democracy, a hopeful antidote to authoritarian rule such as Rome's, will hardly bring an end to paranoidic fears as long as the state and individual goals focus primarily on a projected idea of contentment for the majority. For whether it be classical Greece or modern America, the concept of freedom is still often predicated upon the ability to rule over others, and these "others," even in a prostrate state of repression, cause endless consternation, suspicion, and paranoidic fear among the so-called "free" controllers. As William Blake put it so succinctly, "The bounded is loathed by the possessor."

Sagan's answer to all of this is his belief in the maturation of 10 to 20 percent of the population becoming paranoia-free and no longer engaging in war or racism. This small percentage, therefore, would be qualified to lead. By "paranoia-free," Sagan means paranoidic-free, which can only occur by virtue of the paranoic, a concept he doesn't consider. For only the paranoic allows us to imaginatively project beyond the ills of war and racism.

Unfortunately, Americans specialize in a "paranoid style," as Richard Hofstadter asserted over thirty years ago. And historically, democracy has done precious little to inhibit the soft American mind from fearing whatever has been served up on the fear-monger menu—commies, foreigners, Islamic radicals, illegal immigrants, gays . . .

The modern culture of contentment fosters an inherent tendency to imagine legions of barbarians both inside and outside the sacred gates. And although many cultural and political institutions praise the idea of the paranoic—embracing, for instance, the importance of "thinking outside the box"—in reality, they rarely go paranoic. The contentment dialectic so readily kicks in, which is why in a wealthy, capitalistic, democratic country such as America, "real choice" is usually among things veritably the same. For the contentment fetish breeds banality and repetition. Politicians, musicians, media formats, for instance, all sound and look the same, all cross-checked by the power of the "paranoidic" safely inside the culture of contentment.

In the end, there is no political means for overcoming these paranoidic fears; there is only the paranoic. Therefore the paranoic, rather than contentment-driven democracy, should be the call for the modern individual and the modern state.

Reflection as Paranoic Impulse

And paranoic regeneration begins with reflection . . . upon key moments of reflection, for instance, when paranoic consciousness bubbled to the surface in Western culture; beginning with the Greeks, following the spirit of Hypatia herself, to Alexandria; to Athens, the cultural jewel in the paradoxical crown of Western thought; to Prince Hector himself, suspending the entire Heroic Age, for a prophetic moment, by the frailest strands of paranoic moral thought.

Homer, living during the rough and trying times of the early Iron Age, presents his epic tale the *Iliad* with a certain degree of nostalgia for the supposed glorious times of the Mycenaean kings (1600–1200 BC) at the end of the Bronze Age. And Homer's audience longed to hear of those great days of heroes and conquest. But what Homer's audience didn't expect to hear was the subversive notion, considered by Hector, of suspending the chief values of the Heroic Age for the sake of peace. Hector's climactic moment, therefore, is a precursor to modern moral sensibility.

> Hector, grim and narrow-eyed . . . in his brave heart bitterly *reflected*: "Here I am badly caught. If I take cover, slipping inside the gate and wall, the first to accuse me for it will be Poulydamas, he who told me I should lead the Trojans back to the city on that cursed night Achilles joined the battle. No, I would not, wiser though it would have been. Now troops have perished for my foolish pride. . . . Better, when that time comes, that I appear as he who killed Achilles man to man. . . . Suppose, though, that I lay my shield and helm aside, and prop my spear against the wall, and go to meet the noble Prince Achilles,

promising Helen, promising with her all treasures that Alexandros brought home by ship to Troy. . . . Then I might add a portion of all the secret wealth the city owns . . . share and share alike . . . all that is here within the walls. Ah, no, why even put the question to myself? I must not go before him and receive no quarter, no respect! . . . Better we duel, now at once, and see to whom the Olympian awards the glory . . .

These were his shifts of mood. Now close at hand Achilles like the implacable god of war came on with blowing crest, hefting the dreaded beam of Pelian ash on his right shoulder. (book 22, ll. 115–59, emphasis mine)

Thus, instead of relying upon instinct to know the "good," as Achilles would have (indeed, as nearly all the warriors of Homer's Heroic Age would have), Hector reflects inwardly in order to discover the right thing to do. Such an exercise in moral reasoning is astoundingly off-track and centuries ahead of its time. In fact, the "idea of the good" in the late Heroic Age was still connected with "achievement" or "ability." Thus a good warrior was someone who could kill scores of the enemy (i.e., someone like Achilles). Homer's *Iliad* includes several Greek words for the good: *agathos*—well-born, brave; *kalos*—beautiful, noble; *aristos*—most excellent; *kratistos*—most strong. And it is not surprising that Achilles exemplifies all of these notions, for Achilles is a "good" warrior and the seeming tragic hero of Homer's *Iliad* (the epic work is considered by many to be the first "tragedy" in the Western literary tradition).

The later meaning of the "good"—to espouse specific moral value or the desire to do what is right—would not enter the Greek playing field for at least another hundred years after the time of Homer. In fact, Hector actually practices what ethicists would later term "secondary morality," or relying upon reason to choose the right action. The concept of secondary morality would not materialize in Greece until the sophists introduced it with their rhetorical teachings in the early fifth century BC. In Homer's time, "primary morality," or acting instinctively in accord with accepted and inherited codes of behavior (Achilles), was still the rule of practice.

Achilles' "being" expresses the four essential values of the Heroic Age—courage, strength, pride, and honor. The chief value, however, was that of honor. And it was precisely the notion of honor that Hector paranoically dared to undermine by considering sharing Troy's wealth instead of fighting Achilles. By repudiating the convention of "honor,"

Hector would be overthrowing the "Age" itself and, more precisely, Achilles' exaggerated sense of honor, which caused the great Greek hero to retreat and pout after Agamemnon, King of Kings, took away Briseis, Achilles' Trojan sex prize, in book 1 of *The Iliad*. Without Achilles fighting, the Greek soldiers on the field were doomed to die since, no matter how much they may have outnumbered the enemy, soldiers on the field (in the Heroic Age) can never win without their hero present.

Achilles' fall worsens when he prays to his mother, Thetis, and asks her to intercede with the gods in order to ensure enemy victories. Such an action is unimaginable for a war hero of the modern age. Hypothetically, for instance, could General Schwarzkopf still have been a hero during America's 1991 Gulf War if he had pouted and actually helped the enemy kill American soldiers because he may have been angry at President Bush over an issue of pride? In the Heroic Age, however, even treason is forgiven, because a hero's honor was more important than the loss of soldiers' lives.

Homer, however, paranoically undermines this value system with his subtle portrayal of Hector, the presumed enemy, as the moral hero of the *Iliad*. As perhaps the Western world's first great literary subversive, Homer is very interested in exposing the flaw in Greek heroic culture that allows a hero such as Achilles to acquire sacred status at the expense of human life. In his paranoic "reflection speech," Hector ironically echoes this flaw when he states, "someone inferior to me may say: he kept his pride and lost his men, this Hector!" (ll. 128–29). (It is important to note here that Homer was in all likelihood born in Ionia, an area culturally and demographically aligned with the area of ancient Troy.)

Hector's consideration "to share" and make peace amidst the heroic climax of his life no doubt fits under Plato's later notion, in his *Theaetetus*, of "thinking amiss," which was the first use of the paranoia concept as a verb. Many examples of the paranoia lexicon are also found in Greek drama: in Aeschylus's grandly allusive *Prometheus Bound* (460? BC), Hermes tells Prometheus he is "mad, mad indeed" (l. 975) to accept suffering for the sake of principle, reiterating later that "These are madman's words; a madman's plan: is there a missing note in this mad harmony? is there a slack chord in this madness?" (l. 1053–55); and Euripides employs the paranoia lexicon in *Orestes* (408 BC) with "Sacrilege of madness born!" (l. 822), and in *Iphigenia in Aulis* (405 BC) with "strange frenzy" (l. 838).

Also interesting is the intriguing etymological history that "paranoia" shares with "*petomai*" (I am flying). In Greek literature "petomai" is often used metaphorically to portray life "on the wing," or a life of "uncertain hopes." Such a meaning certainly implies a paranoic risk into the deepest contingency.

In any case, one can conclude that, with the birth of the "paranoia" lexicon, the documentation of self-consciousness begins in the West. And the purest moments that follow, inside the unfolding story of Western thought, are when the paranoic mind recognizes and accepts going beside itself, going dis-tracted, which is nothing less than a fundamental echo inside human consciousness of the eternal "I am." From this, a psychological condition follows wherein the relationship of psyche to the world is one of paranoia, which explains Hector's astounding "reflection" speech, after which he decides to turn and run for his life.

Three times Achilles chases Hector around the perimeter of the city with all of Troy watching. Homer's description of Hector's paranoidic flight is reminiscent of the timeless pursuit the Romantic poet John Keats imagines in "Ode on a Grecian Urn": "As in a dream a man chasing another cannot catch him, nor can he in flight escape from his pursuer, so Achilles could not by his swiftness overtake him, nor could Hector pull away" (book 22, ll. 235–39).

In the end, of course, Hector, knowing he is doomed to lose, and knowing that his action will doom his city and its people, decides to stand and fight the "terrible" Achilles. Thus, although Hector thinks in an enlightened paranoic way, he acts according to the Heroic Age's extreme notion of honor (which is based on the paranoidic).

After killing Hector (with the help of the gods), Achilles strips his armor and ghoulishly drags Hector's naked body about the Trojan plain, an action that marks Achilles not only as a fallen hero but as a truly mad individual (in the paranoidic/Platonic-Hippocratic sense). Although readers may judge Achilles' action as shameless and a sign of his fall as tragic hero, most will not connect it to the Greek classical notion of distracted thinking.

The common Greeks of the classical period, of course, were removed from the rarefied intellectual life and not aware of the paranoia lexicon. But they were aware of the shame involved in fallen (paranoidic) behavior, which is why Hector chooses to fight rather than follow his paranoic vision in his "reflection" speech.

History, Culture, and the Paranoic

Herodotus (485?–425 BC), the West's first historian, relied upon the power of shame to control his audience during public readings in Periclean Athens, and to convince them to pay heed to his cultural judgments. Herodotus neither espoused the use of secondary morality (figuring the "right" through reason), nor did he believe in the sanctity of primary morality (defining the "right" through inherited values and opinions). Rather, Herodotus was a kind of anthropological pluralist; he wanted the Athenians to appreciate the various customs of the world rather than immediately judge foreign cultures as inferior and barbarian because, hitherto, appreciation and absorption is what had made Athens a great culture and people. Indeed, he was paranoic enough to praise the cultural achievements of others (such as the Egyptians) over the Greeks:

> the Egyptians by their study of astronomy discovered the solar year and were the first to divide it into twelve parts—and in my opinion their method of calculation is better than the Greek; for the Greeks, to make the seasons work out properly, intercalate a whole month every other year, while the Egyptians make the year consist of twelve months of thirty days each and every year intercalate five additional days, and so complete the regular circle of the seasons. They also told me that the Egyptians first brought into use the names of the twelve gods, which the Greeks took over from them, and were the first to assign altars and images and temples to the gods, and to carve figures in stone. (*The Histories*, 130)

And he doesn't hesitate to criticize the Greeks for their intellectual arrogance, as noted in his bold peroration on the mystery of the Nile:

> Certain Greeks, hoping to advertise how clever they are, have tried to account for the flooding of the Nile in three different ways. Two of the explanations are not worth dwelling upon, beyond bare mention of what they are. . . . The third theory is much the most plausible, but at the same time furthest from the truth; according to this, the water of the Nile comes from melting snow, but as it flows from Libya through Ethiopia into Egypt, that is from a very hot into a cooler climate, how could it possibly originate in snow? Obviously, this view is as worthless as the other two. Anyone who can use his wits about such matters will find plenty of arguments to prove how unlikely it is that snow is the cause of the flooding of the river. (136–37)

In essence, Herodotus, the world's first multiculturalist, believed that "custom was king," and that the Greeks themselves had acquired many of their customs from foreign people and cultures, especially from Egypt. Moreover, Herodotus believed that success would come to a civilization only if its people were willing to adopt foreign customs, a practice for which he praised the Persians:

> No race is so ready to adopt foreign ways as the Persian; for instance, they wear the Median costume because they think it handsomer than their own, and their soldiers wear the Egyptian corselet. Pleasures, too, of all sorts they are quick to indulge in when they get to know about them—a notable instance is pederasty, which they learned from the Greeks. (97)

It was from this spirit of cultural pluralism that Herodotus became the first to assert that Athens was superior precisely because it was democratic.

Herodotus's "strange" tales of so-called "barbarians" living in distant places eventually gave him the nickname "father of lies" (a moniker forwarded by Plutarch). But ironically, many of his anecdotes of distant cultures were later proven to be true. A more accurate historical appraisal would be that the Greeks instinctively wanted Herodotus's stories to be lies because, culturally paranoid, they feared any perceived disruption to their contentment from outside sources. (In contemporary terms, they feared the influence of "otherness.")

Herodotus, on the other hand, was thinking paranoically: "What is going on outside our environs?" he wondered, and "what are these barbarians really up to? Could they in fact have interesting things to show us?" The word "barbarian" itself can be traced back through the French—who applied it to the Barbary Coast of Africa where the black "barbarians" lived—to the Romans and then the Greeks, who formulated it phonetically to mimic the odd sound of any foreign tongue (bar-bar, bar-bar). Thus the term cast an aspersion on "difference" and reinforced the already institutionalized notion among the Greeks that anyone "other" was inferior.

Herodotus's paranoic capabilities allowed him to think expansively to such a degree that he even dared to undermine the myth of Helen, which was sacred to Greek cultural identity. In book 2 of his *Histories,* Herodotus tells a nearly incredulous story that subverts the entire Homeric tradition (a tradition for which he had no particular affinity).

I asked the [Egyptian] priests if the Greek story of what happened at
Troy had any truth in it, and they gave me in reply some information
which they claimed to have had direct from Menelaus himself. . . .
[The Greeks] were received within the walls of [Troy], and demanded
the restoration of Helen together with the treasure which Paris had
stolen. . . . The Trojans, however, gave an answer which they always
stuck to afterwards—sometime even swearing to the truth of it:
namely, that neither Helen nor the treasure was in their possession,
but both were in Egypt, and there was no justice in trying to force
them to give satisfaction of property which was being detained by the
Egyptian king Proteus. The Greeks, supposing this to be a merely friv-
olous answer, laid siege to the town, and persisted until it fell; but no
Helen was found, and they were still told the same story, until at last
they believed it and sent Menelaus to visit Proteus in Egypt. . . . He
sailed up the [Nile] to Memphis . . . was most hospitably entertained
and Helen, none the worse for her adventures, was restored to him
with all the rest of his property. Nevertheless . . . [Menelaus] took two
Egyptian children and offered them in sacrifice. . . . The discovery of
this foul act turned the friendship of the Egyptians to hatred;
[Menelaus] was pursued, but managed to escape with his ships to
Libya. . . . The [Egyptian] priests spoke with certain knowledge of [the
events] which had taken place in their own country. (173–74)

Iconoclastic statements such as this fueled the defamation of
Herodotus by later Greeks. For his "historia" (reasonable inquiry) into
the cultural past often involved telling the Greeks what they didn't want
to hear, in this case by dis-tractedly (paranoically) stepping outside the
sacred Homeric tradition.

Moreover, the blasphemous notion of "no-Helen-inside-Troy" offers
an existential metaphor centuries ahead of its time. As in Kafka's Castle
where no one is really home, or in the well-planned American raid on a
prisoner-of-war camp in North Vietnam (1971) that was found empty
(the prisoners had been moved), or in the recent American invasion of
Iraq to destroy weapons of mass destruction that were not there,
Herodotus is paranoically suggesting that sometimes war may indeed
be about nothing.

According to Herodotus, Homer did in fact know the Egyptian account regarding Helen's whereabouts but clung to the traditional heroic
thinking.

This, then, is the version the Egyptian priests gave me of the story of Helen, and I am inclined to accept it for the following reason: had Helen really been in Troy, she would have been handed over to the Greeks with or without Paris' consent; . . . Priam was not mad enough to be willing to risk his children's lives and the safety of the city simply to let Paris continue to live with Helen. . . . Surely later on, when the Trojans had suffered heavy losses . . . there can be little doubt that, even if Helen had been the wife of Priam the king, he would have given her back to the Greeks. . . . And it was not likely that Hector would put up with his brother's lawless behavior. . . . The fact is, they did not give Helen up because they had not got her; what they told the Greeks was the truth, and I do not hesitate to declare that the re-fusal of the Greeks to believe it came of divine volition in order that their utter destruction might plainly prove to mankind that great sins meet with great punishments at the hands of God. That, at least, is my own belief. (174)

This last point is in keeping with Herodotus's own sincere faith in divine justice, something for which he was often ridiculed in the latter half of the fifth century.

Ironically, Herodotus, after battling Greek xenophobia in his *Histories,* was himself judged to be a foreign curiosity (he was from Asia Minor) and, after several times being denied citizenship in Athens (a prize of utmost importance to the patriotic Herodotus), exiled himself to the Athenian colony at Thurri. Although the Greeks on the streets of Periclean Athens loved to hear Herodotus's tales (Thucydides would be one of these auditors), the West's first historian was criticized during his own time, and in later centuries, for being "ephemeral and showy."

Yet there were others (at the end of the fifth and beginning of the fourth centuries BC) who loved Herodotus for his colorful depictions and simple prose style (Herodotus was influenced by the Hebrew Chronicles), and many were interested in what he had to say about travel abroad. It wasn't until finally the third century BC when, under the influence of empire and swayed by the retrenchment of Epicurean thought, the majority of Greeks finally began to lose interest in the outside world, and Herodotus fell into paranoidic disrepute.

Thucydides (460?–400? BC), from Thrace, believed by many to be the West's greatest ancient historian, was not gloriously paranoic like Herodotus (he also lacked Herodotus's wit and sense of humor), but neither did he buy into Greek paranoidic fears; in fact, he felt great disappointment in the Athenians for their fierce paranoidic aggression during the Melian massacre of 416 BC. Nevertheless, Thucydides did record some of Greece's most profoundly paranoic moments.

Labeled by later critics as "Mr. Common Sense," Thucydides was the first truly secular historian. The opening fifteen chapters of *The Peloponnesian War* review the evolution of Greek society without any trace of mythology. Moreover, throughout the work, Thucydides consistently interprets events in terms of human nature rather than in terms of fate or the will of the gods. But this great historian, who struggled so diligently to give an objective and even-sided account of the epic war between Athens and Sparta, was never popular in his own day. In fact, his account, which ends in 411 BC (not covering the end of the war), was never seriously praised until Roman times.

Most readers believe the greatest parts of Thucydides' *Peloponnesian War* to be the artful speeches. In all probability Thucydides wrote most of the speeches near the end of his life and added them into the text. (This conclusion can be drawn from changes in language patterns.) None of the speeches is more powerful than Pericles' famous Funeral Oration of 431 BC, one of the truly visionary paranoic moments in Western history. For its dauntless anticontentment message, the Funeral Oration is in keeping with Socrates' statement of high classical idealism in Plato's *Apology*: "a man who is good for anything ought not to calculate the chances of living or dying; he ought only to consider whether in doing anything he is doing right or wrong, acting the part of the good man or the bad" (21).

In his speech, Pericles paranoically steps beyond Athenian contentment neurosis and sounds so expansive and idealistic that he actually tells the Athenians (upon the occasion of their first losses in battle with Sparta) to throw "open the city" and let everyone in because, as a great democracy, Athens has no one to fear. All should be welcome, he asserts, to partake of the Athenian political and cultural experience.

Thus, for Pericles, Athens isn't so much a place to be secured as a state of being. In stark contrast to Sparta, Athens cannot be destroyed even if all the buildings are burned to the ground. (It was rumored that Pericles burned down his own house after the speech in order to prove that Athenians had nothing to fear, even if Sparta sacked the city.)

Certainly this is supreme paranoic thinking. For most, though, it is difficult to imagine a city defined by its ideals and spirit rather than by its land and buildings. Of course, Pericles' political objective was to convince the Athenians that such a rarified spirit was worth dying for, especially since it was infinitely superior to the spirit of Sparta, which was antidemocratic and militaristic. (Garry Wills, in his profound *Lincoln at Gettysburg: The Words That Remade America* (1992), brilliantly explains the connections between Pericles' Funeral Oration and Lincoln's Gettysburg Address.)

Pericles reasoned not only that cultural superiority meant there was nothing to fear from Sparta, but that great sacrifice was sometimes necessary in order for such infinite superiority to survive; and that suffering death, as terrible as it was, would bring a new birth of freedom for the city-state.

> Our constitution does not copy the laws of neighboring states; we are rather a pattern to others than imitators ourselves. Its administration favors the many instead of the few; this is why it is called a democracy. If we look to the laws, they afford equal justice to all in their private differences; if to social standing, advancement in public life falls to reputation for capacity, class considerations not being allowed to interfere with merit; nor again does poverty bar the way—if a man is able to serve the state, he is not hindered by the obscurity of his condition. The freedom which we enjoy in our government extends also to our ordinary life. There, far from exercising a jealous surveillance over each other, we do not feel called upon to be angry with our neighbor for doing what he likes, or even to indulge in those injurious looks which cannot fail to be offensive, although they inflict no positive penalty.
>
> . . . If we turn to our military police, there also we differ from our antagonists. We throw open our city to the world, and never by alien acts exclude foreigners from any opportunity of learning or observing, although the eyes of an enemy may occasionally profit by our openness, trusting less in system and policy than to the native spirit of our citizens; while in education, where our rivals from their very cradles by a painful discipline seek after manliness, we live exactly as we please, and yet are just as ready to encounter every legitimate danger.
>
> . . . And it is only the Athenians who, fearless of consequences, confer their benefits not from calculations of expediency, but in the confidence of free men. . . . In short, I say that as a city we are the school of Hellas. (267–69)

Of course, the Athenians could hardly live up to such demanding idealism. The later plague of 431 BC served to weaken their resolve (they blamed the calamity, which took almost one quarter of the Athenians' lives, on foreigners), and paranoidic fears in general—in conjunction with weak political leadership (Pericles died in 429 BC)—fostered an increasing need to intimidate their neighbors, especially under Cleon, in order to prove their own inner stability and worth. Such paranoidic behavior led not only to the Melian massacre of 416 BC but also to the Sicilian military disaster of 413 BC, which marked the beginning of the end for Athens, for its democracy, and for its high paranoic virtue.

Thus, Pericles' speech by no means represents an overall Athenian sensibility, because the Athenians expressed plenty of fears when it came to outsiders and foreign influence. In fact, the earlier pre-Socratic philosophers ran into resistance when they tried to profess their naturalistic views in Athens at a time when religion and divine myth still held sway. And Attic country dwellers in general were considered non-Athenian and the "idiotes" (from which we derive the term "idiot"), because they were unfortunate enough to live outside the culture of the Athenian "polis," or city-state.

The Paranoic Logos

The pre-Socratic natural philosopher Heraclitus (540?–480) was often jeered at and ridiculed when he gave public speeches regarding his elemental and sublime philosophy. Much of the animosity was brought on by Heraclitus himself. Nicknamed the "Dark One" or the "Obscure One," Heraclitus had nothing but spite for the ignorant masses, and even proclaimed that the logos, or spirit of reason, could not be seen by the common people.

Heraclitean philosophy was based on the unity of opposite forces propelling all things (the first Western dialectic), on the supreme element of fire and the universality of flux, and on the ontological claim for "Becoming" (*genetai*) rather than "Being" (*esti*). But his most paranoic stance was the one he took against mythos and the divine tradition. Heraclitus believed that, through "logos," one was capable of wisdom and divinity on one's own. Such an iconoclastic belief ensured—never mind the fact that Heraclitus was not a "nice guy"—his ostracism in the pre-Socratic Greek world.

Born in Ephesus (on the coast of modern Turkey), the misanthropic Heraclitus gave up his wealth and royal family inheritance to "teach the world" about logos. One of his most famous appearances was at the sixty-ninth Olympiad (504 BC), where historical rumor has it that the public cast stones (and dogs barked wildly) at Heraclitus for repeatedly trying to interrupt the Olympics in order to preach his off-track philosophy. Good and evil were just two sides of the same coin for Heraclitus, and the wise man should recognize this paradox with a sense of calm freedom and strive to know the logos that exists above the ceaseless fire of the universe.

Heraclitus's most splendid paranoic concept, however, was his insistence that an individual should dedicate his life to the conviction of his ideals, even if it should mean poverty and pain, rather than drift along with the motions of circumstance—"Even sleepers are workers and collaborators in what goes on in the universe" (Frag. 124). His belief that the actions of a superior individual could affect the entire universe actually brings his philosophy very close to that of Nietzsche and Hegel. In fact, it is only through a kind of Nietzschean lens that one can make sense of Heraclitus's most obscure and paradoxical statement, "the way up and the way down are one and the same" (Frag. 108), even though he believed that the way upward is better. That is, the superior individual (similar to Nietzsche's Übermensch), through pure will, can actually compel transcendence and achieve "being" in the logos.

Elision of the Classical Paranoic

At the end of the so-called Golden Age (460–430 BC) of classical Greece, Euripides (480?–406 BC) would also earn the nickname the "Dark One." The last of the three great tragic playwrights (the other two being Aeschylus and Sophocles), Euripides was vastly misunderstood and eventually ostracized. (Aristotle didn't like him because he was too pessimistic and unconventional.)

Euripides' *Electra* (413 BC), an irreverent and brilliant reaction to Sophocles' lofty version of the famous story of family curse and murder (in the house of Atreus), presents characters who are shockingly earthy and flawed. This "dressing down" of the wife and children of Agamemnon (Electra herself is unbathed, nasty, and melodramatic) enables Euripides to present some startlingly paranoic moments, such as Clytemnestra's speech to Electra justifying her murder of Agamemnon (because he had sacrificed and killed their daughter Iphigenia in order to win the necessary winds to sail the Greek army to Troy).

Clytemnestra's speech, not often noted in classical scholarship, is actually one of the greatest examples of off-track deconstructive thinking in all of classical literature. The passage suggests the influence of cold sophistical thinking during the twilight years of the Peloponnesian War, but its courageous reversal of Western orthodox notions of sexuality and honor and power, delivered in a seemingly offhand manner by Clytemnestra to her distraught and vengeful daughter, not only debunks the sacred Menelaus-Helen myth, but with it the sacred justification for the Trojan War, which had been the watershed moment for all of Greek cultural history. Indeed, Clytemnestra's paranoic statement is still shocking to those who hold onto archaic sexual assumptions.

> Oh, women are fools for sex, deny it I shall not. Since this is in our na-
> ture, when our husbands choose to despise the bed they have, a
> woman is quite willing to imitate her man and find another friend.
> But then the dirty gossip puts us in the spotlight; the guilty ones, the
> men, are never blamed at all. If Menelaus had been raped from home
> on the sly, should I have had to kill Orestes so my sister's husband
> could be rescued? You think your father would have borne it? He
> would have killed me. Then why was it fair for him to kill what be-
> longed to me and not be killed? (ll. 1035–45)

However, it is Euripides' final work, *The Bacchae*, written just after the playwright had exiled himself to the north of Athens in 409 BC, that may be the most masterful paranoic work of all antiquity.

Euripides, who had never won first prize at the dramatic festivals, had experienced a career in complete opposition to the perennial fa-vorite, Sophocles (495–405 BC), who had earned eighteen first prizes. Be-cause of this alienation, Euripides stands in my mind as the West's ar-chetypal "misunderstood artist," a late-fifth-century BC avant-garde writer whose brutal paranoic truths were too much for Greek society to handle. Thus he was destined to become the reprobate.

Euripides penned *The Bacchae* (408? BC) during the bleak years of Athens's final defeat by Sparta. The "Dark One" had witnessed not only the Athenian demise but also the utter insanity of a generation of de-structive war amidst the blatant hypocrisy of political leaders who hubristically claimed to be the exponents of Reason. Indeed, *The Bac-chae* is a precursor to a notion that we would later realize in respect to the Renaissance: that the belief in the ability of the rational mind to ex-plain all things is a form of clinical paranoia ("delusion of grandeur"). Ironically, *The Bacchae* was posthumously performed in Athens in 405 BC and won first prize.

This daringly paranoic play undermines the very dualisms that purportedly rational beings rely upon to map their way into the terra firma of contentment. The play, simply, cannot be landed, and the maddening paradoxes float the reader/viewer right into the ambiguous and mystical blue.

For instance, critics have been unable to decide whether the work is an indictment of reason or of irrationality, whether it champions justice or incomprehensible suffering, whether it is blasphemous or pious, or whether it is the West's first feminist work or just another Greek expression of misogyny.

One thing is certain, though: the high classical virtue of "reason" cannot stand up to the play's Dionysian attack (represented by revelry, liberation, and madness). And women, who, since Homer, had generally been portrayed as peace weavers (Andromache, Penelope, Athena, Circe), have finally been set free of their looms.

Still the play confounds: has Pentheus had his head cut off (by his own mother) because women, not duly controlled, will necessarily be violent and destructive? Or because the suppression of women in a city-state ruled by male rationalists inevitably leads to extreme consequences?

The play also has eschatological implications, as if the action were occurring not just as a parable about the end of the Hellenic period but as a vision of the end of time itself. And the play's ambiguity suggests an amorality that is hard for contentment-seekers to figure out. The notion of madness becomes especially hard to define—who is mad and who is not, who is on track and who is dis-tracted?

Early in the play, Pentheus appears to be a rational young leader understandably upset with all the women for having fled their domestic duties in the city in order to frolic with the "lecherous" Dionysus up in the mountains. Nevertheless, Pentheus is judged, by the wise Tiresias, to be "grievously mad" and "beyond the power of any drug to cure" (ll. 326–27). Yet, by any standard of judgment, Pentheus seems to act prudently in the face of an incomprehensible threat. And it is Tiresias and Cadmus, parading around in fawn skins and ivy crowns, who appear mad. Inexplicably, though, Cadmus states (to Pentheus), "your mind is *distracted* now, and what you think is sheer delirium" (ll. 332–33, emphasis mine).

Such an irony implies that Euripides intended to indict not just the power of reason but also the classical concept of paranoia. Pentheus is distracted with reason, rather than distracted from reason. For this alone, *The Bacchae* is the classical world's single greatest paranoic work, a work written for the sake of individuals who think beside-their-minds.

Euripides' mental repression entails dancing in fawn skins in the mountains and a mother dismembering her son. This is precisely why Aristotle, with all his tools of classicism, could not comprehend *The Bacchae*, a play that seems to give credence to the very forces that attack Aristotle's idea of contentment-being.

In general, all the ancient Greeks suffered in some degree from an inner conflict between the aspiration for rational self-sufficiency and the tyranny of irrational forces (appetite, emotion). This dichotomy was cemented with a strong gender bias blaming women for the irrational forces in the universe. Soon enough, such a bias opened itself to repressive fears that often ended in personal disorder, a condition that the Greeks labeled madness or paranoia.

Moreover, the gender bias itself was irrational in concept, which is why the natural philosopher Empedocles (484–424 BC) could believe that a monstrous birth resulted from the ruling effect of a woman's imagination. If a mother contemplated a monstrous image at the moment of conception, then her child would be left with the same monstrous imprint. (Twenty-three centuries later, the naturalist Erasmus Darwin [father to Charles] would insist that it was the male imagination that, at the moment of conception, could produce a monster.)

Historically, then, the notion of madness has always been based on a priori notions of contentment to which all people must aspire. But these contentment scenarios, as Euripides suggests, may themselves be products of madness.

Pentheus, after dressing in women's clothing and seeing visions of bulls and spinning suns, is judged by Dionysus to be finally sane. Such a radical reversal (madness as sanity) is usually a product of modern cultural sensibility, yet remarkable exceptions can be found in earlier writers such as Euripides and Shakespeare (*King Lear*).

Such abstruse madness makes me think again of Schreber, as well as Empedocles, and how paranoid one can become of individuals who are paranoic; how we glibly declare them to be living dis-tracted lives in order to feel more comfortable within our own lives.

Take Empedocles, the philosopher from Sicily who postulated the four physical realities—fire, air, water, earth—as the roots of all things. Empedocles dedicated his life to unifying the split between Heraclitus

(Becoming) and Parmenides (Being), finally maintaining that reality is one and fixed but in constantly new forms, a "plurality of unchanging entities" motivating the forces of love and strife.

Such a brilliant and versatile thinker—the man who, Aristotle claimed, invented rhetoric; the man who fathered the schools of medicine and nature in Sicily; the man who envisioned a metaphysic wherein all things were capable of being transformed into all other things—is also a man who was capable of throwing himself into a volcano (Mount Etna) to prove that if we dedicate our life to Logos, we will perforce be transformed into gods. (Empedocles inherited this notion from the earlier mystical Greek philosopher Pythagoras.)

Matthew Arnold (1822–88) penned a poem "Empedocles on Etna" (a closet drama), wherein Empedocles' leap results from his despair over being a "slave of thought." In my opinion, however, Empedocles' tragic action was an attempt to turn a brilliant paranoic fantasy into concrete reality. Such a desire seems, historically, to always be the difference between healthy paranoia—that is, paranoic thinking (which has been repressed in the West since the time of the Greeks)—and paranoid psychosis, wherein the "paranoid" takes what his imagination gives him quite literally, and loses the imaginative filament of expansive consciousness.

Daniel Schreber was guilty of this "madness," of turning his fantasies into a literal reality. In other words, it may have been fine for Schreber to "think" that God was transforming him into a woman; an excellent manner, perhaps, in which to gain paranoic insight into the experience of womanliness. But when he literally gave into God's wish, gave into "voluptuousness" (Schreber's word) and became a woman, a psychotic condition took over.

Schreber, a religious man, was able to surrender to his female sexual wishes only after he became convinced that such an action was his moral duty to God and not simply a surrender to carnal desire. Thus Schreber's actions point to a remarkable unison of hedonism and religion. "I entered into peculiar relations with God," Schreber stated in his diary. By surrendering and embracing his transformation, he successfully cultivated his "voluptuousness" into service for the Divine. Conventional morality thus suspended, Schreber was beyond all limits, a position not unlike that which Abraham experienced on top of his mountain with knife in hand.

Greek mythology often portrays wisdom as contingent upon experiencing both maleness and femaleness, which is why Tiresias lived as both a man and a woman. When asked to settle a dispute between Zeus and Hera regarding which gender enjoyed sex more, Tiresias replied that it was many times better for women, whereupon Hera struck him blind (as punishment for his boldness), and Zeus compensated the wise man by giving him the gift of prophetic vision. And this is the same Tiresias who called Pentheus insane for not dressing up in fawn skin and ivy, and who believed that salvation would come to Thebes only by giving in to Dionysian madness.

Schreber, in his diary, maintained that giving into delusions makes one sane. So maybe Schreber and Empedocles achieved a sanity that most of us will never know. However, it is useful to remember that "delusion" comes from the Latin *"deludere,"* meaning "to play with or to mock." It follows, then, that if one is being played with, like Job, by the gods, one shouldn't take the gods' jokes literally. If one does, the divine-human dialectic collapses and one becomes clinically psychotic. Unless, of course, one has the strength and self-sufficiency of Abraham to withstand literally the metaphor of the spirit.

Nevertheless, Schreber, Tiresias, Empedocles, and Abraham raise an important question in the study of paranoia and history: just where does delusion stop and revelation begin? What makes Abraham a prophet and Jesus God, but Empedocles and Schreber insane?

In other words, it seems to be all right to follow paranoic vision in order to acquire glimpses of ultimate truths. But the minute such glimpses are cemented into spiritual facts, you've tried to build solid land over the paranoic blue, and such a fantasy will likely drown you (unless you are Jesus or Abraham).

Thus the contentment fetish is persistent and insidious, even in the midst of visionary experience. We so much want to concretize the "mental" that we dream of castles in the sea.

Western thinkers often made a habit of scheming up great formulas for contentment. Aristotle's focus on earth-firma to avoid dis-tracted thinking and maintain contentment is in clear contrast to Plato's ethereal forms, as if he were saying: "All right, let's stop kidding ourselves. What we really want is to find a way to achieve happiness and maintain it." And thus the story of philosophy after the fourth century BC in Greece becomes largely a series of variations on the theme of contentment, at the expense of paranoic vision.

At least Socrates demanded expansive consciousness in order to grasp absolute virtue, and at least Plato relied upon transcendent vision in order to outline his ideal state of justice. (Plato's mistake, however, was in trying to make it literal, as evidenced by his disastrous attempt to force-form his utopia at Syracuse.) But after Alexander the Great, the expanding world seemed too much of a burden (especially with the empire rising and then falling). Instead of focusing on "being," thinkers chose methodologies that would ensure the safety of the individual's private earth-space amidst the ever-complicated political world.

53

This is why the history of philosophy from Aristotle through the Romans became largely a battlefield between the Epicureans and the Stoics: the former crying, "Retreat, retreat . . . into your garden, into your pocket of controlled happiness (the safest happiness being intellectual, away from the busy world looming beyond your windows)"; and the latter crying, "Endure, endure . . . venture into the world but don't let what you can't change affect your peace of mind; and, no matter what, don't let your emotions destroy you."

The Romans managed to translate stoicism into a far-reaching cultural and moral code that influenced the burgeoning spirit of Christianity, until the barbarians came, quite literally, crashing in. All of which brings us back to Hypatia, the last salient force of Neoplatonism. But she and the mysteries of paranoic thinking were murdered with pottery shards.

Paranoidic thinking, however, would continue to prosper very much as it had under tyrants such as the Roman Tiberius. Indeed, history is filled with countless destructive paranoids who torture millions of others in order to fulfill their psychotic fantasies of contentment.

Meanwhile, paranoic thinking—the sublime power that is both gift and terror—would continue to simmer beneath the surface of Western history. And, from time to time, individuals in brilliant evanescent moments would float out across the serene electrifying waves, like the Romantic poet Samuel Coleridge in "Kubla Khan," wanting to build in the air his "sunny pleasure-dome with caves of ice!"

Because in paranoic places, meaning means more, the soul struggles with gods, and delusions momentarily meld into revelation.

3

Doom, Providence, Accident

Providence

I've been thinking lately about the catacombs. I can nearly imagine them . . . and the Romans dancing overhead. The subterranean Christians hardly listened, though, to the debauched pagan footsteps. Yet they were ever so grateful for the sound of those footsteps, and for general Roman revelry, the salacious tremors convincing them all the more to risk everything for the "greater goal"—by the paranoic eye beheld.

Most would disclaim such a scenario. Because how could the Romans be dancing overhead if the Roman ordinances decreed that interment must occur outside the city limits? The Romans, like the Greeks, didn't much care for human burial; they cremated their dead. Yet they did allow Christian burials to take place, and underground vaults and galleries to be dug, as long as they were beyond the city gates.

What a splendid irony: the pagans, who shared no belief in spiritual transcendence, were willing to abnegate the body to flame and nothingness; while the Christians, whose persecution resulted from their belief in spiritual transcendence, were reluctant to let go of the body's totemic value. Moreover, it seems the early Christians actually needed to conserve bodily relics in order to make their steely reach for the soul.

So even though the catacombs were not built in secret, they were used in secret for a lot of relic-holding. They were also used, of course, for sanctuary from persecution, as well as to encase shrines to saints and martyrs, and as a site for funereal feasts. But just what were, I wonder, the beleaguered Christians feasting upon? Bone and gristle, while the Romans feasted above on ox and lamb?

Built between the first and fifth centuries, twenty to sixty feet deep, catacombs were dug not only in Rome but in Naples and Syracuse and even Alexandria. Amidst the crumbling earth, Christian corpses were conclusively sealed with slabs of marble. Meanwhile, the catacomb walls were painted, early on, with fresco decorations (the beginning of Christian art), and later with various religious subjects.

Even after Christianity was officially recognized in 313, catacomb burials continued because the members of the newly institutionalized church wanted to lie near the martyrs. With the barbarian invasions (the Goths and Saracens), the catacombs were plundered for the bones of the saints, which were believed to be of "real" value, even to those outside the faith. By the late eighth century, most of the remains had been moved to the early churches, and by the eleventh century, the catacombs, filled with dross and rubble, were forgotten.

In the late sixteenth century, the catacombs were "rediscovered." In fact, the elaborate use of candles during Catholic mass became a permanent acknowledgment to earlier catacombic culture.

Such a chronological account makes for some well-ordered history, but it doesn't satisfy without admitting, at least with the inward eye, that—despite the city ordinance—Christians did tunnel under the empire city, and did hear the dancing and orgies overhead, which they didn't mind, because Roman decadence only served to inspire braver acts of paranoic thought. Of course, such evanescent moments would later perish amidst Christian system-building, and lower paranoidic fears would take their place. But for a while there, the early Christians really had it: the pure feeling of paranoic ecstasy.

Then consider the Romans: astride the pantheon of Western civilization, the single arbiters of the paranoia/contentment dialectic. Consider how, despite their political sophistication and impressive socioeconomic control (dancing in the open air of empire whenever they chose), they were still, nevertheless, trapped by their own paranoidic consciousness. Neurotically fearing any desecration of their "controlled world," maintaining absolute allegiance to Caesar's cultural imprimatur, they danced a dance of paranoidic obsession.

But the Christians, trapped in three-foot tunnels and narrow vaults, amidst a culture of ravaging stoicism and rotting flesh, amidst fasting and weeping and prayer (and maybe occasional feasting), for brilliant and soiled moments, would paranoically imagine a way out—not from the catacombs, but out of the constricting paranoia of Rome itself. (How strangely familiar it is to note here that the physically free so often tend to be the mentally compromised, and the physically trapped—the mentally free.)

So the Christians managed to feed their visionary fires and allow their dreamy minds to wax expansive. By believing in their high-risk paranoic ideals, the Christians—who had abandoned the contentment fetish the minute they descended into the earth—remachinated Rome's culture of contentment.

This tendency toward "remachination" actually began in the middle of the first century with Paul, the "Apostle to the Gentiles," who formed his vision of the "Christian Institution" upon crystalline principles of the Roman Empire. Paul—a Jew and a Roman before he was a Christian—imagined paranoically, yet his imaginings resulted in systematizing the Christian world, even though Paul himself operated by spiritual fervor more than systematic thought. In fact, Paul's public relations work seems to have had little to do with Jesus' preaching, or the bewildering but verifiable facts of Jesus' life and death, and more to do with building a powerful church capable of attracting converts.

By religiously and politically consolidating Christian being, by "landing it," so to speak (Paul's heroic travels took him to Damascus, Jerusalem, Tarsus, Antioch, Cyprus, Pamphylia, Derbe, Troas, Philippi, Salonica, Thessaly, Athens, Corinth, Ephesus, Caesarea, Galatia, Phrygia, Rome, and possibly Spain), Paul, perhaps inadvertently, founded a Rome-like Christian empire. By taking the "Law" of the Jews, mixing in the paranoic faith of the Hebrew Christians, and adding the "universalization" principle of the Roman Empire, Paul astutely scripted a Christian strategy that went beyond ethnicity and race, a system based not on Caesar, but on the newly organized (and revealed) Jewish-Christian God.

Indeed, Paul's iconoclastic argument concerning faith's transcendence of "law" and "works" in his Letter to the Romans is wholeheartedly distracted and paranoically brilliant. Paul is willing to risk it all for the sake of faith. This political and theological gesture made it seem as if he were selling out his own people (the Jews) in order to bring in the outsiders (the Gentiles).

> The promise to Abraham and his descendants, that they should inherit the world, did not come through the law but through the righteousness of faith. If it is the adherents of the law who are to be the heirs, faith is null and the promise is void. For the law brings wrath, but where there is no law there is no transgression. That is why it depends on faith, in order that the promise may rest on grace and be guaranteed to all his descendants, not only to the adherents of the

law but also to those who share the faith of Abraham, for he is the father of us all. (4.13–17)

And that's why I want to be with those catacombed Christians. For just one night . . . to get back to that authentic moment. I want to feel their faith transcending their buried and sullied state; I want to hear their feverish voices whispering of imagined systems (based on their nascent notions of the not-yet-formulated Christian metaphysic), in the earthy and rank underground galleries, voices saying—"yes, the realm of eternity must look like this . . . and the Holy Him will be, and God will be, and there will be no more soul-murder then, but only salvation, accompanied by unearthly music, aspiring to Godliness; because eternal suffering and eternal redemption, through the eyes of God, must look like . . . "

So I know it's true. The Romans really did dance over their heads, and the envaulted Christians didn't strain to hear. That's why I believe some of the lost souls still wander there. And as Edgar Allan Poe said, they had better not dally past midnight—lest "their spirit give them up to quiet the cries of the ancients."

Doom and Accident

And they were all doomed—the Romans by their decaying empire, and the Christians by their exfoliating system. The medieval world even had a word for it—"wyrd," early Germanic for a concept that dates back to the Greeks: doomed to the limits of existence. As Athena says to Telemakhos—"though as for death, of course all men must suffer it: the gods may love a man, but they can't help him when cold death comes to lay him on his bier" (*Odyssey,* bk. 3, ll. 252–53). According to Aeschylus, the only recompense was "blind hope" (*Prometheus Bound*), sowed into mortals by Prometheus to stop mortals "from foreseeing doom" (l. 250).

For most, the doom was even dedicated to a particular time and place (inescapable destiny), as when Polyphemus (the Cyclops) groans after Odysseus tricks and blinds him—"Now comes the wyrd upon me, spoken of old" (bk. 9, l. 530). Oftentimes heroes from the Homeric Age were measured precisely by how well they challenged their inescapable fate (Hector and Achilles fall into this category).

The Greek heroes lived in a naturalistic world enshrouded by a naturalistic religion. Simply put, there was nothing beyond the "nature" metaphysic. Even their afterlife in Hades—or, for the lucky ones, the Elysian Fields—was a sort of filmy, low-calorie version of material existence.

Nor did the gods partake of transcendence. They differed in only two ways: they were more powerful and they were immortal. But they existed in the same natural realm and with the same foibles as humans.

Perhaps this is why the ancients so openly accepted the natural limits of their life, whereas the Christians, bargaining on the spiritual beyond, have been historically reluctant to let go of the corporeal. In particular, this is why medieval Christians were so anxious to replace "wyrd" with eternal salvation, to replace doom with Providence. And this is why Paul's "salvation by faith alone" was such a powerful conversion tool among the gentiles. "Law" and "Empire," and even being one of the "chosen," could no longer do the trick; only faith could.

One would think that doing battle with pagan "doom" would be a wash-out once Providence entered the worldscape, because the idea of divine guidance and care for all humans seems to end all gambits. But doom still has its tenacious appeal. Doom always seems so honest in comparison, and even sexy in a melodramatic sort of way, whereas Providence can seem so colorless and clean. That's why most healthy malcontents can't wait to stick their tongue out at it.

As one might expect, the warm hands of Providence debuted as a paranoic concept, lifting people free from paranoidic fears and pain, from earthy slime and death. But once the bargain for a higher state became secure (nudging doom into the surrounding woods), it wasn't long before Providence churned into nothing more than a higher octane form of contentment. The medieval notion of "Providence" is what all the catacombic fussing came to, in the end.

Meanwhile, biding its time . . . waiting patiently behind curtains and portieres, just beyond the timber of burning castles and huts, screened off ever so subtly and unconsciously, the highest truth of all—contingency—quivered beneath the medieval mindscape. Most purveyors of history are reluctant to believe this, though. They are certain the notion of contingency-awareness—first detectable, perhaps, in the writings of the Greek sophists (fifth century BC) and in the Bible's Ecclesiastes (third century BC)—didn't actually float to the surface until the early nineteenth century. But such a view cheats the medieval folks out of their share of existential dread, which follows quickly behind contingency.

As a cultural phenomenon, dread certainly isn't the sole property of moderns. Despite all the medieval notions of Authority and Order and God and Providence, the medievalists knew dread intimately. Caught as they were in the centuries-old battle between doom and Providence, medieval folks were capable, nevertheless, of paranoically floating free; of recognizing the highest principle—that anything can happen anytime; and of considering that the universe just might be ruled by accident. (Consider here the heightened medieval interest in the Greek myth of three blind women weaving human history.)

Accident is the edict of contingency, and accident-consciousness, to a large degree, prejudiced medieval "being" (even though such a concept makes a mess of traditional intellectual history). In fact, it was doom by accident rather than doom by wyrd that medievalists dreaded most. And it was magisterial "Providence" that dangled over their heads promising divine (if inscrutable) justification for universal suffering.

In this manner, medieval existence seemed to sway at times without the least hint of pattern or logic. And some people actually noticed it, their contingency-consciousness surfacing in auspicious ways. Despite the ubiquity of Christian theology in the Middle Ages, people lived amidst great ontological uncertainty and, in salient moments, were capable of seeing life fracture into thin blue accidental veins. That's the paranoic truth.

Serious medieval minds, however, would not allow vulgar "accident" to rule the universe, and, for the most part, these were the religious ones who controlled the direction of the culture. Refusing to recognize such a nebulous and troubling metaphysic as "accident," they exercised control by adumbrating an increasingly austere and inscrutable "Divine."

Beowulf, one of the earliest medieval works in English, lays out the battleground for the forces of doom, Providence, and accident. Usually seen as a threshold text (between paganism and Christianity), *Beowulf* nevertheless has a strong contingency factor. A paranoic eye will reveal how "accident" unsettles the best of the work's dualistic implications— that is, between doom and Providence.

Since it was widely made available in 1851, *Beowulf* has been seen as that "small light" in the darkness of early medievalism. The "light," of course, is Christian, and so it follows that *Beowulf* is seen as the first recorded evidence of humankind lifting itself up from the chaos and pagan shadows of the Dark Ages.

Set in the sixth century but most probably first composed in the late eighth century (the oldest surviving manuscript roughly dating from the end of the tenth century), *Beowulf* was probably composed by a Christian monk living in England, even though it involves the Germanic tribes of Scandinavia. The cultural fiber by which the tribes survived amidst the "dark" world was the same one Homer examines in his *Iliad*—"*comitatus*"; that is, the intense bonding and series of obligations between men (Achilles and Patrocolus, for example). It was comitatus, many argue, that maintained the fragile membrane of civilization from the preclassical world until the Renaissance.

Comitatus in *Beowulf* is best revealed in the obligatory relationships men express inside the mead hall. A bastion of civilization and frail contentment, Hrothgar's mead hall stands in stark contrast to the accidental evil present in the surrounding natural (and supernatural) world, represented by the monster Grendel.

> This gruesome creature was called Grendel, notorious
> prowler of the borderland, ranger of the moors,
> the fen and the fastness; this cursed creature
> lived in a monster's lair for a time
> after the Creator had condemned him
> as one of the seed of Cain—the Everlasting Lord
> avenged Abel's murder. Cain had
> no satisfaction from that feud, but the Creator
> sent him into exile, far from mankind . . .
> In him all evil-doers find their origin,
> monsters and elves and spiteful spirits of the dead,
>
> (ll. 102–15)

Thus, Grendel descends from the archetypal violator of comitatus, Cain; and as an extreme exemplar of exile and anomie, Grendel luxuriates in destroying the life of comitatus within the not-so-secure mead hall. Grendel is evil, and accidental "doom" is his calling card as he comes to ravage the inner sanctum of contentment (the mead hall).

> Grendel came . . .
> and he found there a band of brave warriors,
> well-feasted, fast asleep, dead to worldly sorrow,
> man's sad destiny. At once that hellish monster,
> grim and greedy, brutally cruel,
> started forward and seized thirty thanes
> even as they slept; and then, gloating
> over his plunder, he hurried from the hall,
> made for his lair with all those slain warriors.
>
> (ll. 118–28)

It is fitting, then, that Hrothgar (the leader of the Danes) turns to Providence, in the form of Beowulf, to dispel the terrifying threat of contingency (Grendel)—"I am convinced that Holy God, of His great mercy, has directed him [Beowulf] to us West-Danes and that he means to come to grips with Grendel" (ll. 378–81).

Beowulf accepts the challenge, claiming that "Fate will often spare an undoomed man, if his courage is good" (ll. 565–66). And after he dispenses with Grendel (fighting without a weapon, he rips off Grendel's arm), the narrator concludes, with an unchristian twist:

> ... Death is not easy
> to escape, let him who will attempt it.
> Man must go to the grave that awaits him—
> fate has ordained this for all who have souls,
> children of men, earth's inhabitants—
> and his body, rigid on its clay bed,
> will sleep there after the banquet.
>   (ll. 991–97)

The narrator suggests here that Beowulf's victory does not mean a victory for "Providence," but only a temporary appeasement before the final wyrd.

John Gardner has some wicked fun with the idea of accidental doom in the face of Providence in his brilliant 1971 work *Grendel,* a rather hybrid retelling of the Beowulf story from the monster's point of view. Through his first-person imaginative portrait, Gardner questions the purpose of the heroic quest and ridicules, from an existential perspective, the bloated values of the "hero."

In the world of Gardner's Grendel, wondrous men become nothing more than "pattern-makers," and the world itself becomes pointless precisely because it is ruled by accident. And since men can't handle the brutality of accident, their "shapers" (the poets) create lies. As the dragon says (a fiery nihilist to whom Grendel goes for advice): "What god? Where? ... The principle of process? God as the history of Chance?" (74).

Beowulf hears the same absurdist philosophy from the lips of the dragon; the difference is that he decides that the assertion of "will" is the only solution. Such a "Schopenhauerian" credence re-dresses the entire heroic tradition of honor and pride.

In Gardner's *Grendel,* the nasty medieval epiphany—which Beowulf whispers into Grendel's ear as he kills him—is that all the meaning in the world comes down to one man's will against another's, amidst an existence shaped by accident and chaos. Try plugging such a stark philosophy into the archetypal battle between Hector and Achilles, and all the gambits regarding heroic significance seem to be off.

In this way, the medieval setting does seem to supply important moments of paranoic achievement. But it is not enough to simply accept the veins of accident in the universe; one must "see" differently, "see better," as Shakespeare's King Lear says. Although *King Lear* is a high-Renaissance work, it is set in the medieval period. In the play, the king starts out "paranoidic"—obsessing about a way to quantify his daughters' love and his kingdom—but ends up quite "paranoic." Nearly naked (both literally and figuratively), Lear is able to see in an off-track way unknown to him before:

> Poor naked wretches, wheresoe'er you are,
> That bide the pelting of this pitiless storm,
> How shall your houseless heads and unfed sides,
> Your [loop'd] and window'd raggedness, defend you
> From seasons such as these? O, I have ta'en
> Too little care of this! Take physic, pomp,
> Expose thyself to feel what wretches feel,
> That thou mayst shake the superflux to them,
> And show the heavens more just.
>
> (3.4.28–36)

Such a visionary (and countercultural) statement of faith by Lear, beyond all else, means that individuals do have the "will" to act in significant ways while inside the accidental moment.

In *Sir Gawain and the Green Knight* (late fourteenth century), the synaptic moment happens in precisely this manner; the hero alters the reality of "fact" by seizing upon the accidental nature of existence.

Sir Gawain wanders aimlessly in the woods searching for the Green Chapel in order to confront the Green Knight. Lost and desperate, he whispers a humble prayer and then looks up into the green scenery; just then, the misty woods resolve, and, like a distant viewing of one of Monet's paintings of Chartres, a magnificent castle gradually comes into focus, right out of the graying green, by the paranoic eye beheld.

The implication, of course, is that the castle had been there all along, but Gawain just hadn't been pure enough to see it. The alternate truth, however, is that he hadn't been able to evolve into paranoic consciousness, where the natural and supernatural are apprehended as an ineluctable oneness. Such a scene is medieval culture at its inspirational best.

Dante offers a muffled version of this scenario in his *Divine Comedy* (1320), which urges the reader to forget about "reality" and get to the meaning. This is why it is so easy for Dante to ignore the issue of evil and focus on the hierarchy of sin, because the meaning of evil is inherent within the "fact" of sin. God is inherent, therefore, in the facts of nature; so if you go against nature you go against God (quite a contrast from *Beowulf*, where nature houses the contingency of evil).

Thomas Aquinas (thirteenth century), a great influence upon Dante, shouldered the notion of "fact and meaning as one" to a paranoic extreme when he asserted that "all is good simply because it is." In Aquinas's thinking, only nothingness is evil. Such an assertion triumphs not only Aristotelian inductive thought, but the paradoxical Christian notion of the "Creator God."

A. O. Lovejoy, in his classic work *The Great Chain of Being* (1936), argues conclusively when he asserts that Western history has been greatly conflicted by the Judeo-Christian tradition, which espouses two simultaneous but greatly contradictory notions of God: a Creator God, who finds his perfection and greatness through the infinite creation of the material universe (to get to Him we must therefore embrace the world below); and God the Absolute, whose greatness and perfection comes from the very fact that He is beyond physical reality (to get to Him, we must leave the world of flesh and vegetation and aspire toward the Transcendent).

Lovejoy's "divine" dualism goes a long to explain the intense medieval moral conflict over nature (was it inherently evil or good?). In medieval times, as is generally true in Christian history, the Absolute God usually wins, and with His victory comes a tyranny of conformist thinking. This is one of the reasons Dante has such a difficult time imagining Heaven in his *Paradiso* (another reason being the impossibility of imagining something outside human experience). As he ascends to God's Imperium, Dante is stripped of all ambient desire. Human beings, it seems, become free from desiring anything other than what God desires as they move closer to Him. But "freely" desiring only God's good will spells death to the paranoic. Therefore, once the notion of the "Absolute" became institutionalized, the struggle by those with paranoic vision became more arduous.

Gawain and the Green Knight is a case in point. The church encouraged circulation of this particular romance not because of its visionary quality, but because Gawain successfully fights off three great temptations of the flesh (embodied in the wife of the nobleman with whom he is staying). Many of the medieval romances are paradoxical in this respect; they were dedicated to the Virgin Mary, yet they were often predicated upon incidents of adulterous sex (which the church obviously deemed problematic).

One of the triumphantly paranoic achievements of medieval thinking is the elimination of this spirit/flesh dualism with the notion of a God who actually dreams a dream of material existence, thus enjoining the Absolute and the Creator. In such a vision of the Divine, human lives become dreamy figments; if God forgets about an individual for just one second, he or she exits the dream. "Real reality," in such a paranoic reversal, is God's dream, and reality as we know it is nothing.

Moreover, if God is paranoically dreaming all of existence, then we can assume that He is not overly concerned with human contentment as a goal. In fact, such a fatuous notion would seem absurd. The "contentment goal" is, therefore, our fabrication and, as such, nothing more than a limp fantasy by a being who himself is being dreamed. If we could accept this stark premise, we could eliminate the foolish "contentment" business once and for all, and focus instead on paranoic journeying.

Meanwhile, the overarching medieval fantasy that dreams are reality goes a long way toward explaining medieval dream-vision allegories such as *The Romance of the Rose* (first composed in the mid-thirteenth century). In *Romance,* the poet falls into a dream and narrates his vision of unified being. The poet-hero "really sees" once inside the dream state, confirming not only that dreams are more real than the world of fact, but that mind and value are more important than corporeal existence.

It would take until the modern era to recover such grand paranoic thinking. The Romantic writers, as well as Freud and his followers, would have to work hard to make up for the damage done by Enlightenment thinkers who pretty much determined dream-consciousness to be a waste of time.

Joan as Paranoic

The burden of being post-Enlightenment, as well as post-Romantic, is having to witness the modern elevation of science and politics to the same precarious pedestal as God and Providence. But at least humans continue to "fail better" (Beckett's term) when it comes to controlling things, leaving delicious dream stories emanating from a paranoic consciousness that nearly made it . . .

Like the girl who left her plow in order to lead the armies of France, because voices told her to, from God, asking more than once. And she never wondered why God would trade off neutrality and transcendence in order to forward a French military victory.

From a modern psychological perspective, Joan of Arc looks like a classic paranoid schizophrenic. Such types are always claiming, in their heightened state, that God's voices are barking at them to save this country or that from barbarians or the devil himself before the painful end of the timed world.

The amazing thing about Joan, though, is that she actually carried it out, actually got people to listen and believe. Most paranoid schizophrenics just work their specter territory alone and then fade away. (Except for Abe, or course, who had the chosen one, Isaac, with him on Mount Moriah, watching him sharpen the blade.)

Like Hypatia, Joan was a martyr and a visionary, but the difference is that Hypatia generated her own dis-tracted thinking, whereas Joan believed she was dis-tracted by God. In Joan's vision, God actually chooses sides in the endless war with England, and Joan is his vassal. Her story, concerning nothing less than the liberation of France, has been greatly mythologized over the centuries, and one must hack away at the kitschlike underbrush to get to the root of her paranoic experience.

Born in 1412, Joan heard her famous "voices" for the first time at age thirteen. In the noon moment, after the church bells rang, standing alone in her father's garden . . . voices coming from the direction of the church behind her, accompanied by a thin bright light and perhaps an aroma of garlic and rosemary.

Joan told no one about the voices—even though it was not uncommon during the waning years of the Middle Ages for individuals to claim to hear voices—until her trial in 1431, at which time she asserted that the voice was actually that of Saint Michael.

Her response when asked how she knew it was the voice of Michael is most interesting. "I believed it immediately, and desired to believe it," she said calmly (*Trial of Joan of Arc*, 120). Joan's words were dutifully recorded at her trial, so we have great reliability on this issue.

Thus, Joan never attempted to turn her visionary experience into indisputable fact. Rather, she merely insinuated a rarified connection between belief and paranoic experience.

There has, of course, been much controversy over the years regarding Joan's voices. Were they hallucinations? Was Joan psychotic? Or was she just a dreamy patriotic adolescent with an overactive imagination? Or was it the voice of miracle?

What complicates most explanations is that Joan doesn't fit the mystical or religious-visionary type; she wasn't starving and fasting, nor was she frail and shy. Joan was a healthy, fleshy, full-figured young woman who loved, with great passion, her beloved saints, and who prayed regularly to the Virgin Mary as most "good" girls her age did.

In fact, she later added Saint Catherine (aka Hypatia) and Saint Margaret to her "voices" list. Clearly, their courageous lives as virgins inspired Joan to emulate them. (Virginity is the operative term here, because in the Middle Ages only a virgin could claim revelatory experiences from God. Revelations from a nonvirgin meant that the girl must be under the spell of Satan.)

Joan's testimony suggests that she was quite willing to enter a "distracted state" whereupon she could "will herself to believe." In this sense, the voices were "real." (Such an act of the "will" is reminiscent of Beowulf's triumph of the will over Grendel, amidst a swirling world of contingency.) In Joan's case, victory over England meant summoning a greater power of will after initially welcoming her paranoic fantasies.

Unlike other saints and martyrs, Joan's voices concerned military matters rather than spiritual ones, which makes some people suspicious. However, the medieval Crusades were often predicated upon similar militaristic callings. But this time it was the English—who were often "called" to the Crusades against the "Heathen"—who were themselves the "evil doers" in Joan's paranoic scenario.

Then there is the gender implication: in medieval culture, hearing voices was one of the only ways women could get people to listen to them. Indeed, there were lots of female visionaries in Joan's day, swearing to virginity and God and claiming prophetic accounts of the future. Yet Joan actually got important people to listen and believe.

And she was neither a wild mystic nor a persuasive shaman, but a healthy girl who loved her country, and who paranoically realized—with the melodramatic fervor of which only an adolescent is capable—that over a hundred years of "attempted" liberation from England (1337–

1453) were enough. The resulting message—that she had been chosen by God for a noble mission—is, again, not improbable, since highly sensitive children are often susceptible to the notion that they are special, in their own heroic existence and in their absolute relation to God.

That she succeeded at a good piece of her mission is what makes Joan truly remarkable. She did have her moments of weakness, though, but most people aren't aware of them. In fact, one terrifying incident demonstrates the supreme dangers of paranoic misapprehension.

While Joan was being held for trial—she had been captured on May 23, 1430, during the siege at Margny—she was overcome by a fit of despair and jumped from her prison tower into a dry moat. Knowing that suicide was a mortal sin, Joan still chose it rather than being handed over to the English to be burned at the stake. (She acutely dreaded death by fire.)

Joan admitted later that divine "voices" were telling her not to jump. But evidently she couldn't handle paranoic vision anymore; she wanted out in a sudden and final way. Amazingly, she survived her leap and didn't even have any broken bones.

After her trial, whereupon she had been found guilty for following the voice of Satan and not God, and because she had kept news of her voices secret and never petitioned for the approval of the church, and because she had disobeyed her parents and paraded around the country dressed like a man, Joan still couldn't face burning at the stake even though it had been the fate of her martyred virgin heroes, Catherine and Margaret. So she recanted her story of the voices in order to win over her inquisitors. But they burned her at the stake just the same.

Joan of Arc died by a slow fire that consumed her clothes and skin. The flames were then raked away to expose her body as truly that of woman and to prove that no evil spirit had stolen her away. A grander fire was then built to reduce her to ashes that were scattered across the river Seine in order to prevent any collection of relics.

Joan's heroes, Catherine and Margaret, were later removed from the church calendar, and their very existence greatly doubted. Meanwhile, Joan herself was canonized in 1920.

But the big question remains: why did Dauphin Charles and the kingdom of France listen to her? Was it because she was telling them what they wanted to hear but were afraid to realize? And was heroic Joan that different from other paranoid schizophrenics such as Daniel Paul Schreber, whose visionary experience included a slow and maddening transformation into a women through the process of soul murder, directed by the big Man Himself?

Schreber the Paranoic

But no one listened to poor Schreber until after Freud's article, published in 1911, the year of Schreber's death. And then everyone jumped on Freud's skittish bandwagon and forgot Schreber's own words.

If only they could have met—Joan of Arc and Schreber of Leipzig, the "virgin" and the "voluptuous" one, the saintly young girl and the famous paranoid. They could have traded stories, Joan basing hers on her court transcripts and Schreber on his *Memoirs*.

Joan and Schreber both heard the voices of God and both had their will directed by the wishes of God, and both crossed over—Joan dressing in the clothes of a man to the dismay of nearly all who saw her, and Schreber describing how his body morphed ever-so-subtly into that of a woman.

Schreber's notions of "soul murder," "soul voluptuousness," and torture by a "ceaseless influx of rays" (into his body) make him a sort of medieval soul mate, in close proximity to Joan's late medieval visionary experience and torture by fire.

Joan and Schreber were only trying to find a way out, which for Joan meant a campaign against England's occupation, and for Schreber meant the sheerest journey of all, the one through paranoic madness.

Great fictional characters have made Schreber-like experiences almost fashionable in a high cultural sense: Shakespeare's Lear, several of Dostoyevsky's characters, and, of course, Gogol's Madman. But until Schreber, few individuals had tried, through nonfiction or autobiography, to write the story of their madness while they were actually mad.

One previous case was that of John Perceval (the son of the British prime minister Spencer Perceval), who published his autobiography of paranoid disorder in 1838–40 in two volumes—*A Narrative of the Treatment Experienced by a Gentleman during a State of Mental Derangement: Designed to Explain the Causes and the Nature of Insanity*. Perceval's incarceration lasted three years, and his account includes visions, voices, inner torment, singing, suicide attempts, fascination with bathing, lascivious scenes, persuasion that the end was at hand, hatred for the hypocrisy of his physicians, an urge to wrestle with his keeper, and the love of another man.

Most interesting, however, is Perceval's conclusion that his madness was caused by his loss of the "spirit of Humour," wherein he took God's levity for the gravity of truth. As James Hillman points out in *On Paranoia* (1986), Perceval forgot that the spirit speaks "playfully, ludicrously" (15). Again, the crucial difference between paranoic seeing and paranoid madness may be one's ability to treat visions allusively.

I agree with Hillman when he concludes that God's "Word may be elliptical, parabolic, jesting" (15). Playing with our defining minds, the spirit's speech may become "psychiatrically delusional when heard as truth, command, mission, prophecy" (15). However, such a conclusion doesn't help to explain Jesus, Abraham, and Joan, who had no sense of humor and who embraced their visions quite literally. Apparently, this was fine since, in their cases, according to most people, the vision was "real."

Thus, claiming that the Almighty thinks in the spirit of humor, "a Trickster God . . . playing with Satan over Job" (Hillman, 15), may be necessary therapy for madmen like Perceval and Schreber but will not assuage the madness of "true" visionaries.

Unlike Schreber, Perceval was cured. Afterward, Perceval still heard voices, but he did not heed them "more than I would my own thoughts, or than I would dreams, or the ideas of others" (Perceval, 329). John Nash, the twentieth-century math genius who won the Nobel Prize after experiencing decades of madness, similarly claimed that he wasn't "cured" as much as he eventually trained himself to ignore all the false voices he heard.

But it was Schreber's account, *Memoirs of My Nervous Illness* (1903), sifted through the uneven hands of Freud, which gave rise to the modern jargon of clinical paranoia, the word itself veritably lost from the time of the Greeks until the eighteenth century.

The line between clinically paranoid and visionally paranoic becomes troublesome with Schreber. His *Memoirs,* a definitive text of the psychoanalytical and psychiatric canon, portrays a man who, though gravely "mad," shares much in common with praiseworthy visionaries such as Socrates, Jesus, and Joan of Arc, who purportedly heard voices and whose messianic roles included some degree of gender-bending: Joan dressed like a man, Socrates was a lover of men, and Jesus, who purportedly died a virgin, may not have been, indeed, a "real" man. (For many Christian traditionalists, the notion of sexual equipment connected to Jesus is simply an inappropriate thought.) Moreover, all four welcomed death, with Joan and Schreber attempting suicide, and Socrates and Jesus expiring as willing martyrs.

Like a true visionary, Schreber had a mission, even if it may have been a delusional one. He believed he was meant to redeem the world and return it to a happier state; this would be preceded by the destruction of the earth and Schreber's transformation into a woman ("unmanning," he called it). Once transformed, Schreber would become God's love mate, and they would produce an improved race of people.

Schreber's paranoic system was not only a psychological one but also a metaphysical and theological one. For instance, he believed that the human soul was contained in the nerves of the body, and that all mental life rests upon the excitability of these nerves by external impressions. In God, however, the "nerves are infinite."

Such an extraordinary system makes for a terrific myth, but for Schreber the system was real, and it became especially terrifying during his second incarceration in the asylum (1893–1902), during which he heroically recorded his experience. Even during periods of severe mental disarray, Schreber kept painful notes on tiny scraps of paper, endeavoring to offer a most "scientific account" of his madness and vision.

The crisis began with what Schreber famously called "soul murder." And who was the perpetrator? His sadistic doctor, Flechsig? God himself? Schreber soon settles upon the latter: "Since God entered into nerve-contact with me exclusively, I became in a way of God the only human being, or simply the human being around whom everything turns" (233).

A classic case of paranoid delusion, one might say, because paranoids are always bringing God into the mix and claiming He asked that the world be saved, etcetera, except that Schreber's account is so poetic, so mythical, so asystematically and paranoically splendid.

Schreber believed that God's nerves were trying to commit soul murder by flooding him with language systems—"God readily *understood* the languages of all nations by contact with their nerves" (27). God's nerve-violation occurred through "rays" that penetrated the nerve boundaries, transforming Schreber by making his nerves the most voluptuous in the world. This was followed by God torturing poor Schreber for voluptuously enticing Him into such a transgression.

One undoubtedly wonders why God would do such a thing. But Schreber has an answer for that as well: "*God did not really understand the living human being* and had no need to understand him, because, according to the Order of the World, He dealt only with corpses" (62). Such static knowledge gives Him endless frustration, so He resorts to soul murder. And Schreber, his primary victim, is so singularly voluptuous once transformation begins that God gets all the more tangled up in Schreber's nerves. The patient's conclusion is that the whole thing amounts to a self-deception on God's part.

At this point, one might consider, at least for a moment, if such an exotic moral and metaphysical system was more than just a paranoid delusion. Was Schreber's vision really that different from that of Joan and Jesus, even though their task was to be the messenger of God, whereas Schreber's task was to fight off God's attempt at soul murder? Yet Schreber really did believe that soul murder would end in the reformulation of the world, the same goal for which Joan and Jesus strived. In this sense, Schreber falls into the classic Hebraic-Christian tradition of the hero "wrestling with God." He is like Jacob in the Hebrew Bible, who wrestles with an angel only to find out later that the angel was really God and that he, Jacob, had actually won.

The Jesuit poet Gerard Manley Hopkins wrote some of his most extraordinary poetry on this subject—"That night, that year / Of now done darkness I wretch lay wrestling with (my God!) my God" ("Carrion Comfort," ll. 13–14). And before him, John Donne with his iconoclastic "Batter my heart, three-person'd God" ("Holy Sonnet," no. 171, l.1). And Rainer Maria Rilke, the modern German poet, in his exquisite *Duino Elegies*—"Every angel is terrifying. / And so I hold myself back and swallow the call-note / of my dark sobbing" ("The First Elegy," ll. 7–9)

And Abraham, climbing his mountain, knowing what he had to do, and Jonah fleeing to Tarshish, and Kierkegaard pacing the graying streets of Copenhagen in full dread, and Joan in her stone tower eyeing the dry moat, and Jesus in Gethsemane, kneeling beneath his God, and Schreber telling himself that his personal misfortune with God may lead to mankind "gaining the knowledge of religious truth in much greater measure than possibly could have been achieved in hundreds and thousands of years by means of scientific research" (68).

If Schreber had lived in the Middle Ages, he would have been better understood. Then he could have turned his torturous experience into a poetic dream-vision. Instead, Schreber's book has been nearly forgotten (out of print until just recently), and people have followed instead the man who made Schreber's story famous, the most feverish system-builder of all—Sigmund Freud.

There is no doubt Schreber was mad; all will admit to that. He bellowed at the sun and called it a whore. But his book, written by an extremely intelligent albeit insane legal mind, is nevertheless truly uncanny. Schreber's curious language and frequent neologisms changed autobiography, psychiatry, and psychoanalysis forever. And his *Memoirs* was composed, as Schreber said, "without having publication in mind" (3).

Since Freud's paper on Schreber in 1911, everyone has had their say on Schreber. But most base their "say" on Freud's analysis rather than Schreber's own book. Such disingenuousness is halting, especially when one considers what might have happened if Freud hadn't written his essay. Schreber may have been forgotten altogether, along with his splendid, truly remarkable, paranoic text.

Schreber on God, nerves, and the Soul:

> The human soul is contained in the nerves of the body; about their physical nature I, as a layman, cannot say more than that they are extraordinarily delicate structures—comparable to the finest filaments—and that the total mental life of a human being rests on their excitability by external impressions. (19)

> *every single nerve of intellect represents the total mental individuality of a human being,* that the sum total of recollections is as it were inscribed on each single nerve or intellect; (20; emphasis in original)

> God to start with is only nerve, not body, and akin therefore to the human soul. But unlike the human body, where nerves are present only in limited number, the nerves of God are infinite and eternal. They possess the same qualities as human nerves but in a degree surpassing all human understanding. They have in particular the faculty of transforming themselves into all things of the created world; in this capacity they are called rays; and herein lies the essence of divine creation. (20–21)

This is supreme paranoic myth-making, and, as such, Schreber's writings seem worthy of being categorized with the writings of other world religions.

Schreber on God and the afterlife:

> Regular contact between God and the human souls occurred in the Order of the World only after death. There was no danger for God in

approaching corpses in order to draw their nerves, in which self-awareness was not extinct but quiescent, out of their bodies and up to Himself by the power of the rays, thereby awakening them to new heavenly life; self-awareness returned through the influence of the rays. The new life beyond is the *state of Blessedness* to which the human soul could be raised. . . . Only pure human nerves were of use to God—or if one prefers, in heaven—because it was their destiny to be attached to God Himself and ultimately to become in a sense part of Him as "forecourts of heaven." (24–25)

Schreber on soul murder:

The idea is widespread in the folklore and poetry of all peoples that it is somehow possible to take possession of another person's soul in order to prolong one's life at another soul's expense, or to secure some other advantages which outlast death . . . the wide dissemination of the legend motif of soul murder or soul theft gives food for thought. . . . The voices which talk to me have daily stressed ever since the beginning of my contact with God (mid-March 1894) the fact that the crisis that broke upon the realms of God was caused by somebody having *committed soul murder;* at first Flechsig was named as the instigator of soul murder. (33–34)

The often sadistic Flechsig, Schreber's attending doctor, would naturally be a suspect for the act of soul murder. But later, Schreber understands that it is God himself.

Schreber experiences miracles as well: talking birds and miracles of pain directed against his head, eyes, abdomen, and even coccyx; miracles of being tied to "celestial bodies"; hot and cold miracles; and defecation miracles—

Like everything else in my body, the need to empty myself is also called forth by miracles. . . . This miracle, initiated by the upper God, is repeated every day at least several dozen times. It is connected with the idea which is quite incomprehensible for human beings and can only be explained by God's complete lack of knowledge of the living human being as an organism, that shitting is to a certain extent the final act; that is to say when the miracles produce the urge to shit the goal of destroying my reason is reached, and so the possibility afforded for a final withdrawal of the rays. Trying to trace the origin of this idea one must assume some misunderstanding of the symbolic meaning of the act of defecation, namely that he who entered into a special relationship to divine rays as I have is to a citation extent entitled to shit on all the world. (205)

This last statement, especially the authority to "shit on all the world," may be construed as a delusion of grandeur, or simply a distinguished moment of scatological humor on Schreber's part; or a grand metaphysical insight, or (and most psychologically pedestrian) an anal fixation. From the sky to the gutter and back again, Schreber's paranoic thoughts fly.

Finally, Schreber regarding his sexual conversion:

For more than six years now my body has been filled with these nerves of voluptuousness through the continuous influx of rays or God's nerves. It is therefore hardly surprising that my body is filled through and through with nerves or voluptuousness to an extent which cannot be surpassed even by a female being. . . . as soon as I am alone with God, if I may so express myself, I must continually or at least at certain times, strive to give divine rays the impression of a woman in the height of sexual delight; to achieve this I have to employ all possible means, and have to strain all my intellectual powers and foremost my imagination. (247–49)

What is most splendidly paranoic (and original) about Schreber's psychotic vision is the profound elimination of the body/soul duality. Since, if the soul rests within the nerves and is in a constant state of voluptuousness (phrases like "nerves of voluptuousness" occur throughout), then the soul—counter to most of Western tradition—cannot be metaphysically elsewhere. (However, one variation of this notion can be found in the poetry of Sappho 2,500 years earlier, where the passion of love emanates from the soul, and then reverberates through the body.)

Moreover, God himself is the perpetrator of Schreber's nerve invasion, implying that God's otherness is somehow dependent on the corporeal. In Schreber's words—"God himself must have known of the plan, if indeed He was not the instigator to commit soul murder on me, and to hand over my body in the manner of a female harlot" (66).

Yet Freud missed all of this paranoic beauty and idiosyncratic splendor of Schreber's vision. Rather than meeting Schreber's myth directly, Freud uses Schreber's *Memoirs* to support a theory he already had in mind; that is, that paranoia in males results from unconscious homosexual wishes based on a frustrated longing for the father. Thus, it was simply a poor "father relationship" that caused all of Schreber's problems. In the face of such a flat and generic conclusion, Freud was, of course, quite glad to discover that Schreber's father did submit his children to the sadistic use of experimental gymnasium machines, posture instruments, and other fiendish contraptions.

In reaching his conclusions, Freud reduced Schreber's language and vision—so exotic and paranoic and original—into the paranoidic fear of homosexuality. And, regrettably, Freud's own paranoidic view of Schreber's *Memoirs* became the basis for much of his theory of psychoanalysis, which thousands of followers have carried through the decades. In fact, Freud is a key culprit in limiting paranoia to the realm of the clinical. By obsessing over "abnormal egos" and paranoidic fears, Freud weakened the lifeline to paranoic expansiveness and to the individual's unique exploration, whether maddened or not, into new symbolic orders.

Freud, who never met Schreber, never once defended his theory that Schreber's fantasy about turning into a woman indicated repressed homosexual love for his father. Moreover, if Schreber was a repressed homosexual, one would think that somewhere in his memoirs he would talk about his attraction to men. But he doesn't. And it can't be because he was afraid to mention it, because how could a man who talked of sexual transformation and defecation theory be reluctant to mention homosexual desire? And even though Freud's reading of Schreber now seems simplistic and even silly, most understandings of Schreber still begin and end with Freud.

Freud, however, may have been right about one thing: delusional systems keep the patient "going" and allow him to hold his world together (as was certainly the case with Schreber). But it is a pity that Freud didn't pay more attention to Schreber's paranoic system, because there is a lot of beauty to it and, perhaps for some, a little truth.

For even "healthy individuals" can involve themselves in delusional mythmaking, and Freud's thinking restores dignity to such visionary capability (even though he was thinking only of the "abnormal"). Most people do need to construe what Freud termed "delusional patches" if they want to live up to their paranoic human potential. This is why Freud remains a modern perennial. Indeed, personal myths can become epiphanies of salvation. As Freud appropriately stated, "the delusion is applied like a patch over the place where originally a rent has appeared in the ego's relation to the external world" (*Standard Edition,* vol. 19, "Neurosis and Psychosis," 149).

Ironically, Freud seemed to unconsciously admit to the "normal" need for delusion when he implied that, in the end, his own theory on Schreber's delusions may indeed be delusionary! "It remains for the future to decide whether there is more delusion in my theory . . . or more truth in Schreber's delusion" ("Psycho-Analytic Notes," 154).

Such an astonishing statement on Freud's part implies that he may have felt guilty over his appropriation of Schreber's *Memoirs,* and that he somehow wanted absolution for his delusional opportunism. In fact, his joking statement to Jung—"the wonderful Schreber, who ought to have been made a professor of psychiatry and director of a mental hospital"—proves that Freud had to be aware of his indebtedness to Schreber (*Freud/Jung Letters,* 311). So Daniel Paul Schreber was more than just a famous psychotic; he was a significant author and visionary, and a potential professor of psychiatry, as well a pseudo-medievalist who, centuries out of time, brought a new variation to the medieval progression of doom-Providence-accident.

In Schreber's realm, Providence becomes depraved the moment God himself enters into soul murder. And since Schreber felt his selection to be arbitrary, Providence was no longer redemption from doom, but the accident of doom itself. This scenario is especially true if, as Schreber claims, God knows nothing of humans and their suffering since He deals "only with corpses."

For this splendid reason (among others), I believe Schreber should be considered a seer—a sort of medieval prophet from the early modern period. Moreover, Schreber anticipates postmodern culture with his sympathy for both sexes, a tradition that stretches back to one of the noblest seers in the Western tradition, Tiresias; the difference being, of course, that Tiresias's paranoic seeing is not self-disclosed. Schreber obviously self-discloses. But, more important, post-Schreber, all autobiography and all use of the figure "I" may be seen as a paranoic act.

Vico on the Paranoic Edge

There were other "seers" who seem to complicate the accepted chronology of Western thought: Giambattista Vico (1668–1744), the Italian Enlightenment philosopher and historian, for one. Many consider him the first "modern historian" precisely because he questioned the Enlightenment notion of history comprised of "bright moments." For Vico, history was about the "development" of societies and institutions, not the biography of great men under God's Providence. And he offered strong credence to the fact that "accident" played a considerable role in societal formation, a daring paranoic view that no one had previously entertained.

Moreover, Vico argued that the study of history—absenting the role of Providence—was valid simply because men themselves had created it. By examining languages and cultural myths, the Italian historian played the role of prophet interpreting "patterns."

Similar to the manner in which Schreber was supplanted by Freud, Vico was supplanted by Hegel and is hardly read anymore. I suppose Vico is less radical than Hegel, and less direct. Unlike Hegel, Vico's genius oscillates between vision and retrenchment, between modernity and Old Worldism. Yet Vico's major work, *The New Science* (1725), nearly breaks into the paranoic blue, before Vico's cloying ideas of divinity drag him back to shore.

In *The New Science,* Vico describes, quite originally, how monotheism and Providence sought to eliminate disorder and paranoia, and how history moved from monotheistic theocracy to monarchy and then to democracy, each new system creating the seeds for its own downfall.

But Vico is unable to follow up on his own ideas, unable to let go of his own need for penultimate divinity amidst the flourishing "new science." Thus Vico moves from the paranoic to the paranoidic as he declares a triumph for monotheism in the end, which will mean a triumph for Providence in all things and therefore the triumph of one moral culture and one moral law. A single history for mankind must be recognized, he argues. And suddenly his positing of an "ideal eternal history" seems a lot like Hegel's historically evolving "Absolute Idea."

Yet in *New Science,* Vico's great Enlightenment mind is equally capable of arguing in the other direction; in favor of ancient Hebraic myth, for example. Mixing religion with science (as many thinkers in his day did), Vico maintains that the Tower of Babel deprived human beings of a single language and culture and therefore of any single institution for communicating with God. Splintered into a multiplicity of languages and forms of self-consciousness, each culture formed its own history.

Behind all this disorder is "the ideal of history," the chief object of focus in *New Science,* which, for better or worse, is a story of God's

Providence. Thus, Vico moves from a prophetic modern stance of arguing the importance of studying human language and culture for its own sake (the first thinker since Herodotus to suggest this), to a more traditional position of reading the Providence of God's historical mind.

In the process, Vico maintains, against Descartes, that science can never produce "certainty" because God made the natural world, and humans, as fallen creatures, cannot figure God's purpose. Thus, the only "authentic" knowledge can be of human creations—namely history, the study of which is noble but a second-class endeavor. (Here he anticipates Alexander Pope's notion [1734] that "the proper study of man is man.")

Thus it seems Giambattista Vico built up human beingness only to undermine it. And even though he said it was noble to study the humanities, to throw ourselves into ancient or "other" cultures, to try to re-imagine them through their literatures, it is providential Being that offers the keys to understanding human history, which offers the chance to "get it right."

Quite paradoxically, one can't make sense of Vico's "modern" ideas of history without his rather antiquated medieval notion of divinity. And Vico critics who have tried otherwise have failed. As Mark Lilla's recent book on Vico substantiates, Vico's philosophy of history won't work without its theological framework.

And that's why I admire Vico. In his moments of weakness, he really does seem to believe that beyond all the puffery of historical "Providence" lies the pulsation of chance, as first conceived by the Epicureans in Hellenistic Greece—random atoms colliding, as Democritus earlier argued, swerving by accident to form the structures of nature, and beings. As the Dragon says, "God as the history of chance." Because Vico is of two minds: as much as he believed in *historia* (the classical Greek notion of "reasonable inquiry"), he knew that we needed "fantasia" (his word for imaginative extrapolation) to understand the darkness of the catacombs, the mystery of Hypatia; to resurrect Being.

Walter Pater, the later-nineteenth-century aesthete, crystallized this notion in his exquisite *Imaginary Portraits*: history without the glowing filament of imagination is quite useless and wan. But long before Pater and the earlier Romantics, Vico opened the modern door of paranoic seeing. Inquiry is just fine, Vico seems to be saying, but it is still only inquiry; without fantasia, the past won't live. (Which means that to understand our own past, we must also summon fantasia.)

The Paranoic in Pittsburgh

Like the time I saw Joan myself, and it wasn't that long ago either, at the old cathedral in Pittsburgh . . . her "being" statued right there where the Sacred Heart used to be, just to the left of the main altar.

She was glorious in bronze; on her knees, more massive than you might imagine; big-shouldered, strong-armed, broad-legged. Joan took up more sacred space than should have been allowed, and almost within reach, right in front and just beyond the white marble communion rail.

Nearly pagan with her sword and armor, suppliant and serene; masculine except for her eyes and hair, and the way her head cast upward, like maybe she was expecting death right there, in Pittsburgh, or maybe even Jesus to walk by—Stand up my child, because you are . . .

Her eyes bearing inside, not out, before her God. And underneath, Joan was all prayer and salvation.

A very large man had ordered her there, from Italy, where Joan had been cast in bronze, for him—his diocese and his cathedral, in the still grayish final postwar year of 1961, with the Catholic president and all. The esteemed Bishop John Wright of Pittsburgh, later cardinal and good friend of Pope Paul VI, the man closest to the Holy Him.

I was only seven, but I remember . . . his voice, his words—"I'm bringing Joan to Pittsburgh," he declared before my parents' Sunday dinner. "The great virgin martyr, Christian warrior . . . she will be our patroness, our special means of intercession and salvation."

Bishop in size and word, this three-hundred-pound towering man under the archway before our living room really was there, beyond the paramnesia (Greek word for the mixing of fact and fantasy in the memory).

And if you investigate, you will find that he came to dinner on a Sunday, when my father invited all his priest friends, because "a man doesn't need anyone else, if he knows the priests," my father used to say. Especially the Jesuits . . . In that late-fifties world that was still his, for a while yet, before the great withdrawal, when the priests stopped coming, and Cardinal Wright was sent to Rome, where he would die.

As I sat beneath the archway in our living room, the big man touched me—his overlarge hand on my head, just like the pope does on TV when he blesses someone who's maybe not even saintlike; with clerical smile, always saying things like "so dear, all of God's creatures." The power was with him, the largest man I had ever seen.

"I hear you're learning your Latin," he said. "Maybe sometime you can serve with me, at the cathedral."

And Joan would be there too . . .

So I learned the Latin, even though the Mass would turn to English and my altar boy labors lost, and my chance at the cathedral, too. But he knew that, the big man with bourbon breath and hands like nothing else no matter how holy, in our house just before dinner, my dad and he drinking bourbons held by too many rings too large for one hand . . . all before me and above. And then his warm fingers no longer touching, he smiled down to see—"There was this girl," he said. "St. Joan. You know the story of St. Joan of Arc, don't you?"

"Of course," my father said. "And he's learning his Latin, aren't you, son? He would love the chance."

Because she was coming from Italy, specially made for our cathedral in Pittsburgh, and our great people, for all to love.

And then it was over. His broad voice passing, his dome of hand retreating . . .

Our dog may have barked as he departed because she didn't like men in uniform, even priests, I can always remember that. Or maybe she just didn't like the way he touched my head.

When I was older, my mother, in her eighties, took me to the cathedral to see Joan, because I never really had, during the more than thirty-some years that had passed. I had never spoken the Latin for her, under his hands, in his cathedral.

And the moment I finally saw her I knew that all of Pittsburgh could collapse around her, and she would still be.

It isn't that hard to remember. You just have to watch out for the invidious voodoo, like I read one time about a skinny old man in Central Africa who could make wide-eyed boys so paranoic that they would forget about their past and leap into another realm, by ecstatic trance removed to a gray expansive state, charioted by rank incense and thick smoke.

And the novelist Malcolm Lowry, so sadly brilliant . . . saying something about it in Haiti, unless he was too drunk to remember. Have you really been to Haiti? I would have liked to ask him. But it doesn't matter, because who can understand voodoo?

That's why in the "New World" all the old African deities were transformed into Christian saints, just like they did with Hypatia centuries before. All because some nasty medievalists suffered from so much guilt and

authority they could hardly think themselves free, and then with Renais-
sance hedonism piled right on top so that after a while you could hardly
enjoy yourself, or remember those moments, with all the sad remember-
ing that goes on . . . One more time, one more time, until you think you've
touched everything, or have been touched, maybe by a bishop one time in
your living room before your father.

Which makes me think of Homer and the goddess Folly—"beguiling
us all . . . her feet soft, from walking not on earth but over the heads of
men." Until after a while you can almost remember that, too.

4

Romantic Elisions

In Blake's Garden

There is always that moment in the garden . . . Again and again, across the centuries and cultures, right out of the milky myths.

Like Eve and her crisis moment, with most people believing that she chose poorly. But the serpent wasn't lying; Eve did put on knowledge with her power. It's just that her "knowledge" included a moral sensibility, which has been making people queasy ever since.

And Jesus in Gethsemane, and Joan, dreamily conscious just past the noon moment, with the church bells ringing, hearing voices in her garden in the village of Domremy . . . and William Blake standing at dawn, in his vegetable garden in Felpham, hearing the lark sing and smelling the wild thyme, as his moment opened spatially . . . into the mystic blue. "In Felpham I heard and saw the Visions of Albion" (*Jerusalem*, pl. 38, l. 41).

Like Rousseau crying himself senseless under an oak tree, Blake fell unconscious for a moment in his garden path and recovered to find his wife standing over him:

> Terror struck in the Vale I stood at that immortal sound.
> My bones trembled, I fell outstretch'd upon the path
> A moment, & my Soul return'd into its mortal state
> To Resurrection & Judgment in the Vegetable Body,
> And my sweet Shadow of Delight stood trembling by my side.
> Immediately the Lark mounted with a loud trill from Felpham's Vale,
> And the Wild Thyme from Wimbleton's green and impurpled hills,
> (*Milton*, pl. 42, ll. 24–30)

Blake's trembling moment, described near the end of *Milton—A Poem in Two Books* (1804), actually occurs in a spatial sense throughout the work. In fact, the poem's most profound unorthodoxy is its spatial metaphysic. Blake's prophetic poem unfolds within the window of his "moment in the garden," and readers will only be endlessly frustrated if they attempt a chronological analysis. As imaginative truth, Blake's vision is beyond temporal constructs entirely.

Moreover, Blake claims to have written down only what he saw and not to have "composed" in any conventional sense. (Many people believe the Bible to have been written in the same inspirational manner.) In a letter to his friend Thomas Butts, April 25, 1803, Blake writes (sounding a bit like Schreber)—"I have written the Poem from immediate Dictation . . . without Premeditation & even against my Will." Three months later (July 6) he writes further to Butts—"I may praise it [*Milton*], since I dare not pretend to be any other than the Secretary; the Authors are in Eternity."

Blake's "moment" involves Milton himself entering Blake through his left foot. Plate 21 of the poem describes the immediate aftermath—"All this Vegetable world appear'd on my left Foot as a bright sandal form'd immortal of precious stones & gold. I stooped down & bound it on to walk forward thro' Eternity" (ll. 12–14).

Blake believed Milton to be England's greatest poet, and he believed himself to be Milton's poetic son. His poem, however, endeavors to correct Milton's errors and establish the true vision of paradise lost and regained. In the poem, Milton admits to doctrinal errors (in his epic *Paradise Lost*), such as his stipulation that the pleasure of sex arose from the Fall. For Blake, sexual activity was the expression of energy, which is "Eternal Delight." Salvation, then, must begin through the flesh. For only by an improvement of sensual enjoyment would creation be "consumed, and appear infinite."

According to Blake's friend Crabb Robinson, Blake acknowledged in 1825 that

> [Milton] came to ask a favour of me. He said he had committed an error in his Paradise Lost, which he wanted me to correct, in a poem or picture. . . . I said I had my own duties to perform. . . . He wished me to expose the falsehood of his doctrine, taught in Paradise Lost, that sexual intercourse arose out of the Fall. Now that cannot be, for no good can spring out of evil. (Symons, 325)

Since Milton's puritan nature caused him to paranoidically fear the irrational power of sexuality, he was incapable of connecting that power to inspiration (as Blake did). This shortcoming led Milton to devalue women, whom he blamed for the flames of sexual impulse.

In Blake's *Milton,* after more than a century in Eternity, Milton descends into the Deep to redeem his relationship with his "Sixfold Emanation" (his three wives and three daughters).

> I will go down to self annihilation and eternal death,
> Lest the Last Judgment come & find me unannihilate
> and I be seiz'd & giv'n into the hands of my own Selfhood
> . . . .
> I in my Selfhood am that Satan: I am that Evil One!
> He is my Spectre!
>
> (pl. 14, ll. 22–31)

A multitude of visionary events follows: the painful dividing of his Spectre self, falling through Albion's bosom into time and space, facing opposition from Los, Enitharmon, and Orc, witnessing the creation of humankind through Urizen. The visionary events culminate in Blake's "moment" in his garden in Felpham.

As in all of Blake's myths, the "action" within *Milton* is propelled by a ceaseless clash of dualistic forces ("without Contraries is no progression"). Blake, nevertheless, remains a monist, and in *Milton* he cleverly invents a spatial poetic structure to suggest the simultaneity of existence. Outside logical order, such a metaphysical oneness offers a powerful sense of immediacy.

My aim here is not so much to analyze Blake's *Milton,* but rather to argue that paranoic vision means no elision. For the visionary must offer a fleshy myth, something one can touch and fall in with. That is why it is not enough merely to claim, epiphanically, that "we see into the life of things," as Wordsworth does in his Romantic lyric "Tintern Abbey." True paranoic seeing results in a painted canvas; it discloses what one sees when one sees into the "life of things."

Reading Blake's incomparable myths, one steps into the paranoic blue (leaving the paranoia/contentment dialectic behind), but one never trades off the concrete for the abstract. Although Blake was a great Romantic system-builder, his systems are no allegorical set-ups. By the paranoic eye beheld, his systems are more real than what most people consider everyday real. His characters (Urizen, Los, Oothoon) are as substantial as the people who sit next to you on the bus. In fact, they are more real—"Vision, or Imagination, is a Representation of what Eternally Exists, Really & Unchangeably" (*Last Judgment,* 604).

Blake's visionary poems give us a way of getting there, and that is why his systems are never "fixed," and why he isn't preaching philosophy or religion, but rather a sort of fluid evolution of "seeing" that begins with the corporeal eye rather than with transcendence. "I question not my Corporeal or Vegetative Eye any more than I would Question a Window concerning a Sight: I look thro it & not with it" (*Last Judgment*, 617).

Blake knows that systems must invariably elide away; that his magisterial myths, which are eternally true in the seeing, will be corrected in time (as Blake corrected Milton's).

In an essay accompanying his grand painting of the Last Judgment (this painting, now lost, was said to have measured seven by five feet and to have included a thousand figures), Blake claims that "Vision is seen by the Imaginative Eye of Every one according to the situation he holds."

Thus, as a master system-builder, Blake never suffered separation anxiety. In every moment he would see and build anew, like his hero Los, who, as the tireless blacksmith, works to build Golgonooza, the eternal city of art, and Jerusalem, the eternal city of liberty. (Ironically, it is often Blake's readers who incline toward delineation of his myths, attempting to do to Blake what is most un-Blakean—that is, to map out a fixed world.)

Blake's fluid visionary systems are in some ways quite antithetical to much of Romanticism. In German Romanticism, for instance, the intellectual charm of buoyant speculation was soon replaced with pontification and absolute systematizing, as when Hegel predicted that the world would end with German philosophy, which is an elision of another kind.

How could I accuse the Romantics of elision, one may wonder, when it was they who were the rebellious ones; they who fostered satanic heroes and revolution, who defended the power of imagination over reason, who gave birth to new literary forms, who offered humane possibilities for passion and sentiment, and who urged the dawning of a new creative spirit? Where is the elision in all of that?

Romantic elisions fire in two directions: the Romantics negated customary thinking (inside the paranoia/contentment playing field) and canceled many of the constraints in the eighteenth century for the sake of revolutionary thought and art; yet many of the Romantics also failed at paranoic seeing, eliding from the "moment" into abstractions and absolutism, especially in their notions of love.

With the exception of certain writers (such as Goethe, Blake, Charlotte Smith, Emily Brontë, and various writers of gothic fiction), most

Romantics shunned away from a fleshy confrontation with love's dark blood and passions, and instead heralded love into a universal transcendental power beyond sight and touch. In this way, the concrete romantic love between two people seems to have been consciously and unconsciously elided.

In Wordsworth, for instance, the power of love is the final epiphany in his epic poem *The Prelude.* Yet this "love" is so vague and airy, the epiphany seems nearly vacant. With a nod toward Plato (the master of the intangible), Wordsworth speaks of "love" only as an abstract force or notion, and his canvas remains, in flesh and blood terms, unpainted.

> ... this love by a still higher love
> Be hallowed, love that breathes not without awe;
> Love that adores, but on the knees of prayer,
> By heaven inspired; that frees from chains the soul,
> Bearing in union with the purest, best
> Of earth-born passions ...
> . . . .
> This spiritual love acts not, nor can exist
> Without Imagination, which in truth
> Is but another name for absolute power
> . . . .
> ... from its progress have we drawn
> Faith in life endless, the sustaining thought
> Of human being, Eternity, and God.
> —Imagination having been our theme,
> So also hath that intellectual love,
>
> (bk. 14, ll. 181–207)

Such a notion of love might seem at first thrilling and glorious, but what is it really? Is Wordsworth's "power of love" that different, say, from what Hesiod offers in his *Theogony* (700 BC) when he speaks of Eros as the universal power of desire that allows all things to be drawn into existence?

Because of this Romantic tendency to universalize love (especially in poets like Shelley and Wordsworth), there is rarely anything close to the brutal honesty of Sebastien Chamfort (1740–94), the French epigrammatist who, shortly before committing suicide during the Reign of Terror, described love as it exists in society as nothing but the exchange of two fantasies and the contact of two epidermises.

In a similar manner to the way in which eighteenth-century writers escaped love's viscidities with wit and satire, many of the Romantics escaped through ringing notions of transcendence. And the man who seemed to frame it all—the great exponent of the Enlightenment and the Father of Romanticism, Jean-Jacques Rousseau—suffered a lifelong split between the ideal and real aspects of love, between Mademoiselle Vulson (an older woman who supported his work and who was his intermittent lover) and Therese Le Vasseur (a servant by whom he had five children, all consigned to a home for foundlings). Such a split increased an already bipolar pathology that afflicted Rousseau his entire life. (He talks about this openly, and perhaps honestly at times, in his *Confessions.*)

But at least the Romantics were not seduced by the ruse of contentment. For most of them, that fetish elided away. Unlike the literature of the previous age, the works of Goethe, Rousseau, Blake, Coleridge, Wollstonecraft, Mary Shelley, and Emily Brontë never give contentment the time of thought. Something else beckoned, paranoic and beyond.

Wuthering Heights, the astonishing 1847 novel by Emily Brontë, is so supremely paranoic that no reader can ever quite "get it." Like the Bible and much of Blake's poetry, *Wuthering Heights* is ultimately mystical and elusive. No hook can capture it, no theory can contain it.

Moreover, the two protagonists, Heathcliff and Catherine, are not the least interested in the social or ethical notions of love wherein happiness reigns triumphant. Instead, the "love" connection between them seems primal, nearly incestuous, and demonic. With Heathcliff and Catherine, all of the polarities of love—animism and animalism, the spiritual and the physical, the Apollonian and the Dionysian—are united in a hybrid mystifying manner that can neither be admired nor repeated (as evidenced in the more "normalized" mirror figures of the next generation, Hareton and Cathy).

Trapped in human bodies, Heathcliff and Catherine express a paranoic love that can only be viewed, through a human lens, as overly dramatic and perverse, albeit intense and vital. And because their love exists on an amoral plane, it is necessarily dangerous, which is one reason that the book's two narrators, Nelly and Lockwood, as well as the book's readers, don't know what conclusions to draw. In fact, Brontë herself was probably trying to depict a vision of love that she could only imagine, but not understand.

At the end, the book impossibly unites the polarities of love through a naturalistic conjoining of eros and thanatos (love with death) in the intermingling of Heathcliff and Catherine's decomposing bodies and timeless selves between the open sides of their coffins inside the "quiet earth." Such an erotic mixing after death mystically liberates their earthly spirits.

And that's what the moment in the garden is all about. It has nothing to do with contentment pursuit, and everything to do with imagining the abstract and concrete in new and brilliant paranoic unities. That's why most people fail at having their "moment." They are expecting something else, within time's nasty exigencies, and miss their chance. Eventually, by unconscious will, they invent their "moment," culled from muddled memories and unreliable intentions. They convince themselves they've "been there."

And what about my "moment," one may ask . . . Maybe I never had it. Or perhaps I invented it in order to eliminate the paranoia/contentment dialectic once and for all, to prove to myself that paranoic seeing is really something.

In Kilkenny's Garden

In my moment there wasn't any lark singing, which Blake heard, and which Aristophanes claims was there at the Beginning, just as Chaos and Night closed in, its song of inspiration intervening and bringing order and light to all existence; the lark, the oldest of things, Aristophanes says, sang amidst the ancient forces.

No, there wasn't any lark for me when I was feeling lost inside Ireland's Kilkenny. I may have heard a dog barking, though, faint and nearly indistinguishable inside the fog and twilight as I wandered the famous castle grounds and strolled under the ancient cypress trees that stood along the River Nore. It was almost a garden there, under the thick branches and the closing canopy of night, with the diabolical fog thick as rain, and nearly as insipid.

In my paranoic aloneness I considered, for no consequential reason, that maybe I was at this place—in this moment—because He was going to communicate with me, on the castle grounds of Kilkenny where one could hardly see. He was going to indicate some important words that I didn't want to recognize because I didn't want to know if He existed, since then I would have to spend the rest of my life explaining.

And so I cursed Lehman Lemahn, the old man I had met by accident earlier over breakfast at the guest house where I was staying; cursed him even though he was the Doorkeeper to the Pope, the man just below the

Holy Him; Lehman Lemahn . . . fleshless looking, droop-headed, in a too-large old wrinkled suit and wearing glasses that kept slipping down his nose as he talked, or whispered rather, telling me of his two identities—Lehman in Germany and Lemahn in Holland, and his home on the border somewhere in between. I cursed myself, too, for telling him I was interested in philosophy because otherwise he never would have made me follow him back to his room where the faded charts and colored maps were taped to his walls, and a mess of books on the bed (I recognized two of them as Teilhard de Chardin's The Phenomenon of Man *and a little blue book—*Our Lady of Fatima*), and a large worn-out leather satchel stuffed with files and clippings from which he pulled various papers of identification to prove to me that he really did work as Doorkeeper to Pope Paul VI, and that he really was on holy assignment to do eschatological research on uniting all of the world's doomsday scenarios into one magnum opus, so that the pope could deliver an encyclical on doom. Lehman Lemahn's doom-point was calculated based on a corrected date for Christ's birth, and marked on the time chart by a symbol I didn't recognize but which seemed vaguely familiar; and his words never sounded passionate but only calm and methodical, the weak-looking man whispering instead of talking for a reason I didn't understand, with a breath that smelled like sour lumber which I never would forget; making me listen like the wedding guest in Coleridge's poem "The Ancient Mariner," who "cannot choose but hear" the supernatural tale of trespass and redemption told by the world-worn old mariner; every now and then my eyes wandering upward to stare again at Lehman Lemahn's chronologically calculated doom-point in a year I didn't want to know about.*

After leaving his room, I avoided Lehman Lemahn for the rest of the day, which is how I found myself strolling the famous castle grounds in Kilkenny as the dusk and fog settled in, the sky turning chalky and then brownish-gray, and the castle itself seeming to lose dimension, its silvery mass somehow unreal, like in an old movie.

For a moment I thought it was raining and considered turning back to the guest house and risk seeing Lehman Lemahn, but it was only the fog; so I continued along the path between the line of trees and the River Nore, the castle appearing between the interstices every time I turned back to check on it.

The mist seemed to fall like rain, just like Democritus said, all the tiny atoms raining downward, from the beginning of time which had no father; all things determined by accident, by motion of the immeasurable small bodies downward . . . we are not free, unless, if Epicurus is correct, we can will the particles to swerve. I remembered all of that, which helps to explain the sudden rush of things until after a while you hardly notice it, like gravity.

But Lehman Lemahn was still with me; tingling at my hands and skin. I pulled my room key out of my pocket and thought about throwing it into the river, that way I wouldn't be able to go back to the guest house. But I never do things like that. Instead, I used the key to carve my initials into a tree, shaping the cork-like bark until the three letters appeared as I willed them. When I finished I wiped the key on my pants and put it back in my pocket.

Nearly inside my "moment," under the cypress trees and castle fog, I actually prayed for a miracle not to happen; it was a twisted prayer.

And no message followed.

Maybe He had listened, and decided not to show Himself, and "no message" was the message; "notmoment" the moment; which is why I was glad I had carved my initials into the tree, just to prove that I was there, and had nearly seen, before my elision . . .

In my weakness, I considered the epiphany to be the fact that there was no epiphany. And then I noticed that I was shivering, and probably had been for quite a while. I didn't think it got that cold in Kilkenny.

Amidst the dark chill, the recessive castle depressed me in a way I had never felt before, which made me wonder if maybe I had lost hold of the strands of time while inside the garden of Kilkenny.

Had I entered paranoic being and translated it otherwise? Had my moment opened, and had I been afraid to enter?

It was raining after all (the fog had been a lie). I noticed it while running across the damp lawn, hearing the faraway sound of the dogs which seemed almost like voices, beyond the God Knows Whom . . .

Lehman Lemahn was gone by the time I got up the next morning, and a year and half later Pope Paul VI would be dead, in August 1978, before ever delivering any encyclical on doom, which made me wonder if Lehman Lemahn and his charts and books had ever existed. But I did see him, I did smell his voice.

When I returned to the castle grounds twenty years later, I couldn't find my initials, and none of the trees resembled the ones I remembered. In fact, everything was out of place; the entire park seemed reconstituted. Tourists were strolling in groups, picnickers and children sat playing games, and a young man lay feeling up his girlfriend beneath a tree.

This was no place for paranoic seeing, I decided. My "moment" could never have happened here. And I had never carved my initials, or sensed the doom of Him upon me, amidst the arching trees and dark river and spreading gray lawn.

Unless I am still inside it, across all the years . . . and that's why I can't go back to see.

High Paranoic Romanticism

In 1766, Jean-Jacques Rousseau traveled to England at the invitation of the philosopher David Hume, and there he began work on his *Confessions*. Paranoia was thick with him during those years, and after a short while Rousseau believed that Hume, like many of his erstwhile friends, was in conspiracy against him. So he returned to France where the *Confessions* was completed in 1770 (though not published until 1780, two years after Rousseau's death).

In Paris in 1775, Rousseau—convinced that everyone was against him—tried to sneak part of his manuscript onto the altar at Notre Dame (so it could be received by God Himself). An iron gate prohibited his entry, however, and Rousseau concluded "even God is against me."

Simmering beneath this latent paranoia, of course, was a man wondering at his own misery, but also a man who had dedicated his life to repudiating contentment scenarios. Despite his periodic bouts of sybaritic behavior in Paris, Rousseau never wavered when it came to his soul: it belonged in the paranoic blue. Meanwhile, his wistfulness for the ordinary never ceased.

> I should have passed a peaceful and quiet life, such as my disposition required, in the bosom of my religion, my country, my family, and my friends, in the monotony of a profession that suited my taste, and in a society after my own heart. I should have been a good Christian, a good citizen, a good father of a family, a good friend, a good workman, a good man in every relation of life. I should have loved my position in life, perhaps honored it; and, having spent a life—simple, indeed, and obscure, but calm and serene—I should have died peacefully in the bosom of my family. Though, doubtless, soon forgotten, I should at least have been regretted as long as anyone remembered me.
>
> Instead of that—what picture am I going to draw? Let us not anticipate the sorrows of my life; I shall occupy my readers more than enough with this melancholy subject. (*Confessions*, 43–44)

In this greatest of "should have" passages, from the end of book 1 of the *Confessions,* Rousseau reveals a self-reflexive narrator questioning his life with simultaneous cynicism and sincerity. Moreover, the passage defines a Romantic archetypal polarity that largely defines modern existence: in the choice between contentment and creative (paranoic) being, which will we embrace?

And should we believe Rousseau? Would he really have given up his dark life of genius, his authorship of astonishingly original works in social and political theory, in education and autobiography, for the sake of a secure and ordinary Christian existence? Conversely, how many people today would be willing to give up their secure existence, their house on the hill, for paranoic journeying?

This is the critical question handed down to us by the Romantics: how much contentment turf are we willing to sacrifice, and would we double back on ourselves, like Rousseau, and undermine our choice of being?

William Blake (1757–1827) believed that he forfeited his chance for success on the world stage in order to illuminate his maddening myths. From inside his house, and with the assistance of his wife, Catherine, Blake employed an original engraving process that he claimed had been whispered to him by his brother Robert after Robert's death.

In his early years, though, Blake doubted himself, as he admitted to his friend George Cumberland in his letter of July 2, 1800—"I myself remember when I thought my pursuit of Art a kind of criminal dissipation & neglect of the main chance, which I hid my face for not being able to abandon as a Passion which is forbidden by Law & Religion, but now it appears to be Law & Gospel too, at least I hear so from friends." Paranoically committed, Blake wasn't interested in the world's contentment prescriptions (and neither was the world ready for Blake's visions).

Seventeen years later, heavy under the influence of Rousseau, Mary Shelley (at the age of twenty) published her remarkable novel *Frankenstein.* Like Blake and Rousseau, Mary Shelley felt the need to apologize for her off-track (paranoic) writings, which is why she called her novel a "work of fantasy" in her 1817 preface. And in her introduction to the 1831 edition, she willingly entertained the so-called problem of "how I, then a young girl, came to think of, and to dilate upon, so very hideous an idea" (5).

As she searched for the source of her artistic inspiration, Mary landed on the influence of her parents, William Godwin and Mary Wollstonecraft, "two persons of distinguished literary celebrity." She also admitted to a childhood love of scribbling stories and a "dearer pleasure than this, which was the formation of castles in the air—the indulging in waking dreams. . . . My dreams were at once more fantastic and agreeable than my writings" (5).

Twenty years earlier Coleridge had broken through literary tradition in "Kubla Khan," a poem drawn from a dream (an artistic choice not practiced since the Middle Ages). Yet he backed away from actually calling his idiosyncratic work a poem by adding the subtitle "A Vision in a Dream. A Fragment."

In Shelley's *Frankenstein*, the dream vision enters fully into the nightmare pages of modern literature, and, like Blake and Schreber, Mary Shelley admits that she didn't so much write the novel as see it and record it:

> When I placed my head on my pillow, I did not sleep, nor could I be said to think. My imagination, unbidden, possessed and guided me, gifting the successive images that arose in my mind with a vividness far beyond the usual bounds of reverie. I saw—with shut eyes, but acute mental vision—I saw the pale student of unhallowed arts kneeling beside the thing he had put together. I saw the hideous phantasm of a man stretched out, and then, on the working of some powerful engine; show signs of life, and stir with an uneasy, half vital motion . . .
>
> He sleeps; but he is awakened; he opens his eyes; behold the horrid thing stands at his bedside, opening his curtains, and looking on him with yellow, watery, but speculative eyes. (9)

The novel's protagonist, Victor Frankenstein, suffers a Rousseau-like polarity: he is conflicted by his extrinsic goals of contentment and his intrinsic attraction to unholy creativity. This division is represented geographically through the dualistic worlds of Geneva and Ingolstadt.

In Geneva (Rousseau's home city), Victor has everything Rousseau pined for—a Christian life, security, family, a virtuous wife, domestication, health, "approved" social intercourse—while in Ingolstadt, everything is antithetical: unbridled creativity, loneliness, disease, flirtation with evil and amorality. His creation of the monster, then, predicated as it is upon the free consciousness he experiences in Ingolstadt, is a paranoic act, while the later creation of the second "companion" monster is a paranoidic act, since it is predicated on Victor's fears for his family's safety.

In truth, Victor is bored by the domestic amiability of Geneva and excited by his dark work at Ingolstadt. For this he is punished with a mysterious illness and mental breakdowns that only the purifying qualities of nature will cure. (Ironically, nature is also the source of his monster, suggesting that nature, too, is ambiguous, both beneficent and malicious.)

Victor's polarity is most profound, however, in his relationships with Elizabeth and the monster. His apparent attitudes are rarely born out by his actual behavior to them. He seems committed to Elizabeth and her world, yet he frequently acts in accord with the world of the monster.

From a biographical perspective, the novel's ambiguities may result from divisions within Mary Shelley herself. And it is certainly not surprising that a nineteenth-century novel dealing with self-division would be penned by a woman. Nevertheless, the book's polarity is a universal one (one that most people try to mediate). Fittingly, the novel actually begins and ends at the North Pole and concludes with an image of fire and ice.

In Freudian terms, the book is a battle between the conscious and the unconscious; in philosophic terms, a battle between Rousseau and Nietzsche. Since Nietzsche would not even be born for another twenty-eight years, the novel is astoundingly prophetic. In fact, Mary Shelley not only anticipates Nietzsche's thinking, but her monster is one of the purest literary examples of the Übermensch (Nietzsche's Superman): the monster comes from beneath the earth and out of primordial time; he is born large (over eight feet) but is extremely quick and agile; he is an "individual" in the fullest sense—resourceful and intelligent; he is free from the whole context of guilt and morality (indeed, he is born with an amoral consciousness), and he speaks from an ethical orientation that has nothing to do with civilized life—"Evil henceforth became my good."

All these conditions are in keeping with Nietzsche's "transvaluation of values" wherein "so-called evil" becomes good, and wherein the values of the West become merely the revenge-thinking of resentful slaves and weaklings.

Slave, I before reasoned with you, but you have proved yourself unworthy of my condescension. Remember that I have power; you believe yourself miserable, but I can make you so wretched that the light of day will be hateful to you. You are my creator, but I am your master;—obey! (167)

In terms of the perplexing moral-aesthetic question the book forces—namely, is the monster ugly because he's evil, or evil because he's ugly?—one needs Nietzsche to feel satisfied. In a Nietzschean sense, the monster appears ugly because his freedom, nonconformity, and primal urges are a threat to slave consciousness. Thus the monster defies what Nietzsche terms "slave morality," which is also the morality of the culture of contentment.

At the novel's end, the monster, free and strong, makes his way to the North Pole, a place that epitomizes the harsh and cruel face of nature that Nietzsche believed in, rather than the beautiful and serene face of nature to which Rousseau and Wordsworth subscribed.

Overall, the sections of the novel when the monster is not present seem "enervating," to use Mary's word. This is why, from a literary standpoint, the monster's sections are the best parts, not unlike the Satan sections of Milton's *Paradise Lost*. (Blake claimed that "Milton wrote in fetters when he wrote of Angels & God, and at liberty when of Devils & Hell, because he was a true Poet and of the Devil's party without knowing it" [*Heaven and Hell*, pl. 5].)

Quite fittingly, the monster's self-education includes a careful reading of *Paradise Lost*, along with *Plutarch's Lives* and *The Sorrows of Young Werther*, which produced an "infinity of new images and feelings that sometimes raised me to ecstasy, but more frequently sunk me into the lowest dejection" (128). In Werther, in particular, he finds a character who contained "no pretension," and whose extinction caused him to weep.

Written more than forty years before *Frankenstein*, Goethe's *The Sorrows of Young Werther* immediately gained world notoriety. The book was translated into a multitude of languages, and people everywhere aped Werther's dress, ideas, and even his melodramatic suicide (carried out in countries as far away as China). *Werther* was actually banned in Italy, and for years Goethe had to travel incognito. He regretted his reputation as "the man who wrote *Werther*," and I expect he cursed the fact that his paranoic vision had become transmuted (by portions of the frenzied public) into a perverse solution to the tyranny of the culture of contentment. The misappropriation of Werther's hypersensitive being included the gnashing of teeth, throwing oneself at the feet of one's lover in tears and trembling kissing, and, in extreme cases, self-immolation.

Nevertheless, *The Sorrows of Young Werther* is much more than a wildly celebrated "period piece" from the Age of Sensibility. A great psychological achievement and a milestone in the development of Romanticism (a clear affront to eighteenth-century rationalism), Goethe's *Werther* introduces the possibility of living an intense emotional life amidst nature, even if such a life leads to paramount moments of self-torture and doom. If Victor Frankenstein acted dangerously on his paranoic urges, then Werther felt his paranoic dizziness coming on and collapsed in the face of it. Contrasted to this paranoic experience, of course, is Werther's "other" life back in town where he struggled paranoidically against a numbing bureaucracy and vapid aristocracy.

Perhaps most important, though, is the crucial role *Werther* plays in the evolution of the idea of modern love. Rather than being shunted into the realm of abstraction, love plays itself out on a complex canvas and includes a mixture of aesthetic, sexual, platonic, spiritual, moral, emotional, and psychological tones.

Indeed, *Werther* is high paranoic Romanticism at its finest. No elision here. Goethe's canvas of love is set before the modern world for embarrassing and ineluctable recognition. And even though Goethe claimed that he didn't intend to portray extreme emotionalism as a desirable way of life, he did admit to wanting to find a new way to talk about the spiritualization of love; he did want to paint a youth drawn passionately to nature and to love, a youth open to all impressions and cashing in on the "living moment."

What Goethe didn't realize, at least to the full extent, was the important role Werther played in validating a new "irrationalism" predicated upon fresh relationships to art, nature, love, death, and eternity. This new combustible mix of "being" had the potential to explode Rousseau's polarity problem. Speaking through his fragile protagonist, Goethe actually re-machinates the polarity into a positive Romantic vitalism and paranoic energy, which would later be championed by Blake, Coleridge, Shelley, and Hazlitt (among others).

> That the life of man is only a dream has already occurred to many, and I also am always haunted by this feeling. When I see the restrictions by which the active, speculative powers of man are hemmed in, when I see how all activity is directed toward the satisfaction of needs which themselves have no other purpose than to prolong our wretched existence, and that the only way to meet certain speculations is by a dreamy resignation, in which we paint the walls of our prison with colored figures and bright prospects—all this . . . makes

me dumb. I turn in upon myself and find a world! But again more with presentiment and obscure craving than plastic power and vital force. Everything seems before my senses and I continue on my way through the world with a dreamy smile. (*Werther,* pt. 1, letter of May 22)

For Blake, "energy" is always good (a concept that would later be part of Nietzsche's thinking). But such a view can seem problematic, especially when people question the "energy" that leads to aggression and suffering. Blake's paranoic answer: evil results from "misdirected" energy, which is why even "the cut worm forgives the plow."

In just twelve lines, Blake's poem "The Clod and the Pebble" (from *Songs of Experience,* 1794) deals with love's central polarity—selfishness versus selflessness, as well as with the moral ambiguity that results from such divided energies.

"Love seeketh not Itself to please,
"Nor for itself hath any care,
"But for another gives its ease,
"And builds a Heaven in Hell's despair."

So sang a little Clod of Clay
Trodden with the cattle's feet,
But a Pebble of the brook
Warbled out these metres meet:

"Love seeketh only Self to please,
"To bind another to Its delight,
"Joys in another's loss of ease,
"And builds a Hell in Heaven's despite."
(211)

Standard moralistic interpretations of this gemlike poem focus on the clod of clay and stipulate that the course of "true love" must be selfless giving, symbolized by the clay that allows itself to be trodden for the sake of another's survival and contentment. To the clay, "being" means connecting to the surroundings; its modus is cooperation and annihilation of selfhood.

According to this reading, the pebble performs a cautionary function: it warns people of "false love," which tempts with promises of autonomy and power. Appropriately, the pebble is hard and fixed and unto itself, and binds "another to its delight."

The problem with this view is that Blake is not a moralist, and "The Clod and the Pebble," like Blake's other poetry, actually resists such categorical thinking. Moreover, the poem certainly doesn't reveal love's truth by pointing out false love. Rather, the poem, by its very dualism, suspends. (The fact that the pebble's view ends the poem might even point to the opposite interpretation, that the essence of love is selfishness.)

Ultimately, the poem's meaning lies in its literalness: both views are presented, so both views are valid. Moreover, with some dis-tracted thinking (paranoically stepping outside Western morality), one can courageously admit that the poem isn't about morality at all, but about truth. And until we can see the truth about love's paradoxical energies, no good will be achieved.

It may make one uncomfortable to admit it, but possession and self-interest are frequently the goals in even the most heralded relationships. People will often justify marriage by stating that this particular person "makes them happy," or "I need this person," or "I can't live without this person," thus binding another to his or her delight.

This doesn't mean, of course, that we don't have unselfish motivations, that we wouldn't sacrifice ourselves. Someone in love always professes that he/she wants the other's happiness. But would a man finding his wife in adultery ever say, "Go ahead, dear, if it makes you happy"?

Blake simply wants us to admit that, when we profess to love someone, we are also saying that we desire that person for our own. Likewise, it's not so much that we would throw ourselves in front of a train for someone, as challenge the speed of the train in order to have what is ours.

There is no abstraction in this, and no elision. Blake's message of love is fleshy and real, as real as any pebble and clod of clay, by the paranoic eye beheld.

In his *Visions of the Daughters of Albion* (1793), Blake's prophetic work that deals most directly with love's dark desires, we again enter a mythical world that, like *Milton,* is more spatial than temporal. In word and illumination, *Visions* paints timeless images of love, desire, aggression, jealousy, bitterness, and lament. Most poignantly, though, the poem anticipates modern views on female sexual expression.

Oothoon (instinct), the central character in *Visions,* has fallen in love with Theotormon (desire). However, as she freely makes her way toward him through the world of experience, Oothoon is captured and raped by Bromion (reason), who proclaims: "this harlot [is] . . . mine . . . Stampt with my signet" (pl. 1, ll. 18–21). With this depiction of Bromion, Blake

seems to remarkably anticipate the rather recent sociocultural understanding of rape more as an expression of power rather than of sexual
desire. Indeed, Bromion's associations are complex; he stands not only
as the male power of reason controlling female passion but also as a vi-
cious slaveholder and enemy of the abolitionist movement.

After Oothoon is raped by Bromion, she is forsaken by Theotormon.
Trapped in the nets of religious hypocrisy and judgment, Theotormon
can no longer take joy in her, so he chains Oothoon and Bromion back
to back in Bromion's cave. As a sort of eternal tableau, such an image offers more about the dark truth of love and desire than any collection of
Romantic abstractions. Meanwhile, as Theotormon sits and cries over
his loss, Oothoon rejoins:

> And does my Theotormon seek this hypocrite modesty,
> This knowing, artful, secret, fearful, cautious, trembling hypocrite?
> Then is Oothoon a whore indeed! and all the virgin joys
> Of life are harlots, and Theotormon is a sick man's dream,
> And Oothoon is the crafty slave of selfish holiness.
>
> (pl. 6, ll. 16–20)

Typical of Blake's fluid dualisms, the opposing forces in Bromion and
Theotormon seem to mix and then reverse. That is, Bromion starts out
as the power of reason, yet is undone by his own violent desire; Theotormon moves from desire to a figure of cold reason and bitter judgment.

At the end, Oothoon attempts to rise above the paradox in her lament
against a world that restrains love:

> I cry, Love! Love! Love! happy happy Love! free as the mountain wind!
> Can that be Love, that drinks another as a sponge drinks water?
> That clouds with jealousy his nights, with weepings all the day,
> To spin a web of age around him, grey and hoary! dark!
> Till his eyes sicken at the fruit that hangs before his sight.
> Such is self-love that envies all! a creeping skeleton
> With lamplike eyes watching around the frozen marriage bed
>
> Arise you little glancing wings, and sing your infant joy!
> Arise and drink your bliss, for every thing that lives is holy!
> Thus every morning wails Oothoon, but Theotormon sits
> Upon the margind ocean conversing with shadows dire.
> The Daughters of Albion hear her woes, & eccho back her sighs.
>
> (pl. 7, ll. 16–22; pl. 8, ll. 9–13)

Such unelided love is predicated upon energy, immediacy, and instinct, making *Visions of the Daughters of Albion* a fleshy prophecy but also one that is richly allusive. Some readers see it as a complaint against the measured world of reason and restraint, while others see it as an allegory about slavery and the soul of America in chains. Collectively, perhaps, the poem is a prophetic cautionary fable about women who are unable to celebrate life and desire because they are enslaved by male self-love.

This argument seems especially relevant when one considers the publication of Mary Wollstonecraft's *A Vindication of the Rights of Woman* one year earlier (1792). Blake certainly reacts to *Vindication* in *Visions*; the question is, to what degree? (Blake had known Wollstonecraft for some time, having illustrated her children's book *Original Stories from Real Life* in 1788. He was also a good friend of Mary's husband, William Godwin, the political theorist and social thinker.)

In *Vindication,* Mary Wollstonecraft (1759–97) argues that marriage is a legal custom and not a natural custom, and therefore very much like slavery. Britain had outlawed slavery in 1772, but the slave trade was not abolished until 1807. The abolitionist movement was at its height in 1790s England. And, mostly led by women, the movement boycotted products of the slave trade such as sugar.

Wollstonecraft also bemoaned the thousands of prostitutes who nightly roamed the streets of London. For this reason, although a feminist in her time, Wollstonecraft was against the kind of free love that Oothoon expresses in *Visions*. With free love, Wollstonecraft believed, women would only end up pregnant and abandoned—"I cannot discover why . . . females should always be degraded by being made subservient to love or lust" (136). But with marriage, they were little better than slaves. Instead, she wanted women to become "rational agents" who could participate in egalitarian relationships with men.

In this light, Blake's vision of female liberation from sexual modesty and repression seems problematic. But Blake's "correction" upon Wollstonecraft is certainly not a sexist one, as some feminist critics have argued (Anne Mellor, for example). Rather, Blake is simply a different kind of feminist. And he is not so much attacking Wollstonecraft as taking aim at any theology that restrains sexual expression.

Ultimately, both *Visions* and *Vindication* are revolutionary statements outside the bounds of accepted thought, and both avoid elision by paranoically presenting a stirring new canvas on the subject of love and desire. Wollstonecraft would eventually be demonized for her writings and especially for her scandalous and tragic life. Because of the sexual climate of her day, the "incidents" in Mary Wollstonecraft's life—the abuse by her father, her best friend dying in her arms, extramarital relationships, an illegitimate child, two suicide attempts, and an early death (after giving birth to Mary Wollstonecraft Godwin Shelley)—overshadowed her profound achievements in writing and thought.

Meanwhile, Blake, whose poetry was generally unknown, would continue to speak regularly to his visionary characters: Jesus, Gabriel, Socrates, Ezekiel, Milton, and his brother Robert. Blake saw, with his corporeal eye first, the eternal states of "desire" and "selfhood" through which the human soul must pass. He tried to recall that soul from generation and death to the free paranoic glory of imaginative being. But he always stood by the notion that his visions were not transcendent, but built from the flesh outward.

During his three years in Felpham on the south coast of England, Blake encountered the sea for the first time and fed on the energy of that paranoic blue. At Felpham, Blake claimed he had his "first Vision of Light" while sitting at the beach where his wife and sister liked to bathe. At Felpham, he witnessed a fairy funeral one night inside his small vegetable garden enclosed by its low flint wall. And at Felpham, at dawn, he experienced the stupendous mystical vision recorded in *Milton*.

> For when Los join'd with me he took me in his fi'ry whirlwind;
> My Vegetated portion was hurried from Lambeth's shades,
> He set me down in Felpham's Vale and prepar'd a beautiful
> Cottage for me, that in three years I might write all these Visions
> To display Nature's cruel holiness, the deceits of Natural Religion.
> Walking in my Cottage Garden . . .
>
> (pl. 36, ll. 21–26)

Known during his life only as a journeyman engraver, Blake suffered neglect and even ridicule. Yet he labored amidst the antipathy of his epithet and wrote his incorruptible verse. Forgotten for forty years after his death, Blake was reborn in 1863 with the publication of Alexander Gilchrist's biography. And he has been with us ever since, in flesh and in spirit.

As he told his wife one day, "I will never leave you." And he remained true; coming often to visit her after his death, sitting right down in his usual chair for several hours a day and conversing with her.

Critical interest in Blake escalated greatly with the publication, in 1947, of Northrop Frye's trenchant work *Fearful Symmetry,* the first full-scale attempt to understand Blake's symbology and myth, and also a book that used Blake as a general "illustration of the poetic process."

Mary Wollstonecraft suffered neglect as well. In the Victorian era, the notion of her scandalous life was so secure that even writers sympathetic with the women's cause elided away, including John Stuart Mill, who, in his influential work *The Subjection of Women* (1869), failed to mention her even though Wollstonecraft's radical ideas are present throughout his essay. It wasn't until recent decades (with the birth of feminist criticism) that *Vindication* has been recognized as "great," as a feminist work, as social argument, and as literary expression.

In fact, *Vindication* avoids a narrow polemical status precisely because Wollstonecraft's argument for women's rights is predicated upon her social analysis. That is, as members of an oppressed class, women are condemned to lowly vocations—servants, governesses, and nurses; experience a multitude of indignities; and are denied political rights. (As nonpersons in a legal sense, for example, women would lose all their property upon marriage.) Furthermore, it was because they were denied respect and power that women were forced to seek their goals through "coquetry and cunning."

After such an intrepid and paranoic argument, one might expect Wollstonecraft to have backed off (after all, the year was 1792). Instead, she went further and, anticipating Marx and modern sociopolitical theory, claimed that the oppression of women or any social class corrupts the oppressor as much as it distorts the life of the oppressed. (Blake similarly believed that the oppressor loathed the oppressed precisely because the oppressor knew he was dependent upon his control of the oppressed in order to know who he was.) For Wollstonecraft, the situation leads to an astonishing conclusion: an unbalanced social condition prevents both the oppressed and the oppressor from becoming fully human.

Thus Wollstonecraft envisioned without elision. And her "nothing is sacred" approach included even Rousseau. Untouchable and almost a god to Romantic writers, Wollstonecraft subsumed Rousseau into her thought and utilized him positively if it would enhance her argument, and negatively if it would not.

It is farce to call any being virtuous whose virtues do not result from the exercise of its own reason. This was Rousseau's opinion respecting men:

I extend it to women, and confidently assert that they have been drawn out of their sphere by false refinement . . . [and] the illegitimate power, which they obtain, by degrading themselves, is a curse, and they must return to nature and equality. (129)

She even "corrected" Rousseau if that served her needs:

"Educate women like men," Rousseau says, "and the more they resemble our sex the less power will they have over us." This is the very point I aim at. I do not wish them to have power over men; but over themselves. (179)

And she castigated him in one of the greatest "what nonsense" passages in Western literature:

Rousseau declares that a woman should never, for a moment, feel herself independent, that she should be governed by fear to exercise her natural cunning, and made a coquettish slave in order to render her a more alluring object of desire, a sweeter companion to man, whenever he chooses to relax himself. He carries the arguments, which he pretends to draw from the indication of nature, still further, and insinuates that truth and fortitude, the corner stones of all human virtue, should be cultivated with certain restrictions, because, with respect to the female character, obedience is the grand lesson which ought to be impressed with unrelenting rigour.

What nonsense! when will a great man arise with sufficient strength of mind to puff away the fumes which pride and sensuality have thus spread over the subject! If women are by nature inferior to men, their virtues must be the same in quality, if not in degree, or virtue is a relative idea; consequently their conduct should be founded on the same principles, and have the same aim. (134)

But as bold and ingenious as Wollstonecraft could be, it is nevertheless sad that she, of all people, was waiting for "a great man [to] arise" in order for things to change. As political nonpersons, women hadn't the strength to foster change on their own.

At the end of chapter 4, Wollstonecraft returns to the subject of love and again utilizes Rousseau's nature arguments, only in an inverted manner, claiming that the relationship between the sexes shows the "fair defects in nature."

> Women appear to be created not to enjoy the fellowship of man, but to save him from sinking into absolute brutality, by rubbing off the rough angles of his character and by playful dalliance to give some dignity to the appetite that draws him to them. (185)

Like Wordsworth, she turns to God as the ultimate authority on love and human relations:

> —Gracious Creator of the whole human race! hast thou created such a being as woman, who can trace thy wisdom in thy works, and feel that thou alone art by thy nature exalted above her,—for no better purpose?—Can she believe that she was only made to submit to man, her equal, a being, who, like her, was sent into the world to acquire virtue?—Can she consent to be occupied merely to please him; merely to adorn the earth, when her soul is capable of rising to thee?—And can she rest supinely dependent on man for reason, when she ought to mount with him the arduous steeps of knowledge? (185)

Her audacious questioning of God's purpose (in His creation of women) is really a clever repudiation of men's usurpation of God's role in their domination of women. Thus, in her brilliant rhetorical stance, men are guilty of prohibiting women from rising (in Aristotelian fashion) through reason and virtue to God.

Wollstonecraft invokes the concept of "universal love" upon which Wordsworth meditates so abstractly at the end of *The Prelude* (published more than fifty years later). But unlike Wordsworth, her plea for universal love is predicated concretely on the necessary facts of education and social opportunity.

> Yet, if love be the supreme good, let women be only educated to inspire it, and let every charm be polished to intoxicate the senses; but, if they be moral beings, let them have a chance to become intelligent; and let love to man be only a part of that glowing flame of universal love, which after encircling humanity, mounts in grateful incense to God. (185)

This soaring passage echoes Plato's notion of love's two levels, the one fleshy and the other spiritual, as well as Plato's notion of the "ascent" from the first level to the second.

Although Wollstonecraft's rhetorical device of bypassing men in order to plea to God works splendidly, it would result in increased alienation for Wollstonecraft. For such a side-step violated Milton's dictum that women must find their way to God through men; in Eve's case, through God's handler—Adam. "Hee for God only, shee for God in him" (*Paradise Lost*, bk. 4, l. 299).

Thus, Wollstonecraft experienced the clever loneliness of the high paranoic, through all of the pale hallways that tilt into the next dimension.

Cleverness

The German philosopher Friedrich Hegel (1770–1831), a contemporary of William Blake and Mary Wollstonecraft, believed that cleverness resided within the "world soul," and that individuals enter precarious territory when they try to predict the progress of this world soul, which is beyond human ken. According to Hegel, we perpetually face "the cunning of history." Thus, if we ignore history's dialectic we are swept up in it, and if we try to figure the dialectic we inevitably err (except in the rare case of the Hegelian hero who sees correctly, but who remains outcast and misunderstood). One way or the other, then, history, through the world soul, makes individuals serve its purpose.

This is why history's cunning elisions leave most people in a morass of paranoia. And the more clever one thinks one is, the more brutal the slips and turns of history. Then there is the paranoic irony that Hegel's notion of the "cunning of history" may itself be a misreading since history, by his definition, would be too cunning to allow anyone to see it as cunning. Yet, despite such maddening paradoxes, Hegel's paranoic goal is for one to become conscious of the form of life one is involved in, and then attempt to transcend it.

Meanwhile, individual Romantic elisions (away from conformism and constraint) are denied their rebel status in Hegel since, unbeknownst to the Romantic hero, all rebel acts are readily subsumed into the logical dialectic of history.

In Hegel's universal dialectic, as presented in his *Phenomenology of Spirit* (1807), history results from the constant state of "becoming," a synthesis resulting from the conflict between various aspects of being (thesis) and nonbeing (antithesis). This universal process is the logical, active principle of all existence.

In Hegelian terms, the Absolute Idea (the closest proximity to God in Hegel's thinking) moves through the dialectic of history into greater levels of self-knowledge, and the world soul is only part of this developing consciousness (and self consciousness).

From hydrogen to monkeys, then, existence developed as a quest for consciousness, as a story of the primal blind mind evolving "through matter and men," the goal being the Absolute Idea's eventual self-consciousness through the mind of a human being who just happened to be Hegel himself, since it was Hegel who first adumbrated the notion of the Absolute Idea.

Philosophy, therefore, transcends religion for Hegel, since philosophy enables the comprehension of the Absolute Idea through the study of the "history of philosophy," which is no different, in Hegel's mind, from studying the "philosophy of history."

Thus, it is paramount to see the Absolute Idea as not separate from the world (unlike the Good of Plato or the Absolute God of Hebraic-Christian myth). Rather, the Absolute Idea is actually predicated upon the changing reality of the world. In this sense, appearance is reality, and "thought" connects all. Indeed, this is one of Hegel's fundamental similarities to Blake: both men are absolute idealists; for both, "thought" defines reality. Yet for Hegel, this "thought" must be logical, while for Blake it must be imaginative.

In Hegel's view, then, human beings think in accordance with the logical structures of nature through which the Absolute expresses itself. And the history of the world is actually the progress in the consciousness of the ideal—freedom—in the mind of the Absolute Idea.

Although I love the paranoic beauty of such giddy notions, Hegel's Absolute Idea always seems to elide away just as I am about to imagine it, like mercury sliding beneath a warm finger across a marble table . . . and my mind slips into a thin gray space where it is hard to see.

For there is nothing like the "logical march of history" to drive the flesh away. Which explains why the British poet and thinker Samuel Taylor Coleridge had such a difficult time trying to synthesize German idealism and British empiricism.

Coleridge (1772–1834) lived during nearly the same years as Hegel and traveled twice to Germany (1798 and 1828). He attempted, as his lifelong goal, to bring German abstract philosophy down from the sky and British scientific empiricism up from the soil. Such a desire for intellectual and philosophic holism became the mark of his being, and the mark of his life's protracted torture.

Viewed by many as one of the greatest talkers who ever lived, Coleridge never thought of himself as a poet, an identity he reserved for his friend Wordsworth. Ironically, however, the closest Wordsworth came to paranoic thinking was in his prose, not his poetry.

In Wordsworth's *Preface to the Lyrical Ballads* (1800), there is a truly prophetic passage that seems to refer more to the world of the year 2000 than to that of 1800. Wordsworth paranoically rants about the "multitude of causes" that are acting to "blunt the discriminating powers of the mind," reducing it "to a state of almost savage torpor." For this he blames the "increasing accumulation of men in cities," the "uniformity of their occupations," which produce a "craving for extraordinary incident which the rapid communication of intelligence hourly gratifies" (*Poetical Works,* 792). (Wordsworth's idea of "rapid communication" was the sudden proliferation of daily newspapers.)

All of these cultural-social changes, Wordsworth argues, will lead to society's unending thirst for "outrageous stimulation," which will eventually ruin the human mind, unfitting it for subtle explorations and exercise, such as that which poetry employs.

Wordsworth's dark paranoic prophecy, however, is not what most readers focus on in his *Preface.* Rather, the focus has always been on Wordsworth's stressing of the importance of the pastoral and rustic life, which was actually not that original since Rousseau had argued, years earlier, for the importance of a simple life close to nature. Moreover, Mary Wollstonecraft argued similarly in 1797, three years before Wordsworth wrote his *Preface,* in an essay entitled "On Poetry and Our Relish for the Beauties of Nature." Wollstonecraft's essay, which is not found in general anthologies and is therefore mostly unknown, stresses the importance of the poet being close to nature, for the "the sublimated spirits [that] combine images, which [rise] spontaneously" and for the poet being a person of "strong feelings" (*Wollstonecraft Anthology,* 171).

Thus the revolution for which Wordsworth is credited—namely, returning poetry to the "language of real men" who write from passion and live close to nature—was actually first adumbrated by Wollstonecraft. And it was Coleridge, I believe, not Wordsworth, who was actually the paranoic poet.

Coleridge's sublime poetic achievement begins with one of his earliest poems, "The Eolian Harp" (1795), the first "greater Romantic lyric" poem. "The Eolian Harp" pre-dates Wordsworth's "Tintern Abbey" by three years, yet it is Wordsworth who generally gains the credit for inventing the form. Written in blank verse, the greater Romantic lyric relies upon shifts between description and meditation, and is often in the mode of a conversation addressed to a silent auditor.

"Eolian Harp" opens with Coleridge and his wife, Sara, sharing a picturesque moment sitting outside their cottage on a fine October day in Clevedon, a village overlooking the Bristol Channel. Coleridge muses upon "emblems" of "innocence and love," but the love he refers to is mostly poetic and pastoral, and certainly not passionate. (Indeed, Coleridge would soon regret his marriage to Sara. He had originally proposed to her as part of a plan to move to America to set up a small utopian community with friends. After the plan fell apart, Coleridge, who had never loved Sara, nevertheless married her out of guilt.)

Coleridge's thoughts are soon drawn to the sound of the window harp, a favorite symbol for the Romantics. For Coleridge, the harp seemed to organically produce nature's own music, thus enabling the poet to hear nature's paranoically inspirational voice. And because the music is spontaneous and uncensored, Coleridge can't help but slip into the demonic:

> How by the desultory breeze caressed,
> Like some coy maid half yielding to her lover,
> It pours such sweet upbraiding, as must needs
> Tempt to repeat the wrong! And now, its strings
> Boldlier swept, the long sequacious notes
> Over delicious surges sink and rise,
> Such a soft floating witchery of sound
>
> (ll. 14–20)

Coleridge's own fantasies soon begin to operate in the same inspirational manner, and he sees himself outstretched upon a hill at noon:

> Whilst through my half-closed eyelids I behold
> The sunbeams dance, like diamonds, on the main,
> And tranquil muse upon tranquillity:
> Full many a thought uncalled and undetained,
> And many idle flitting phantasies,
> Travers my indolent and passive brain,
> As wild and various as the random gales
> That swell and flutter on this subject Lute!"
>
> (ll. 28–35)

The poem climaxes in the next stanza with a grand "what if" passage, as Coleridge paranoically shifts from status quo thinking about the human mind in favor of the imagination itself as harp:

> And what if all animated nature
> Be but organic harps diversely framed,
> That tremble into thought, as o'er them sweeps
> Plastic and vast, one intellectual breeze,
> At once the Soul of each, and God of all?
> (ll. 36–40)

Immediately, then, the poem collapses as Coleridge—caught by "the more serious eye [of Sara] a mild reproof"—elides from his own paranoic moment. Having risked his ordained place walking "humbly with . . . God" in order to fantasize about the grandeur of the imagination, Coleridge now repudiates his vision and castigates his whimsical endeavor:

> These of the unregenerate mind,
> Bubbles that glitter as they rise and break
> On vain Philosophy's aye-babbling spring.
> (ll. 47–49)

Coleridge's self-censorship keeps step with Christianity's expected condemnation of amoral expression, and the poem ironically ends with Coleridge retreating back to "Faith" and "saving mercies" and "Peace" and his "heart-honored Maid." Such a finale is the obverse of Victor Frankenstein's, who would choose Ingolstadt and amoral creativity over a safe Christian life with Elizabeth, his time-honored maid.

However, in "Kubla Khan," Coleridge's most famous poem, the poet's imagination does not elide back on itself but rather follows where paranoic vision leads:

> But oh! that deep romantic chasm which slanted
> Down the green hill athwart a cedarn cover!
> A savage place! as holy and enchanted
> As e'er beneath a waning moon was haunted
> By woman wailing for her demon lover!
> (ll. 12–16)

Although "Kubla Khan" displays no elision, Coleridge's attitude toward the poem surely does. Hesitating to call the work a poem, he added the subtitle—"A Vision in a Dream. A Fragment"—precisely because he feared public reaction to his seemingly demonic (amoral) fantasies. Moreover, in a note written to accompany the work, Coleridge claims that he published the poem "as a psychological curiosity" rather "than on the ground of any supposed poetic merits."

At the center of Coleridge's uncertainties was his doubt over whether great art could be generated from the stuff of dreams, especially in a poem that, as he admits, was "composed in a sort of reverie brought on by two grains of opium." Yet the resulting work had just that "strange effect," and it helped to open Western artistic expression to the mysterious channels of the paranoic unconscious.

Such imaginative liberation is one of the distinguishing legacies of the Romantics. They ventured toward the paranoic blue and away from culture's landed restraints upon the mind. As "Kubla Khan" symbolically represents with its staggering image of the "mighty fountain" from which "huge fragments vaulted like rebounding hail," and as Coleridge would specifically argue in his brilliant work of literary criticism *Biographia Literaria,* the true source of creativity is to be found in the individual's primal energies, which are essentially amoral and paranoic.

From this premise, the Romantics served up a new image of the artist that the modern tradition has inherited: a demonic visionary at odds with conventional religious values and whose sole being seems to violate society's bourgeois pieties. Indeed, the artist's very existence often stands in opposition to societal goals of goodness and restraint. This is why, as Coleridge projected at the end of "Kubla Khan," the world's citizens will inevitably cry out: "Beware! Beware! His flashing eyes, his floating hair!"

With this in mind, it is ironic that Coleridge's greatest poem seems to be his least revolutionary. "Frost at Midnight" (1798), a nearly perfect greater Romantic lyric, achieves the paranoic level of Blake's works by the way it subtly imagines a serene mystical unity between nature's universals and particulars, as the "Frost performs its secret ministry" until, by poem's end, the "silent icicles" are "Quietly shining to the quiet Moon" (l. 74).

"Frost at Midnight" unfolds as an accidental paranoic moment that begins with the narrator drifting away from the contentment realm inside his cottage late at night. In this way, the poem achieves an astounding oneness of form and content—the thoughts of the narrator making an associative journey through meditation and memory until his past and his present, his child's present and future, and the universals and particulars of Nature all become "one" through the process of the poem. And it all begins with the narrator's paranoic self-consciousness while the "inmates" of his cottage are "all at rest" (including his infant by his side), which leads him to "abstruser musings" until the power of "quiet" itself "vexes meditation," and he becomes aware of the sputter of grease on the fire grate, which

111

> Still flutters there, the sole unquiet thing.
> Methinks its motion in this hush of nature
> Gives it dim sympathies with me who live,
> Making it a companionable form,
> Whose puny flaps and freaks the idling Spirit
> By its own moods interprets, everywhere
> Echo or mirror seeking of itself,
> And makes a toy of Thought.
>
> (ll. 16–23)

Coleridge's elastic lyricism and mythy mind would fire up the aspirations of such great prose writers as Carlyle, Ruskin, and Pater in the later nineteenth century. Yet Coleridge's exasperating failure to write about "everything" (in one magnum opus) would at the same time act as a cautionary tale. In fact, the later-nineteenth-century writers had to give up all hope of writing about all things, facing as they did the imminent fragmentation of learning into disciplines and specialization, and the headlong rush of science and technology.

Thus Coleridge would be one of the last to test a philosophic means by which to penetrate the mysteries of creation, while simultaneously obsessing with the mystery of the Trinity and the various claims of traditional Christian theology. He was perhaps the last thinker to mix epistemology and logic with a personally amorphous philosophy aimed at drawing in all the achievements of modern science and art.

Near the end of his life and in the face of despair, Coleridge's passion for holism was still inextinguishable, no matter the magnificent lament in his late sonnet "Work without Hope" (1825).

> All Nature seems at work. Slugs leave their lair—
> The bees are stirring—birds are on the wing—
> And WINTER slumbering in the open air,
> Wears on his smiling face a dream of Spring!
> And I the while, the sole unbusy thing,
> Nor honey make, nor pair, nor build, nor sing.

And would you learn the spells that drowse my soul?
Work without Hope draws nectar in a sieve,
And Hope without an object cannot live.

(ll. 1–6, 12–14)

After a life of procrastination, self-laceration, and guilt, Coleridge would die with only one regret: "I wish life and strength had been spared to me to complete my Philosophy."

Eros

The call of the paranoic tortured and seduced many of the Romantics, and resulted in many elided constructs alongside the venues of love. And since the Romantic era was one of chaos and change (revolution, war, urbanization, industrialization), philosophies predicated on notions of love and strife were ever more appealing. Such philosophies can be traced back to Pythagoras (582–507 BC) and Empedocles (495–435 BC), as well as to Plotinus and the later Neoplatonists.

Collectively, these philosophies imagined a universe that experienced alternate dominations of Love and Strife: Love resulting in a coming together, predicated on a balanced mixture of the universe's various forces; Strife resulting in a falling apart, whereby the various forces fragment into warring components.

In Blake's grand myth, the eternal human form continually fragments into self-interested beings whose desire to dominate the corporeal world results in the torturous cycles of history. Blake blames the "Urizen principle," or the tyranny of reason, for the misery and cruelty of his own time.

For Blake (as well as for the Neoplatonists), self-love was responsible for the breakdown of harmony into separate forces. This is why, in Blake's *Milton* for instance, selfhood is the force that Milton must destroy through the renewed vigor of his moral imagination.

Many Romantic writers conceived of "love" as the transcendent power behind the moral imagination. "Love," as Percy Shelley said, "connects man with everything which exists." Yet Shelley, as well as Wordsworth, was unable to connect transcendent love with passionate human love. In fact, Wordsworth, whom many consider to be a poet of love as much as a poet of nature, never directly deals with love as physical passion but rather only as the power of connectedness, wherein love passes from "earth to man, from man to earth."

Such an argument is also evident in Percy Shelley's *Defense of Poetry* when Shelley speaks of the imaginative manner in which love transcends selfhood, and therefore the passions of selfhood:

> The great secret of morals is love; or a going out of our own nature, and an identification of ourselves with the beautiful which exists in thought, action, or person, not our own. A man, to be greatly good, must imagine intensely and comprehensively; he must put himself in the place of another and of many others; the pains and pleasures of his species must become his own. The great instrument of moral good is the imagination. (424–25)

John Keats (1795–1821), as well, worried about excessive selfhood and the influence of what he termed the "Wordsworthian egoistical sublime." And he seemed to find an answer to this problem in his great ode "To Autumn," composed shortly before his death. In this magisterial work, the poetic self is not so much annihilated as imagined right into the spirit of autumn.

In Wordsworth, Hegel, and Shelley, universal love harmonizes the disparate parts of the universe. Hegel, in fact, believed the power of love to be the ultimate force capable of undermining his universal dialectic and "excluding all oppositions." And Wordsworth, at the end of *The Prelude,* relies upon the generalized power of "love" to complete his vision—

> ... this love by a still higher love
> Be hallowed, love that breathes not without awe;
> Love that adores, but on the knees of prayer,
> By heaven inspired; that frees from chains the soul,
> Bearing in union with the purest, best
> Of earth-born passions ...
>
> (bk. 14, ll. 181–86)

Amidst all of these grand effusions over "universal love," it is the flesh that, consequently, suffers elision. And M. H. Abrams, the great critic of Romanticism, seems to notice this when he argues, in *Natural Supernaturalism* (1971), that the Romantic poets "differ markedly in their choice of the specific type of relationship which serves as the paradigm of all the other types [of love]" (297). And the chosen type is often not one of passion and flesh.

In Coleridge, for example, Abrams argues that friendship tends to be the paradigmatic form, and that Coleridge "represents sexual love as an especially intense kind of confraternity" (297). For Wordsworth, the favored model is "maternal love," as "the babe in his mother's arms [leads] to the all-inclusive 'love more intellectual'" (298).

Percy Shelley, at the end of "Queen Mab," offers a vision of uninhibited love, mixed with a dose of reason and natural evolution, that redeems earth and actually turns it on its axis, melting the polar cap and producing an eternal summer. Although such an exuberant vision may be chalked up to poetic immaturity (Shelley was only twenty when he wrote "Queen Mab"), much of Shelley's poetry seems to rely on sexuality as a metaphor for the struggle of love in a cosmic sense. Because of this elision, some people speculate (unfoundedly) that Shelley suffered from a sense of sexual repression, which is why he was unable to deal with the feelings and "ludicrous images" that sexual love awakens.

I believe the answer lies in Shelley's belief, stated in his 1818 "Discourse on the Manners of the Ancient Greeks Relative to the Subject of Love," that "gratification of the senses . . . soon becomes a very small part of that profound and complicated sentiment which we call Love" (106). This is the reason Shelley is most poetically comfortable when love is apprehended mystically, as a power we can just barely imagine.

Such a mystical vision of love, in fact, is at the center of his grandiloquent poem "Hymn to Intellectual Beauty" (1817). In the poem, Shelley, the unsettled atheist, aims his poetic invocation at his notion of a universal God—the "Spirit of Beauty." The shadow of this spirit passed over him when he was and young boy, and Shelley "shrieked, and clasped [his] hands in extacy!" (l. 60), like one under the influence of some great religious passion. At a later moment of high emotional pitch, Shelley addresses his universal power as—"O awful LOVELINESS" (l. 71).

For Shelley, "love" is the power behind the power, very much like the power Wordsworth envisions at the end of *The Prelude* (which Shelley could not have seen, since *The Prelude* was first published thirty years after Shelley's death). In Shelley's "Hymn," the universal command to "love all human kind" emanates from behind the "Spirit of BEAUTY, that dost consecrate / With thine own hues all thou dost shine upon / Of human thought or form" (ll. 13–15).

Moreover, in the poem's most boldly paranoic passage, Shelley claims that earlier poets misread the Spirit's sublime message, and "therefore the name of God and ghosts and Heaven remain the records of their vain endeavor." The truth for Shelley, however uncomfortable to accept, is that the universal spirit is elusive and mysterious, and its edict—as earlier paranoic visionaries ascertained—is "accident." And it is the poet's responsibility to clue in to the Spirit's whimsical visits and interpret the meaning.

> Frail spells—whose uttered charm might not avail to sever,
> From all we hear and all we see,
> Doubt, chance, and mutability,
> Thy light alone—like mist o'er mountains driven,
> Or music by the night wind sent
> Through strings of some still instrument,
> Or moonlight on a midnight stream,
> Gives grace and truth to life's unquiet dream.
>
> (ll. 29–36)

Thus, the call of the Spirit of Beauty (which Shelley heeded his entire life) is also a call for paranoic vision, which visits like the voice of some distant and arcane God. As Shelley makes clear in his great poem of the same year, "Mont Blanc," the call not only "teaches awful doubt" (regarding all landed beliefs) but also has the power to paranoically annul: "Thou hast a voice, great Mountain, to repeal / Large codes of fraud and woe; not understood / By all, but which the wise, and great, and good / Interpret, or make felt, or deeply feel" (ll. 80–83).

In this light, Shelley's famous claim at the end of his *Defense of Poetry* (written, in one sense, to repudiate the increasing hegemony of nineteenth-century contentment culture that Shelley viewed as a threat to the fragile world of poetry and prophecy) that poets are "the unacknowledged legislators of the World" (448) is one of the great paranoic claims in Western literature.

This notion was never so archetypally portrayed as at the end of Coleridge's "Kubla Khan," wherein the paranoidic public finally desires to protect the paranoic voice of the poet-prophet: "Weave a circle round him thrice, / And close your eyes with holy dread, / For he on honeydew hath fed, / And drunk the milk of Paradise" (ll. 51–54).

Despite such profoundly paranoic moments in Coleridge and Shelley, both writers (and Wordsworth as well) had trouble adumbrating a notion of love both visionary and fleshy. Blake is the exception here, as he was able to illuminate a vision of eternity witnessed through his corporeal eye: "I look thro it & not with it." For the body is not separate from the soul, according to Blake, but rather that "portion of Soul discernd by the five Senses" (*Heaven and Hell*, pl. 4), the universe itself appearing "infinite and holy . . . by an improvement of sensual enjoyment" (*Heaven and Hell,* pl. 14).

Blake's fleshy vision makes him a unique paranoic hero, along with, of course, Hypatia, who was no virgin, but a lover of men and of Neoplatonic truths; and Jesus, who realized his godliness through his manliness (not by eliding from it); and Joan, who wasn't ascetic and frail, but broad-shouldered and strong, and who became a warrior in the flesh in order to attain her spiritual vision; and Schreber, who not only believed that the soul rested within the body (the nerves), but whose vision of world-reformulation would begin by his sexual mating with God.

Yet, even though some Romantics tended to elide into metaphors away from the flesh, they still produced startling insights into love. In Shelley's "Discourse on Love," for instance, he argues that homosexuality was prevalent in ancient Greece because Greek women were so degraded. (Women were, in fact, considered little more than slaves; the word "*damar*" was used to denote both slave and wife.) For this reason, Shelley believed, women were incapable of inspiring romantic love, and the highest practice of love therefore had to be between men. This situation would last until the Middle Ages, when the chivalric code liberated heterosexual love, and, as Shelley would state in his "Defense of Poetry," women would inspire a "poetry of sexual love."

Still the most integral work in the Western tradition in terms of the paradoxical powers of love is Plato's *Symposium* (perhaps his greatest work, along with the *Apology*). Most readers tend to view the *Symposium* (Shelley shares some responsibility for this) as a wonderful example of platonic ascent, much like the famous cave myth in Plato's *Republic*. In the *Symposium*, however, instead of ascending from darkness into light by the power of reason (as in the *Republic*), one ascends from the physical to the spiritual by the power of love to eventually achieve a vision of the Eternal Good.

The problem with such a reading is that the *Symposium* doesn't actually end with Socrates' description of the ascending power of love (from the physical to the mental to the intellectual to the spiritual). Rather, there is the "knock at the door" (one of the most significant "knocks at the door" in Western literature), followed by the disruptive entrance of a drunken Alcibiades, whose earthy presence serves to undermine Socrates' elevating speech on love. The result of this great literary moment is impasse.

Consequently, the telos of love depends upon mediation between body and soul, flesh and vision. And if anyone attempts to transcend the flesh, Alcibiades will always be there, drunk and crowned with ivy, charming with his words, adding weight to one's feet, making it ever so difficult to climb the ladder of love.

Such an idea of passion undoing the noble goals of the soul is, of course, a prominent legacy of the Greeks. And any classical subversion of this body/soul polarity would probably have occurred outside the cultural arena of Athens, which it did, in fact, in the case of Sappho, the female poet and teacher who flourished on the island of Lesbos during the first half of the sixth century BC.

Because of Sappho's supposed bisexual nature, the early Christian Church took an active role in destroying her writings. (Pope Gregory in the fourth century played a particularly key role in this endeavor.) So most of Sappho's works survive only as papyrus fragments. Ironically, the greatest number of Sappho papyri have been excavated from ancient Egyptian waste dumps. Somehow, these "thrown away" writings survived longer than other texts the ancients tried to preserve. (Other papyric fragments have been found encasing Egyptian mummies, and even stuffed inside Egyptian crocodiles.)

Sappho's astounding poetry is in keeping with high paranoic Romanticism in the very sense that it undoes the flesh/soul dichotomy. In fact, Sappho, one of the first lyrical poets of the Western world, may also be one of the first to suggest that not only are passion and soul not dichotomous, but that the power of passionate love (Eros) actually emanates "from" the soul and is the soul's purest form of expression. Furthermore, when love manifests in ecstasy, both body and soul are nearly shattered, as described in one of the two poems by Sappho to survive in entirety. (This poem was preserved through the Roman writer Longinus, first century AD, who described it as expressive of a "concourse of passions.")

> . . . it breaks my spirit;
> underneath my breast all the heart is shaken.
> Let me only glance where you are, the voice dies,
>   I can say nothing.
> but my lips are stricken to silence, under-
> neath my skin the tenuous flame suffuses;
> nothing shows in front of my eyes, my ears are
>   muted in thunder.

And the sweat breaks running upon me, fever
shakes my body, paler I turn than grass is;
I can feel that I have been changed, I feel that
   death has come near me.

(no. 2, ll. 5–16)

Such a paranoic seizure of the soul would not appear again until the late eighteenth century in the person of Goethe's Werther. Like Sappho, Goethe seems to suggest that, as irrational and destructive as the consequences of love might be, experiencing the grip of Eros is the essence of life.

The sonnets of English Romantic writer Charlotte Smith (1749–1806) also express the tortured voice of a passionate soul. Subversive in her own right—especially because of her bleak tone and intense emotion, and for a long time noncanonical (like Sappho)—Smith often depicts a kind of tragic impasse. A key difference, however, is that in Sappho's poems one always feels the narrator will eventually go on to love again, while in Smith's sonnets (and in the case of Werther as well), one senses there will be no rebirth of love.

Ah! poor humanity! so frail, so fair,
Are the fond visions of the early day,
Till tyrant passion, and corrosive care,
Bid all thy fairy colours fade away!
Another May new buds and flowers shall bring;
Ah! why has happiness—no second Spring?

("Close of Spring," ll. 9–14)

The publication of Smith's *Elegiac Sonnets* in 1784 not only helped to resurrect the English sonnet, but the description-meditation format that Smith employed influenced Coleridge in his creation of the greater Romantic lyric ("Eolian Harp," 1795).

Lyricism

The Romantic period's greatest lyrical poet, John Keats, negated the flesh/soul dichotomy by eliding from Romantic transcendence altogether. In fact, Keats's great odes are actually "anti-ascent," since Keats again and again refuses to give up the verdant earth below for the sake of vision and immortality above. Any meaning that Keats has to offer, then, comes through a sensuous grasping of his intense and lush images, which is why one cannot actually "learn" Keats but can only tune up one's aesthetic skills so as to experience fully the sensory truths he offers, to acquire a "strenuous tongue / [which] Can burst Joy's grape against his palate fine" ("Melancholy," ll. 27–28).

In his exquisite greater Romantic lyric "Ode to a Nightingale," the promise of transcendence through imagination and "poesy" is actually repudiated by the narrator because he will no longer be able to see what flowers are at his feet:

> . . . what soft incense hangs upon the boughs,
> But, in embalmed darkness, guess each sweet
> Wherewith the seasonable month endows
> The grass, the thicket, and the fruit-tree wild;
> White hawthorn, and the pastoral eglantine;
> Fast fading violets cover'd up in leaves;
> And mid-May's eldest child,
> The coming musk-rose, full of dewy wine,
> The murmurous haunt of flies on summer eves.
>
> (ll. 42–50)

At the end of the ode, Keats actually deconstructs key Romantic tenets such as imagination ("Adieu! the fancy cannot cheat so well / As she is fam'd to do, deceiving elf" [ll. 73–74]) and the role of the poet-prophet ("Was it a vision, or a waking dream? / Fled is that music:—Do I wake or sleep?" [ll. 79–80]).

Keats offers the reader a kind of "fleshy immorality." Instead of ascent, he focuses on the intensity of beauty, on experiencing the moments of life sensuously rather than imaginatively. Instead of escaping into spirit, he wants to die into life where pleasures turn "to poison while the bee-mouth sips" ("Melancholy," l. 24).

Walter Pater's later-nineteenth-century variation on the Keatsian moment—"to burn always with this hard, gemlike flame, to maintain this ecstasy, is success in life" (*Conclusion to Renaissance*, 60)—led to accusations of decadence and hedonism. But Pater's paradox of the "gemlike flame" poses a most brilliant and condensed symbol for achieving the simultaneity of flux and permanence, the key philosophic problem since the time of the pre-Socratic philosophers and the ancient debate between Heraclitus's fiery Becoming (*genetai*) and Parmenides' sublime Being (*esti*). This debate filtered into the philosophic differences between Aristotle and Plato, setting up the most fundamental ontological and metaphysical dichotomy the West has faced . . . which all becomes so maddening that after a while you want to retreat back to a garden somewhere and spend some quiet time, maybe with Jeremiah, even if he never tired of his lamenting.

In Jeremiah's Garden

Jeremiah, that good man, performing his ministry during the late seventh/early sixth century BC (just a couple of generations before Heraclitus and Parmenides), mostly in Egypt, where all the ancient men of days had to go; where you could act quiet and there was no soul murder or elisions of any kind, above or below.

Egypt, where you could walk upon the sandy canopsis, the site of Alexander's yet-to-be-erected namesake city, against the brown gleaming waters at the mouth of the Nile . . . waters that would later retreat right over the place once known as Alexandria.

Egypt, where under the ancient sky so grand anyone with a paranoic eye could see that blue really was the color of infinity.

And there must have been some fine gardens there, where Jeremiah could rest his swollen feet, before making his way to Jerusalem.

Some claim that Jeremiah didn't actually write the Lamentations, that the biblical work is just a collection of laments by several authors evoking their paranoidic dread over the destruction of Jerusalem by the Babylonians (587 BC), when the Lord of Zion seemed to have deserted his own people—"The Lord has become like an enemy" (2:5). Then, like an enemy, He elided away.

But I believe that Jeremiah did make it to Jerusalem, and there were still some glorious gardens there, and he did write his truly paranoic Lamentations over the ruined city. Because I have seen him there, which is all right since Vico said we need "fantasia" to make the paranoic truth live; Jeremiah, always in the same scene, always walking away from the smoldering ruins just as my eyes close in . . . Jeremiah, the only one who could say:

> I am the man who has seen affliction
> under the rod of his wrath;
> he has driven and brought me
> into darkness without any light;
> surely against me he turns his hand
> again and again the whole day long.
>
> (3:1–3)

In ancient Hebrew, Jerusalem meant "city of peace." But for William Blake, in his final visionary work of the same name, Jerusalem was the "spirit of liberty" and the great female emanation of Albion.

So while Jeremiah lamented Jerusalem, Blake redeemed her; that is the paranoic truth. And Blake's *Jerusalem* may be the grandest paranoic vision of all, which explains why Robert Southey, when he called on Blake to see for himself Blake's *Jerusalem,* remarked that it was "a perfectly mad poem." Because how could Southey figure Blake's mind? A mind that, in *Jerusalem,* could envision

> Los . . . in London building Golgonooza,
> Compelling his Spectre to labours mighty; trembling in fear
> The Spectre weeps, but Los unmov'd by tears or threats remains.
> "I must Create a System or be enslav'd by another Man's.
> "I will not Reason & Compare: my business is to Create."
> (pl. 10, ll. 17–21)

No, he could not, and neither can we. Because Blake's paranoic vision always seems beyond us, even if we were to stand right next to him, in his garden in Felpham's Vale.

5

The Jutland
Heath

Stark Black Dearth

In Robert Browning's poem "Childe Roland to the Dark Tower Came"
(1852), there is no garden, but only a place where "the grass . . . grew
scant as hair / In leprosy; thin dry blades pricked the mud / Which underneath looked kneaded up with blood" (ll. 73–75).

A late Romantic writer, Browning offers, prophetically and paranoically, the first eschatological "wasteland" in modern Western literature, out of time and place; and his Childe Roland is one of the West's
first antihero heroes. In a hybrid language tinged with disgust and
doubt, Childe Roland speaks of his bleak quest beginning with the
"hoary" and "hateful cripple" whom he asks for directions, and whom
he paranoidically believes to have "lied in every word, / . . . with malicious eye / Askance to watch the working of his lie on mine" (ll. 1–4).

In this subversion of the medieval knight-quest scenario, Browning's
Roland is no longer searching for a means to greatness amidst a dangerous landscape. Rather, he is—even at his early stage of knighthood
("Childe" connotes that Roland is still untested)—questing for the Dark
Tower for which "neither pride / Nor hope rekindling at the end de-
scried, / So much as gladness that some end might be" (ll. 16–18). In
fact, Roland's desire to have his moment of failure and be done with it
repudiates the previous three centuries' obsession with humanistic triumph and goal-oriented consciousness.

> For, what with my whole world-wide wandering,
> What with my search drawn out through years, my hope
> Dwindled into a ghost not fit to cope
> With that obstreperous joy success would bring,

I hardly tried now to rebuke the spring
My heart made, finding failure in its scope.

(ll. 19–24)

Such grimness explains why this grandly mythical poem is historically problematic in light of the middle- and later-nineteenth-century
inclination toward social theory and utopianism. With everyone trying
to erect their "crystal palace" where suffering would be no more and enlightenment shared by all, Roland's "joy" at knowing failure is at hand
appears culturally antithetical.

123

Moreover, Roland's ancillary question—will I be fit to fail?—is unimaginable as human measurement amidst the nineteenth-century
fetish for progress, and inconceivable even as a garden whisper. (Years
later, Samuel Beckett would have expressions such as "fail again, fail better" uttered by figures who seemed to exist outside any mainstream socioeconomic sphere.) Nevertheless, Roland utters to himself, just before
falling inside the dimension of the Dark Tower, "Here ended, then, /
Progress this way" (ll. 171–72).

Browning's "Childe Roland" de-romanticizes the individual's relationship with nature and the world, and any attempt to re-animate the
fallen landscape with energy and vision is out of the question. And the
farther Browning's knight continues into the arcane darkness, the more
the Romantic dream of Nature fritters away—"I think I never saw / Such
starved ignoble nature; nothing throve . . . You'd think; a burr had been
a treasure trove" (ll. 55–60).

Yet Browning's de-romanticizing doesn't lead in the direction of other
later-nineteenth-century writers who cultivated a "new realism" (writers such as Dickens, Flaubert, and Tolstoy). Browning's surreal and
nearly postmodern landscape, more prescient than Matthew Arnold's
"Dover Beach" (written the same year), leads paranoically into Roland's
eschatological realization that only "the Last Judgment's fire must cure
this place" (l. 65).

Thus, in the world of the poem, de-romanticization surprisingly
leads to the paranoic unexpected, outside the controls of the conscious
mind, which doesn't "see" until it's too late: "[there] came a click / As
when a trap shuts—you're inside the den! / Burningly it came on me all
at once, / This was the place!" (ll. 173–76).

Roland's final paranoic vision is nothing like his expected images of
terror served up by paranoidic consciousness, especially the Tower

itself, with its "round squat turret, blind as the fool's heart, / Built of brown stone, without a counterpart / In the whole world" (ll. 182–84). The diminutive and nondescript Tower, so undramatic and supremely banal, is the true edifice of evil, by the paranoic eye beheld.

And the Tower seems to have come to Roland, rather than any physical motion on Roland's part taking him there. Indeed, the Tower seems very much to "appear" as the Green Knight's castle finally appears to Gawain, only after Gawain is worthy enough to "see" it. For Roland, the Tower appears only after his altered consciousness allows him to sanction the notion of failure. This shift in consciousness is what the journey of the poem is all about. ("Should I be fit [to fail]?" [l. 42])

In this way Browning's "Childe Roland" stands as an astonishing precursor to modern existential literature, in which the external quest toward worldly goals often seems ludicrous (especially a chivalric one toward a shining Grail). Browning's poem un-means the very notion of a purposeful journey, and to see this unmeaning during the process of the poem is the poem's meaning. To see this unmeaning is to understand that in Roland's final existential moment, when he reaches to blow his slug-horn, there is no goal attained, but merely a statement of endurance inside a dimension where triumph doesn't even exist.

Robert Langbaum, in *The Poetry of Experience* (1957)—his study of later Romanticism—concludes similarly that Browning's poem questions the viability of the so-called noble quest and that the blast of the slug-horn is "of defiance in that it contains both the knight's praise of himself for having endured . . . and his dispraise of what has been endured" (195).

Because of this existential condition, Childe Roland's "end" involves no cataclysmic violence. Rather, his "end" is psychological and outside time itself, amidst an increasing apocalyptic noise that tolls "like a bell"; suddenly, Roland finds himself inside a graying dimension surrounded by a multitude of valiant peers who previously had found failure, even though Roland heard nothing but how "one was strong, and such was bold, / And such was fortunate, yet each of old / Lost, lost!" (ll. 196–98). In Roland's final moment, they stand

> . . . ranged along the hillsides, met
> To view the last of me, a living frame
> For one more picture! in a sheet of flame
> I saw them and I knew them all. And yet

Dauntless the slug-horn to my lips I set,
and blew. *"Childe Roland to the Dark Tower came."*

(ll. 199–204)

Thus the poem ends with Roland's psychological duration inside his
heroic moment of failure, and the surreal annihilation of the world's
meaning.

125

Browning later explained that the poem came to him in a dream and
that he wrote it mostly at one sitting, a claim similar to Coleridge's regarding "Kubla Khan" (1797). But in Coleridge's dream-poem the poet
follows his paranoic vision into imaginative transcendence until he as-
pires to "build that dome in air," whereas in Browning's dream-poem, at
the moment of death, imagination fails and meaning vanishes.

(Because both poems are written in first-person, the reader is welcomed into the dream. The key difference, of course, is that Browning's
poem is a "dramatic monologue," which means that the reader must fil-
ter out Browning's personal vision from the anxiety-driven words of his
character, Roland.)

Written ten years after one of the great coincidences in Western literary history—namely, the simultaneous fashioning of the "dramatic
monologue" by both Browning and Tennyson, the former in Italy and
the latter in England—"Childe Roland" confuses its reader by eliciting a
mix of emotions, which is precisely the goal of most dramatic mono-
logues. The format allows the poet to narrate his torturous inner experience in an objectified manner by projecting through a dramatic per-
sona (such as Childe Roland), and it avoids guilt over such explicit
egoism since the poet remains behind the character. (Poetical egoism
was a concern ever since Keats first adumbrated it in his letter of October 27, 1818, when he distinguished himself from poets of "the
wordsworthian or egoistical sublime.")

After 1842, Browning and Tennyson wrote almost exclusively in the
dramatic monologue form. Tennyson often used it—in his lengthy *Idylls
of the King* (1871), for example—to nostalgically lament the chivalric
Arthurian world forever lost amidst the increasingly industrialized and
utilitarian world; Browning altogether questioned the teleology of the
past chivalric world amidst a premodern landscape evermore wastelike,
a landscape that ultimately undermines the Wordsworth/Shelley dualism of nature (that is, nature as serene and joyful versus nature as cold
and indifferent, "Tintern Abbey" versus "Mont Blanc"), in favor of an

increasingly sterile landscape fashioned out of some nightmare collective consciousness, in which the poet can no longer envision a "sunny pleasure dome with caves of ice" ("Kubla Khan"), but only "stubbed ground, once a wood, / . . . a marsh . . . now mere earth / Desperate and done with . . . Bog, clay and rubble, sand and stark black dearth" ("Childe Roland," ll. 145–50).

Waste Black Mud

. . . and I can see those knightly peers, ranged along the stark dearth hillsides, and the horses' heads drooping, and the men's eyes burning clear in the near-dark. Because they were dressed for me once, but as slovenly Russians in oversized winter coats and hats, with steamy breath too much for the rain-drizzled early morning just past five o'clock, when I was nineteen . . . the rest of my housemates asleep in stuporous beds, while I quested without purpose; deciding, peradventure, to walk the entire perimeter of the lake where we lived, because no one had done that before, not after staying up all night; and no one would be awake to see, as I stepped across their properties; never considering just how large the lake really was and the impossibility of making it; and that's why I derided myself when I stopped less than halfway.

Under a thin gray sky the lake mocked me: still and blackened, congealing like oil and wanting to inch closer. I remember seeing a patch of mushrooms sprouting near and thinking—botulism, a quickening disease amidst a tightening land, and how the lake refused to reflect the lightening air of the sky, bluish-black with vague sparklings. The lake was awful then: dark and recessive, low and marsh-black, surrounded by waste black mud; and nothing moved except in league with the oily mist and sticky webs.

I sat on the water's edge even though I knew my pants would get damp. Go ahead, I thought, because who cares . . . But eventually I weakened and tried sitting on my hands for a while. And when they started feeling numb I held them against the margin of the lake; bony, light brown hands, blueveined, cold, and fragile against the opaqueness. I reached back and grabbed hold of a large branch swung horizontal over the lake; the bark was loose and moldy and crumbled at my touch. But by pulling downward I was able to arch my body in the air, with only my feet still touching the ground, and my pants hung loose from my legs and the dampness went away . . . The rib-like fingers of the branch swooshed across the black water creating silver ripples in the lake's swampy skin.

After a while, I let go, and again my body felt the dampness of the lake mud. Above, the branch rocked slowly to a halt. And then it would move slightly from time to time, sort of nodding at me. Meanwhile, the lake vanished into silver streaks flashing upward into a dull white sky. I turned my head to the right and looked up the hill through the trees, and there they were—the damn Russians in their heavy coats and smoky breath, their faces all the same and their coats various shades of brown and gray; four or five of them standing shoulder to shoulder in silhouette at the top of the hill, as still as the trees. I wondered how long they had been standing there, and what they wanted . . . And then I knew—nothing more than to watch me hang from my tree limb in absurdity, because I felt sad. And that's when I noticed the noise, because it had been quiet for so long, before the gradual brightening.

I didn't believe in the noise at first, because their bodies remained so still. But their feet must have been stamping in unison on wooden planks I couldn't see; but I could hear the noise getting louder, like people in a stadium increasing toward madness. And so I acquiesced, and lay my head back into the moist lake mud, and tried to be as still as I could to stop the shivering, and closed my eyes like a gate, refusing to open them even when the stamping became so loud it was hard to catch my breath.

Then, before I could notice, the sound churned into a banal hum, a background static that most of the world forgets to hear. And when I turned to look for the Russians, they were gone—hats, smoky coats, shadows, wooden reviewing stands, and all.

I got up to leave when the trees started crouching around and some disturbed dog began barking. I walked resolutely past all of the depressing lake houses, which appeared out of the damp grey air in insipid demand of Sunday morning.

The Aesthetic-Existential

The sound of Roland's slug-horn disturbs more than just the nineteenth century's obsession with utility and progress; the horn's timbre undermines the century's intoxication with imagination and aesthetics (the poem's final landscape can be neither imaginatively transcended nor aestheticized).

Born out of Wordsworth's "spots of time," and Coleridge's theories of the imagination, and Blake's spatial visions, and Keats's idealized "Grecian Urn," and Shelley's belief that poets are the "unacknowledged legislators of the world," and Ruskin's moral aesthetics in his five volumes of *Modern Painters,* and Pater's claim that the artist must "burn always with that hard gemlike flame," and Wilde's remorse over the "decay of lying," and Joyce's desire to "forge in the smithy of my soul the uncreated conscience of my race"—the aesthetic movement was an attempt to perceive beauty in a personally holistic way, and, as such, it directly affronted Enlightenment culture with its assumptions of universal objectivism and order. Darwin's mid-century writings, disturbing the world's "sea of faith," would make aestheticism even more seductive.

And so what began with a Romantic emphasis on the artist's imagination led to the "work itself" defining its own reality. And once art was separated from so-called "objective truth," it was just a matter of time before doubt would set in and one would wonder if art was really "something," or merely nothingness in disguise. Such questioning is highly paranoic and can lead to new ways of thinking about the self and world, which is why the "sycphatic" condition is at the center of existential thought. ("Sycphatic" is my term for the anxious awareness that nothingness may be parading around as something.)

Many cultural historians don't see it this way. They believe that aesthetics and existentialism arose as separate cultural and intellectual phenomena. But Browning's "Childe Roland" proves otherwise: the poem's sterile final landscape is a repudiation of aestheticism; the scene cannot be transmogrified. Hence, the existential trap—"click . . . you're inside the den!" "Child Roland," then, represents one of the best examples we have of the later-nineteenth-century shift from aesthetics to existentialism.

Another example of this shift would be Dostoyevsky's *Notes from Underground* (1864), where the narrator, at a traumatic moment earlier in his life, is accused of sounding "just like a book." This leads him to realize later that we can no longer escape the existential underground through aesthetics. And after ranting for pages about his rejection of the "good and the beautiful," he proclaims that he will not offer us literature: "I don't want to let considerations of literary composition get in my way. I won't bother with planning and arranging; I'll note down whatever comes to my mind" (122).

At the end of part 2, the narrator reiterates that his "shame" for writing his story proves that he isn't offering "literature," but a punishment and an expiation:

> Of course, spinning long yarns about how I poisoned my life through
> moral disintegration in my musty hole, lack of contact with other

men, and spite and vanity is not very interesting. I swear it has no literary interest, because what a novel needs is a hero, whereas here I
have collected, as if deliberately, all the features of an anti-hero.
These notes are bound to produce an extremely unpleasant impression. . . . Why, we've reached a point where we consider real life as
work—almost as painful labor—and we are secretly agreed that the
way it is presented in literature is much better. . . . Why, today we
don't even know where real life is, what it is, or what it's called! Left
alone without literature, we immediately become entangled and
lost—we don't know what to join, what to keep up with; what to love,
what to hate; what to respect, what to despise! (202–3)

For Tennyson and Arnold, closing in on the existential "edge" resulted
in them eventually eliding away from the existential condition. Tennyson, after expressing levels of religious doubt and loneliness in his
epic poem "In Memoriam" (1850), added the prologue, which under-
mined his impending existential crisis and replaced it with religious certainty. And Matthew Arnold, after offering the existential and surreal
image of a "darkling plain" where "ignorant armies clash by night" at the
end of his great prophetic poem "Dover Beach" (1852), would soon give
up writing poetry altogether to focus on critical prose instead, where he
would argue aesthetically for a "touchstone" tradition in Western literature. Through this great cultural tradition Arnold would hope to find
meaning, in the same way that others find meaning in religion.

In the early twentieth century, T. S. Eliot, who was greatly influenced
by Browning, chose to end his brilliantly innovative poem "The Love
Song of J. Alfred Prufrock" (1917) with a repudiation of both Romanticism and aestheticism. After the language shifts ironically into a contrived Romantic lyricism—"I have seen them riding seaward on the
waves / Combing the white hair of the waves blown back" (ll. 126–27)—
the poem ends with a modern/existential wake-up call: "We have lin-
gered in the chambers of the sea / By sea-girls wreathed with seaweed
red and brown / Till human voices wake us, and we drown" (ll. 129–31).

Conceptually, both aestheticism and existentialism are paranoic
(both elide from the two-plus-two world of utility and the paranoia/
contentment dialectic). And both, therefore, really are "something." Yet
the holism of the former led to the fragmentation of the latter precisely
because the personal projection of beauty, as a justification for existence, couldn't hold up, not amidst the modern world's chaos and loss

of belief in objective reality and divine providence. And so, personal aesthetic reality—just like the objective world it replaced—started looking like delusion, making one wonder if beauty itself was just a screening off from the dread of contingency.

Of course, one is still free to embrace Beauty's sublime power, but after the existential "moment" it is hard to trick oneself into believing in aesthetics as metaphysical triumph. Just ask, if we could, the great poet/priest Gerard Manley Hopkins (1844–89), whose stone tablet rests in Poets' Corner in Westminster Abbey between two Victorians, Tennyson and Browning, and two moderns, Auden and Eliot. Hopkins was born a Victorian and then reborn a modern, since his poems were not published until 1918, twenty-nine years after his death. Fittingly, a bust of John Dryden (1631–1700), the last Catholic writer to be admitted to Poets' Corner, looks down on Hopkins, the only priest ever enshrined among the Greats of English literature.

Hopkins was tutored at Oxford by Walter Pater, the most important thinker in the British aesthetic movement. Pater, who coined the phrase "art for art's sake," had been greatly influenced by John Ruskin's aesthetic theories (it was Ruskin, in fact, who introduced the term "aesthetic" into English usage). All three nineteenth-century writers (Ruskin, Pater, Hopkins) strained to embrace the notion of beauty as life's valued meaning, but it was Ruskin and Hopkins who would suffer a lifelong battle between the lure of beauty and the strict religious assumption that too much love of beauty was an insult to God and a direct affront to salvation.

The contemporary intellectual critic Denis Donoghue, in his impressive biography *Walter Pater—Lover of Strange Souls* (1995), argues in the end that the aesthetic movement is ultimately sad because it is an acknowledgment that life cannot be understood, but only lived. However, the idea of art becoming a retreat because we don't know where we are going adds fuel to the notion that the aesthetic movement did in fact lead us into an existential condition.

For Hopkins, the conflict between his avowed Jesuitical asceticism and his passion for sensuous beauty was never resolved, and much of his exquisite poetry records the ongoing spiritual and mental anguish that he experienced as a result of this conflict. Increasingly for Hopkins (perhaps second only to Keats in terms of the sublime power and beauty of his lyrical poetry) the battle between aestheticism and asceticism, nature and God, beauty and piety, led more and more into existential anguish, the kind that the Danish theologian Søren Kierkegaard had experienced a generation earlier, which became the centerpiece of his magnificent theistic existential works.

For Gerard Manley Hopkins, the drift into existential dread began with paranoic separation from his body. For most of his short life, Hopkins was sickly and weak. He felt cursed with a body in which "nature in all her parcels and faculties gaped and fell apart, like a clod of earth sticking together and holding fast only by strings of roots" (Pick, 110). His failing body was linked, in Hopkins's mind, to his perceived failure as a priest, teacher, and poet. In Poem 74 ("Thou are indeed just, Lord"), Hopkins notes, reminiscent of Coleridge in "Work without Hope," that "birds build—but not I build; no, but strain, / Time's eunuch, and not breed one work that wakes. / Mine, O thou lord of life, send my roots rain" (ll. 12–14).

Hopkins's body let him down to such an extent that he despised its flesh and referred to it at various times as a burden, a bad joke, a fragment of broken pottery, an ill-matched patch of cloth, a useless splinter of wood, a coffin of weakness and dejection. In poem 75, written shortly before his death, Hopkins offers a startling threnody to his failing body:

> But man—we, scaffold of score brittle bones;
> Who breathe, from groundlong babyhood to hoary
> Age gasp; whose breath is our *memento mori*—
> What bass is *our* viol for tragic tones?
> He! Hand to mouth he lives, and voids with shame;
>
> (ll. 5–9)

The shortcomings of Hopkins's physical frame led him to idolize not only the resilience of nature, with its "dearest freshness deep down things," but the sinewy beauty of Harry Ploughman (in a poem of the same name), with his "Hard as hurdle arms . . . rack of ribs; the scooped flank; lank / Rope-over thigh; knee nave; and barreled shank—" (ll. 1–4).

In many of his late poems, Hopkins's failing body acts as a metaphor for the trap of temporal time itself, and as a reminder of man's need to escape through faith. But the nearer Hopkins moved toward death, the more this escape seemed crowded with despair.

"Spelt from Sibyl's Leaves" (1886), a poem Hopkins considered to be the longest sonnet in the English language, traces a pattern of time that oscillates between the flux in nature and a strained hope in the transcendent apocalyptic moment. But by poem's end, Hopkins's attempt to leap from temporality to eternity resolves into an existential condition in which the speaker is framed in a time that is neither temporal nor apocalyptic, but rather psychological—"selfwrung, self-strung, sheathe- and shelterless, thoughts / against thoughts in groans grind."

The astonishing seven adjectives that open "Sibyl's Leaves"—"EARNEST, earthless, equal, attuneable, vaulty, voluminous, / . . . stupendous"—describe the aura surrounding the flux of evening. Yet there is something atemporal occurring, something more than day succumbing to night. "Earthless" suggests that evening not only blots out day, it dissolves the material world itself. The fourth word—"attuneable"—points to some harmonizing effect wrought from this metaphysical occurrence, a unison of body and soul. And the culminating adjective—"stupendous"—locks in the sense of immanent transcendence.

Hopkins interprets the truth of the straining evening much as the Cumaean Sibyl of the poem's title deciphered the judgment of the gods from natural signs per order of the Roman Senate. Hopkins, taking a leaf out of Sibyl's book of prophecies, spells out the implications within the order of nature:

> . . . For earth her being has unbound, her dapple is at end, as—
> tray or aswarm, all throughther, in throngs; self in self steeped and
>   pashed—quite
> Disremembering, dismembering all now. Heart, you round me right
> With: Our evening is over us; our night whelms, whelms and will
>   end us.
>
> (ll. 5–8)

The fading of all light forms, the merging into a shadowing mass, coupled with the notion of the self being "pashed" and then forgotten—"disremembering," speaks of a world that is becoming undone, and of a self that is losing the ability to order experience.

John Ruskin, whose works Hopkins read at Oxford, believed nature to have a moral and aesthetic purpose. In fact, for Ruskin, aesthetics was the basis of morality. As he stated emphatically in "Traffic," the second lecture of *Crown of the Wild Olive* (1870), "Taste is not only a part and index of morality, it is the ONLY morality!" (*Complete Works*, 41).

In Hopkins's apocalyptic reading of evening's metaphysical grandeur, morality is the undisputable quotient. The straining of the aestheticized evening results in a moral imperative: all human actions will be judged. And Hopkins's apocalyptic moment is hardly a beautiful one; his "Dies Irae" is signed with "beak-leaved boughs dragonish" that "damask the tool-smooth bleak light; black, / Ever so black on it" (ll. 9–10). Fierce symbolic shapes—beaks of vultures, dragons' claws—etch the cold sky like blades of justice. This is the dark sibylean tale that Hopkins tells.

This austere tale also speaks of Hopkins's lifelong conflict of body/soul. In "To What Serves Moral Beauty?", most probably composed shortly after "Sibyl's Leaves," Hopkins addresses an ancillary problem: what purpose has the world's beauty, which sets "dancing [the] the blood," if it will be eventually dissolved? In "Mortal Beauty," Hopkins concludes that one must "Merely meet it [beauty] . . . then leave, let that alone" (ll. 12–13). In "Sibyl's Leaves," however, the speaker is cursed with tragic reluctance.

> . . . Let life, waned, ah let life wind
> Off her once skeined stained veined variety upon, all on two spools;
>   part, pen, pack
> Now her all in two flocks, two folds—black, white; right, wrong; . . .
>
>   (ll. 10–12)

For John Ruskin, the conflict paranoically resolved itself. His severe evangelical prejudice allowed him to accept the full riches of the natural world after a momentous experience in Turin, Italy, when he encountered in 1858 the Veronese painting *Solomon and the Queen of Sheba.*

> Certainly it seems intended that strong and frank animality, reflecting all tendency to asceticism, monachism, pietism, and so on, should be connected with the strongest intellects. . . . Homer, Shakespeare, Tintoret, Veronese, Titian, Michael Angelo, Turner . . . are all of them boldly Animal. Francia and Angelico, and all of the purists, however beautiful, are poor weak creatures in comparison. I don't understand it; one would have thought purity gave strength, but it doesn't. A good stout, self-commanding magnificent Animality is the make for poets and artists. . . . One day I was struck by the Gorgeousness of life which the world seems to develop. . . . can it be possible that all this power and beauty is adverse to the honor of the Maker of it? has God made faces beautiful and limbs strong, and created these strange, fiery, fantastic energies, and created the splendour of substance and the love of it . . . that these things may lead His creatures away from Him? And

is this mighty Paul Veronese, . . . this man whose finger is as fire, and whose eye is like the morning—is he a servant of the devil; and is the poor little wretch in a tidy black tie, to whom I have been listening this Sunday morning expounding Nothing with a twang—a servant of God? It is all a great mystery. . . . It is all very well for people to fast who can't eat; and to preach who cannot talk nor sing; and to walk barefoot who cannot ride, and then think themselves good. Let them learn to master the world before they abuse it. (*Modern Painters*, vol. 5, Cook, xl–xli)

Thus Ruskin's conversion to the acceptance of created beauty as leading to, rather than away from, the Creator came about suddenly and epiphanically, his paranoic vision in Turin finally breaking down his evangelical paranoidic fears. Fittingly, in letters to friends, Ruskin referred to his Turin moment as his "unconversion."

Ruskin's acceptance of the "animality" of art and the purging of his religious scruples prepared him for the later splendor he describes in *The Queen of the Air* (1869), his rich imaginary portrait of Athena and her sensuous manifestations. But although the "moment in Turin" had taught Ruskin to be "a little wicked and a man of this world," it did not alter his lifelong belief that "taste" and "morality" are essentially one.

In his *Lectures on Art* (1871), delivered during his appointment at Oxford, Ruskin concludes, rather unplatonically, that the purpose of art is to "perfect the moral state of man." He then extrapolates upon the imaginative purity of the passion of love and shifts the source of moral sentiment from the conscience to the imagination, thus mixing the desire for beauty with the desire for love (enabling the integration of his social philosophies with his moral aesthetic). Ruskin preaches a religion of aesthetics in which life demands industry, industry demands art, and art demands morality, because "little else except art is moral."

You cannot have a landscape by Turner, without a country for him to paint; you cannot have a portrait by Titian, without a man to be portrayed. I need not prove that to you I suppose, in these short terms; but in the outcome I can get no soul to believe that the beginning of art is in getting our country clean, and our people beautiful. (*Lectures on Art*, Cook, 107)

As a result of his "moment in Turin," Ruskin was able, in *The Queen of the Air*, to bring to life his lovely Athena in all her physical splendor and yet also to view her as a fresh source of moral truth. In fact, Ruskin's passion and adoration for the creative forces of Athena surpassed any feeling he once may have had for discovering the Christian God in nature. His Athena is the spirit in the air, the fire in the soul, a guide to moral passion, a just companion to the Madonna. Spiritually, Athena is the queen of all glowing virtue, "the unconsuming fire and inner lamp of life."

As the breath of the air, Athena becomes emblematic of the dove or universal spirit; as the omnipotent earth, she becomes the infernal serpent, the source of all man's woe.

> [Athena] . . . the divine hieroglyph of the demonic power of the earth,—of the entire earthly nature. As the bird is the clothed power of the air, so this is the clothed power of the dust; as the bird the symbol of the spirit of life, so this of the grasp and sting of death. (*Queen*, Chesterfield, 55)

In the third lecture of *The Queen of the Air*, "Athena in the Heart," Ruskin's goddess becomes the directress of human passion and will. His aesthetic continues to be morally defined, however, because her new function is to make work "right" by directing "virtue of character." The idea in Ruskin's *Modern Painters*—that "good men produce good art"— reappears with a slight variation: "Great art is the expression of the mind of a great man, and mean art that of the want of mind of a weak man" (78).

Ruskin's moral aesthetics also encouraged him to prevail upon his Queen in order to find fault with Enlightenment culture and science for dividing the world of myth from its phenomena, rendering the images lifeless and eliminating the wonder and truth from primitive beliefs, ultimately separating man from nature.

> Ah, masters of modern science, give me back my Athena out of your vials, and seal, if it may be, once more, Asmodeus therein. You have divided the elements, and united them; enslaved them upon the earth, and discerned them in the stars. Teach us, now, but this of them, which is all that man need know,—that the Air is given to him for his life; and the Rain for his thirst, and for his baptism; and the Fire for warmth; and the Sun for sight; and the Earth for his meat and his Rest. (vii)

Thirty years later, the American writer Henry Adams, in his influential autobiography, would make a similar argument by comparing the

dynamo, which represented the impersonal forces of an emerging in-
dustrial society, to the Virgin Mary.

Unlike Ruskin's momentary flash in Turin, which enabled him to fuse
aesthetic intensity with morality, Hopkins's "unconversion" never fully
arrived. Transported from the rhythms of nature to the cusp of eternity,
where there is a momentary and sobering embrace of the apocalypse,
Hopkins returns, at the end of "Sibyl's Leaves," to the tortured rack of his
inner self.

As in the Dark Sonnet, poem 65, where the "mind has mountains;
cliffs of fall / Frightful, sheer, no-man-fathomed," Hopkins wrestles, at
the end of "Sibyl's Leaves," with himself for the sake of his God. This theistic existential anguish vanquishes the awesome beauty of nature and
the grand order of the apocalypse.

Charlotte Smith, in her sonnet "To Night," published in 1784, anticipates by nearly one hundred years the notion of nature as something
that can no longer be romanticized or aestheticized. Yet, in the spirit of
Browning and Hopkins, Smith nevertheless continues to address her
lament to nature's landscape in spite of its existential indifference:

> In deep depression sunk, the enfeebled mind
> Will to the deaf cold elements complain,
> And tell the embosom'd grief, however vain,
> To sullen surges and the viewless wind.
> Though no repose on the thy dark breast I find,
> I still enjoy thee—cheerless as thou art;
> For in thy quiet gloom the exhausted heart
> Is calm, though wretched; hopeless, yet resign'd . . .
>
> (ll. 5–12)

In "Sibyl's Leaves," alienated by his own worm of conscience, Hopkins's mind gnaws and feeds inwardly—"thoughts / against thoughts in
groans grind." And in this way, his poem remarkably and paranoically
moves away from a concern with late-nineteenth-century aesthetics
and toward a vision of the modern existential condition.

It is Hopkins's mind that cheats him of the eternal moment, whereas
in the Dark Sonnets it is Hopkins's failing body as well as his mind and
his troubled soul that deprive him of the comfort of immortality.

Ironically, the Cumaean Sibyl suffered a similar fate. Loved by Apollo,
she was granted the gift of prophecy and as many years of life as grains
of dust she could hold in her hand. But she forgot to ask for youth as

well, and she shrunk smaller and smaller until, according to Virgil, her entire body was contained in a tiny jar. The fate of the Cumaean Sibyl illuminates the paradox of "natural" perception: those most gifted at reading Nature may not recognize the existential fate of the self in the natural world. Reading nature, although an unnatural ability, does not free one from the forces of entropy. Thus, the simplest scheme for transcending the terror of disintegration becomes a trap.

Knowing that Hopkins was a Jesuit priest, the reader might expect the hellish mental nightmare depicted in "Sibyl's Leaves" to be particularly Christian. Yet, like Ruskin's pagan dance with Athena in "Queen of the Air," "Sibyl's Leaves" may be the most pagan poem Hopkins ever wrote. It has none of the salient religiosity found in many of his other works, and the strongest source of its paganism is Virgil's *Aeneid*, which Hopkins believed anticipated Catholic eschatology. Like Saint Augustine and Thomas Aquinas before him, Hopkins in "Sibyl's Leaves" attempts a synthesis of Christian revelation and pre-Christian metaphysics. In this sense, the poem is the most archetypal and paranoic Hopkins wrote.

As in Kierkegaard's theistic existential dialectic, the personal anguish in the poem evokes universality. This universality rests upon the collective recognition that human anguish is subjective and psychologically a matter of duration—"selfwrung, selfstrung, sheathe- and shelterless." It is by virtue of this existential truth that the poem is most moving, most paranoic, and most credible.

Like Tithonus in Tennyson's poem of the same name, the Cumaean Sibyl's mental and physical anguish is such that she desires only death (which is what she tells Aeneas during his descent into hell). In the Dark Sonnet "Carrion Comfort" (poem 64), Hopkins barely refrains from evoking the same desire:

Not, I'll not, carrion comfort, Despair, not feast on thee;
Not untwist—slack they may be—these last strands of man
In me or, most weary, cry *I can no more.* I can;
Can something, hope, wish day come, not choose not to be.

But ah, but O thou terrible, why wouldst thou rude on me
Thy wring-world right foot rock? lay a lionlimb against me? scan
With darksome devouring eyes my bruised bones? and fan,
O in turns of tempest, me heaped there; me frantic to avoid thee and
     flee?
Why? That my chaff might fly; my grain lie, sheer and clear.

Nay in all that toil, that coil, since (seems) I kissed the rod,
Hand rather, my heart lo! lapped strength, stole joy, would laugh, cheer.
Cheer whom though? The hero whose heaven-handling flung me,
   foot trod
Me? or me that fought him? O which one? is it each one? That night,
   that year
Of now done darkness I wretch lay wrestling with (my God!) my God.

Composed after the Dark Sonnets (and shortly before his death), Hopkins's eschatologically sublime poem "That Nature is a Heraclitean Fire and of the Comfort of the Resurrection" mixes Christian mythology with Greek natural philosophy. Yet, in "Heraclitean Fire" Hopkins manages to "hold on," through paranoic vision of the apocalyptic moment, to Christ's victory over temporal time.

   Across my foundering deck shone
A beacon, an eternal beam. Flesh fade, and mortal trash
Fall to the residuary worm; world's wildfire, leave but ash:
   In a flash, at a trumpet crash,
I am all at once what Christ is, since he was what I am, and
This Jack, joke, poor potsherd, patch, matchwood, immortal
   diamond,
   Is immortal diamond.

                                        (ll. 17–23)

Paranoic Existentialism

The notion of "holding on" can be understood as the active state of "waiting"—a fundamental existential condition. As seen in Browning's "Roland," holding on amidst the banal modern landscape may have to be enough, or like Hopkins holding onto his frail body—"a clod of earth sticking together and holding fast only by strings of roots."

In William Faulkner's great existential novel *The Sound and the Fury* (1929), it is Dilsey, the aged black female servant, who holds on through all the destructive tragic winds of the Compson family. Faulkner once claimed that among all his works, Dilsey was his favorite character, which is why, in his appendix to the book, he heroically says of Dilsey, "she endured."

In Beckett's *Waiting for Godot* (1952), for many the most influential play in the latter half of the twentieth century, Didi and Gogo's heroic ability to hold on for one more day (for the coming of Godot) is their supreme act against the universe's absurd panorama. Yet their reason for holding on is pragmatic rather than principled, as evidenced at the end of the play when they stand before their nearly barren tree and decide not to hang themselves only because one of them would be left behind, alone. This is how, in Beckett's world, "not choosing not to be" prevails.

"Holding on" can even be, in some paradoxical scenarios, a kind of paranoic "letting go" into the face of danger. An example of this is Joseph Conrad's story *The Secret Sharer* (1912), in which a nameless sea captain finally acquires his courage and identity by "holding on" steady to the wheel while the ship sails closer and closer to the rocky coast (to give his "double," a man who is wanted for murder, a chance to secretly swim ashore). By "letting go" of all sense and risking the ship and the lives of those aboard, the captain proves his "being" inside the paranoic blue.

Most profound, however, is the fact that the captain's dangerous "moment" may exemplify our tie to a primordial paranoic state, wherein human consciousness is only capable of completely fulfilling itself while inside a reality of uncertainty. (In ancient times uncertainty was ever-present, brought on by the relentless elements of nature and assorted wild beasts, which had to make our ancestors quite anxious.)

Perhaps after thousands of years of primal paranoic consciousness our brains somehow became pre-figured, and a danger-filled paranoic state became our natural state. And then perhaps, in one lost moment, back in the ancient of days, we quick-silvered away . . . and became paranoidically desirous. This elision in consciousness may be why human civilization has focused so singularly on erecting the walls of contentment in order to be safe from life's contingencies, making one wonder, once again, if we have despoiled ourselves. Because full "being" through paranoic consciousness can be realized only inside the con- tingency. And if we choose to eliminate contingency in order to achieve contentment, we will, by necessity, find ourselves increasingly neurotic, obsessive, and paranoidic.

Thus, the question returns: which is better—to be free and paranoic, or content and paranoidic?

Søren Kierkegaard (1813–55), the Danish theologian and philoso- pher, in his remarkable essay "Dread as a Saving Experience by Means of Faith," offers a quintessential example of paranoic freedom experi- enced in the midst of contingency on the Jutland Heath:

When one or another extraordinary event occurs in life, when a
world-historical hero gathers heroes about him and accomplishes
heroic feats, when a crisis occurs and everything becomes significant,
then men wish to be in it, for these are things which educate. Quite
possibly. But there is a much simpler way of being educated much
more fundamentally. Take the pupil of possibility, set him in the
midst of the Jutland heath where nothing happens, where the greatest event is that a partridge flies up noisily, and he experiences everything more perfectly, more precisely, more profoundly, than the man
who was applauded upon the stage of universal history, in case he
was not educated by possibility. (*Concept of Dread*, 142–43)

To be educated by this "possibility" (or contingency) is to know paranoic being, and such knowledge can't be taught. One must spend time
on the heath until the idea of possibility makes one feel dread. Because,
for Kierkegaard, "Dread is the possibility of freedom." Therefore, "he
who is educated by dread is educated by possibility," and such a man
is educated "in accordance with his infinity." That is why possibility is
the "heaviest of categories."

Considered by many to be the "father of existentialism," Kierkegaard
was actually a "theistic" existentialist, which is why, for him, dread becomes a "serviceable spirit which against its will leads him whither he
would go." This journey, for Kierkegaard, leads to the passionate experience of faith, but in a manner that no one hitherto conceived: a journey not through dramatic revelation or dogma or prayer or good works
or Bible meditation, and not through a faith complacently propped up by
bourgeois culture and middle-class comfort. In fact, Kierkegaard inwardly
raged when he paced the streets of Copenhagen and viewed his fellow
"Christians" mindlessly and complacently going about their business
confident that the issue of faith and God had already been settled, rele-
gated as it was to a controlled sequence of gestures and prayer on Sunday
mornings. Meanwhile, the truth of faith lay paranoically beyond them.

For Kierkegaard believed that to be a Christian and an "individual"
was the "hardest of things," experienced as a lifelong struggle outside
the culture of contentment. Fittingly, "The Individual" is the epitaph
carved on Kierkegaard's gravestone. And as Kierkegaard made clear in
all his writings, the struggle to exist as an individual is actually predicated upon contentment's opposite and declared enemy—anxiety and
dread.

And dread has no object, which makes it quite different from fear. "Nothing begets dread," Kierkegaard says. So the individual, paranoically free and anxious in being, through dread experiences the passion of faith, but only by virtue of the absurd because, for Kierkegaard, "faith begins where reason leaves off." And it is because the Kierkegaardian quest for faith is predicated upon passion that faith is open to all: "Faith is a marvel, and yet no human being is excluded from it; for that which unites all human life is passion, and faith is a passion" (*Fear and Trembling*, 67).

By defining the "essentially human [as] passion," Kierkegaard—despite his theistically existential emphasis on dread—is still, at the core, a nineteenth-century Romantic. Rejecting Hegel's universal dialectic in favor of a personal existential dialectic, Kierkegaard claims that "truth is subjectivity" and dread itself a state of being. For this reason, Kierkegaard maintains that true dread is located inside the individual rather than out in the world as "Grimm's Fairy Tales would have it." Dread results from the realization of the possibility of freedom and "is" the condition of humankind.

> I would say that learning to know dread is an adventure which every man has to affront if he would not go to perdition either by not having known dread or by sinking under it. He therefore who has learned rightly to be in dread has learned the most important thing. (*Concept of Dread*, 139)

For Kierkegaard, there is no equivocation; if we want to be free we must suffer dread. And the greater the dread, the greater the person.

In *Fear and Trembling* (1843), a hybrid text that most scholars believe to be Kierkegaard's greatest work (Kierkegaard himself said that *Fear and Trembling* was "enough for an imperishable name as an author"), Kierkegaard meditates upon Abraham's near-sacrifice of his only son on a mountaintop in the land of Moriah. But what Kierkegaard is most interested in is Abraham's dread. Because without dread Abraham could never have achieved his greatness, could never have achieved his unique status as father of the Jews, Christians, and Muslims. Without his dread, Abraham would not have become a "knight of faith," Kierkegaard's term for the rare figure who transcends conventional heroism in an incomprehensible moment of paranoic experience (placing him in absolute relation to the Absolute).

Indeed, the notion of the "hero" goes out the window when one confronts Abraham's ramifications as madman, child abuser, and willing murderer; and God's ramification as sadist. This is why most readers never want to come to terms with this paradoxical story, and why they choose to elide away into kitschlike encapsulations of Abraham as that "good man, who loved God more than anything, even more than his only son," or "Abraham, the great patriarch, the supreme Father of Faith."

But no kitschlike response will eliminate the troubling notion of Abraham as murderer, which is why one needs Kierkegaard's notion of the knight of faith "in order to perceive the prodigious paradox of faith, a paradox that makes a murder into a holy and God-pleasing act, a paradox that gives Isaac back to Abraham again, which no thought can grasp, because faith begins precisely where thought stops" (*Fear and Trembling,* 53).

As a knight of faith, Abraham offers something higher and infinitely rarer than any hero possibly can. For heroes choose to sacrifice, whereas the knight of faith is chosen by God; heroes act in support of society's ethics, while a knight of faith momentarily and teleologically suspends ethics to become in "absolute relation to the Absolute." And whereas tragic heroes die, the knight of faith lives (Abraham and Isaac return home after their journey up the mountain). And while a tragic hero's actions are understood and sanctioned, the knight of faith is never understood (in fact, Abraham can never explain his experience atop the mountain because he himself never understands it).

> Abraham I cannot understand; in a certain sense I can learn nothing from him except to be amazed. If someone deludes himself into thinking he may be moved to have faith by pondering the outcome of the story, he cheats himself and cheats God out of the first movement of faith—he wants to suck worldly wisdom out of the paradox. (37)

Moreover, a knight of faith is rewarded in this life (Abraham is given land, wealth, and numerous descendants), and the tragic hero is offered a promise of reward only in the life beyond.

But Abraham's reward comes only by virtue of the absurd:

> He had faith by virtue of the absurd, for human calculation was out of the question, and it certainly was absurd that God, who required it of him, should in the next moment rescind the requirement. . . . he had faith by virtue of the absurd, for all human calculation ceases long ago. (35–36)

And Abraham's work is his dread, especially the dread he feels during his three-day journey to the top of the mountain when he anguishes over having to take the life of his only son, whom he loves beyond all things. Most paradoxically, Abraham's willing gesture must be carried out with love; otherwise he is merely God's cold executioner. Indeed, Abraham must love both God and Isaac during the moment of his knife's descending arc: "He must love Isaac with his whole soul. Since God claims Isaac, he must, if possible, love him even more, and only then can he *sacrifice* him, for it is indeed this love for Isaac that makes his act a sacrifice by its paradoxical contrast to his love for God" (74).

Thus, since Abraham's actions cannot be understood, the only way to get to him is through passion. "I cannot think myself into Abraham; when I reach that eminence, I sink down, for what is offered me is a paradox" (33). One must feel Abraham's dread, which is why, in *Fear and Trembling*, Kierkegaard keeps re-imagining the story. The truth lives passionately and inside the individual and comes to life only through anxiety and dread.

As an initial step, one must fight the tendency to abstract or reduce Abraham's experience. As Kierkegaard states: "It is supposed to be difficult to understand Hegel, but to understand Abraham is a small matter. To go beyond Hegel is a miraculous achievement, but to go beyond Abraham is the easiest of all" (32–33).

Fear and Trembling, however, proves just the opposite: to understand Abraham is the hardest of all endeavors. And this most important aspect of the story, the "terrible human content," we tend to leave out.

> I for my part have applied considerable time to understanding Hegelian philosophy and believe that I have understood it fairly well; I am sufficiently brash to think that when I cannot understand particular passages despite all my pains, he himself may not have been entirely clear. All this I do easily, naturally, without any mental strain. Thinking about Abraham is another matter, however; then I am shattered. I am constantly aware of the prodigious paradox that is the content of Abraham's life, I am constantly repelled, and, despite all its passion, my thought cannot penetrate it, cannot get ahead by a hairsbreadth. I stretch every muscle to get a perspective, and at the very same instant I become paralyzed. (33)

In Hegel's theories of history, human beings become merely spectators to the universe's unfolding; in Kierkegaard's thinking, human beings are actors, and to know the truth we must first subjectively feel the truth. Abraham must be as real as ourselves; we must feel his dread and his alienation. In fact, Kierkegaard was the first to argue that the individual's anxious sense of "alienation" actually suggests God's existence. Our sense of alienation proves we are in need of something else, something beyond the bourgeois world of fact, beyond the thinking of the "crowd." The "crowd is untruth," Kierkegaard says. For it is easy to win over the crowd, but to win over the self is the real quest, which is precisely what Abraham had to do. And Abraham's dread was his education.

Inside Abraham's moment on the mountain, with the knife rushing down, not only are ethics and reason momentarily and teleologically suspended (as Kierkegaard makes clear), but the paranoidic world itself is dismissed. Abraham's arm creasing the realm of time and fact is one of the greatest paranoic moments in Western cultural history; it is a gesture by a man who not only never understands what God asked him to do, but who returns afterward to his wife and people to live as a good man, a good father, and husband, and Jew.

And if all of this makes one think, "maybe I should visit this kind of man so I can learn from him," to actually travel to him would, again, be paradoxical.

> The instant I first lay eyes on him . . . I jump back, clap my hands, say half aloud, "Good Lord, is this the man, is this really the one—he looks just like a tax collector!" But this is indeed the one. . . . I examine his figure from top to toe to see if there may not be a crack through which the infinite would peek. No! He is solid all the way through. . . . He belongs entirely to the world: no bourgeois philistine could belong to it more. Nothing is detectable of that distant and aristocratic nature by which the knight of the infinite is recognized. . . . He attends to his job. . . . Sunday is for him a holiday. He goes to church. No heavenly gaze or any sign of the incommensurable betrays him; if one did not know him, it would be impossible to distinguish him from the rest of the crowd. (38–39)

Friedrich Nietzsche (1844–1900), to most readers' surprise, never read Kierkegaard, yet he nevertheless imagined his own elusive figure—the Übermensch (overman)—who is as different from the "herd" as a World War I flying ace is from those in the trenches. Unlike the herd, who desire a life without pain, Nietzsche's Übermensch rejects happiness and welcomes suffering as the condition for his creative and dizzy-

ingly free existence. Most important, Nietzsche's concept of the Übermensch liberates paranoic being from the underground, where it
dwelled with Dostoyevsky for instance (or where it dwelled literally with
the early catacombic Christians). With Nietzsche, the alienation included in the paranoic movement away from the culture of contentment leads to soaring and dangerous heights.

As Nietzsche suggests in *Thus Spoke Zarathustra* (1885), the existence of the Übermensch is predicated on the dread-filled acknowledgment that "God is dead." Yet when Zarathustra comes down from his
mountain, after spending ten years in the high paranoic air, the people
in the village reject this claim. For they lack the animal strength to believe that there is something beyond the human (an Übermensch), or
that life's greatest experience is to paranoically repudiate happiness as
well as any existence based on reason and passivity.

> Man is a rope, fastened between animal and superman—a rope
> over an abyss. A dangerous going-across, a dangerous wayfaring, a
> dangerous looking-back, a dangerous shuddering and staying-still.
> What is great in man is that he is a bridge and not a goal; what can be
> loved in man is that he is a going-across. . . . I love him who lives for
> knowledge and who wants knowledge that one day the superman
> may live. And thus he wills his own downfall. (*Zarathustra, Nietzsche
> Reader,* 239)

Similar to Kierkegaard's emphasis on "the individual," Nietzsche's
Übermensch is forever involved in the Dionysian pain of individuation,
which eventually offers the promise of salvation from a declining civilization obsessively caught up in overrationalization. For Nietzsche, this
salvation depends upon the "coming of age" acceptance of the death of
God and of the ruling idea of "becoming" (made prescient by the evo-
lutionism of Hegel and Darwin). If "everything evolves" then nothing is
permanently true, and the Übermensch must be able to face this uncertainty and still pursue his creative life amidst the blue-gray paranoic
air. Most cannot handle this, and the resulting collapse of morale through
a growing consciousness of purposelessness would lead to the modern
wars and catastrophes, which Nietzsche seems to have prophesized.

Ultimately, there are two doors to Nietzsche's philosophy: the first
leads into contingency and dread (because everything is permitted if
God is dead), and the second leads to transcendence (for the spirited
few). This transcendence is not metaphysical, however, the way most

Western thinkers have believed transcendence to be. Rather, transcendence for Nietzsche occurs by the power of "Will"; and not the will over others, but the will over the self. In this way, the Übermensch's journey is life-affirming; it stresses strength and freedom, and it is only for those with the courage to reject the morality of the herd in order to generate individuated morality. The Übermensch, perhaps the Western world's most extremely paranoic figure, risks all to pursue his journey inside the blue contingency.

The price of even "thinking" oneself into such painful transcendence is great, which is why Nietzsche spent most of his life ill and flirting with madness, and terrifyingly lonely. (Like the Übermensch, Nietzsche had no God or dogma to console him.) Lou Salome, a Jewish intellectual and the only woman Nietzsche ever loved, decided to leave him in 1885 (when he was working on *Thus Spoke Zarathustra*) because Nietzsche was, in her words, "too difficult." This led to Nietzsche's further retreat into an ascetic and lonely life. (Ironically, Salome admitted in 1894 that Nietzsche was more important than she had thought, and she tried to redeem herself by publishing a biography of him.)

A few years after Salome's desertion, Nietzsche would have his own "moment in Turin," a moment quite unlike Ruskin's 1858 "Turin moment" when he encountered the mighty Paul Veronese's painting *Solomon and the Queen of Sheba* and was "struck by the Gorgeousness of life," realizing, in an astonishingly Nietzsche-like manner, that "a self-commanding magnificent Animality is the make for poets and artists."

Nietzsche's moment in Turin was in 1889, the same year Hopkins lay weak and dying, disgusted by his "useless splinter of wood" body. Turin, a unique medieval Italian city that shows almost no trace of the Renaissance, was where Nietzsche would write, between bouts of madness, his last works—*Twilight of the Idols, The Anti-Christian, Ecce Homo*—works written with such an uncanny presenticity one can almost feel Nietzsche thinking.

In *Ecce Homo*, "Why I Am a Destiny," Nietzsche ponders his fate and, true to Ruskin's vision of "a magnificent animality" and Hopkins's life-long dream for a healthy body and Blake's emphasis on seeing first with the "corporeal eye," Nietzsche's vision is grounded in his nostrils:

> One day there will be associated with my name the recollection of something frightful—of a crisis like no other before on earth, of the profoundest collision of conscience, of a decision evoked *against*

everything that until then had been believed in, demanded, sancti-
fied. I am not a man, I am dynamite.—And with all that there is
nothing in me of a founder of a religion—religions are affairs of the
rabble. . . . I have a terrible fear I shall one day be pronounced *holy*. . . .
The truth speaks out of me, but my truth is *dreadful*: for hitherto the
lie has been called truth.—*Revaluation of all values*: that is my formula
for an act of supreme coming-to-oneself. . . . It is my fate to have to be
the first decent human being, to know myself in opposition to the
mendaciousness of millennia. . . . I was the first to discover the truth,
in that I was the first to sense—smell—the lie as lie. . . . My genius is
in my nostrils. . . . I contradict as has never been contradicted and am
nonetheless the opposite of a negative spirit. I am a *bringer of good
tidings* such as there has never been, I know tasks from such a height
that any conception of them has hitherto been lacking; only after me
is it possible to hope again. With all that I am necessarily a man of fa-
tality. For when truth steps into battle with the lie of millennia we
shall have convulsions, an earthquake spasm, a transposition of val-
ley and mountain such as has never been dreamed of. The concept
politics has then become completely absorbed into a war of spirits,
all the power-structures of the old society have been blown into the
air—they one and all reposed on the lie: there will be wars such as
there have never yet been on earth. Only after me will there be *grand
politics* on earth. (*Nietzsche Reader*, 24–25)

In his final weeks in Turin, however, journeying into the paranoic
blue became increasingly a journeying into a maddened self. His writing became unreadable (except to his mother and sister); he had constant headaches, sudden attacks of weeping, severe trembling, uncon-
trollable facial grimaces.

Nietzsche's moment in Turin had been developing for years. He experienced periods of madness and despair dating back to the early
1870s. The source for this was probably the syphilis he had contracted
in a brothel in 1865. By 1889, the syphilis was consuming his brain, and
he spent his final conscious days in Turin talking to no one except shop
clerks and attendants.

Departing his apartment one rainy morning, Nietzsche fell into embracing a cab horse after he saw the driver whipping it. When the driver
finally pulled him away, Nietzsche collapsed on the street. And so . . .
Nietzsche lost himself from the world.

He would live another eleven years, mostly under the care of his increasingly paranoidic anti-Semitic sister against whom he had railed in a Christmas letter of 1887: "You have committed one of the greatest stupidities—for yourself and for me! Your association with an anti-Semitic chief expresses a foreignness to my whole way of life which fills me again and again with ire or melancholy. . . . It is a matter of honor with me to be absolutely clean and unequivocal in relation to anti-Semitism, namely, *opposed* to it, as I am in my wrings" (*Portable Nietzsche*, 456–57).

Until his death in 1900, Nietzsche would remain paralyzed and mostly silent. (Ironically, Ruskin, who would also die in 1900, spent his last decade in mental seclusion and dumbness.)

There are those who like to deride Nietzsche because they resent his writings. They argue that his "revaluation of values," which undermines Western ethics and the Christian tradition, inevitably led to his deserved madness. Thus the terror of Nietzsche's end becomes a fitting morality tale.

Yet, because of the syphilis, we will never really know what brought on Nietzsche's madness. More so than with Hopkins and Kierkegaard (and even Schreber), Nietzsche's rejection of the culture of contentment seemed to bring on the worst consequences. And that's what makes Nietzsche the tragic prince of the paranoic.

But all of their lives ended alone: Hopkins, because of his Jesuitical dedication to God; and Kierkegaard, because of his passionate embrace of the religious, which included breaking off his engagement to Regine (explained in his work *Either/Or,* written just before *Fear and Trembling*), telling her that he could not marry her because it would mean giving up the nothingness that he was. (Regine would later marry the German philosopher Friedrich von Schlegel.) And Nietzsche, because he was paranoically too difficult for the world, enclosing himself inside a loneliness unbearable, perhaps, for even the Übermensch. As he said in a letter to Franz Overbeck, August 1886:

> For the lonely one, even noise is a consolation. . . . If only to give you an idea of my loneliness—I have no one among the living or dead to whom I feel related. And it is indescribably horrible. (*Self Portrait*, 90)

And from one of his last letters:

> I call myself the last philosopher because I am the last man. Nobody talks to me but myself, and my voice comes to me like that of a dying

person . . . through it I conceal my loneliness from myself. . . . The terrible loneliness of the last philosopher! . . . And I make my way into the multitude by lies, for my heart cannot bear the terror of the loneliest loneliness and compels me to talk as if I were two. (Jaspers, *Nietzsche,* 55)

For me, Nietzsche's life was an internally violent process of tearing himself loose from his own moral and spiritual roots. And his torment occurred at the same time that many thinkers and writers in the Western world were contemplating the same fate. The difference is that Nietzsche didn't arm-chair his thinking; he actually made the paranoic journey. This is why in his writings Nietzsche pictures himself as a madman. To lose God equates with madness because all former assumptions of human beingness vanish. And as the values that heretofore gave life meaning begin to disappear, life itself becomes colder and night closes in.

And no one else is "in the madness" with you, because no one else has really discovered and accepted that God is dead.

My time has not yet come, some are born posthumously.—One day institutions will be needed in which people live and teach as I understand living and teaching: perhaps even chairs for the interpretation of Zarathustra will then be established. (*Ecce Homo, Nietzsche Reader,* 21)

Thus, Nietzsche is the loneliest of men because only he is paranoically inside the human predicament. "Those who manage to have a god never experienced what I know as loneliness." And so he longs for relief from his loneliness, and for his cold truths to be untrue: "I wish someone could cause my truths to become incredible. . . . I have neither god nor friends."

The importance of Nietzsche, it seems then, is not really a result of whether he was wrong or right (regarding, for instance, whether most of Western values are falsehoods). Rather, his importance lies in urging us to think that what he is saying "might" be true. Instead, many want to morally condemn Nietzsche, or smile smugly, or use him for a game of intellectual marbles or philosophic gymnastics. Most toy with him as they would a ferocious-looking doll, but never allow him to live.

In the end, most are afraid to really think through Nietzsche, afraid to really go that far, because maybe the earth really would drop out, and maybe they, too, would find themselves faithless, tormented, and alone.

Thus the danger in Nietzsche is not in his "revaluation of values" but in wondering if we really are capable of thinking in an ultimately free paranoic manner. In this way, Nietzsche's great virtue is in challenging us, daring us to think the unthinkable, to feel the thrill and dizziness of paranoic journeying.

Might we walk out just a bit onto the Nietzschean rope, suspended between animals and superman, a rope woven of the thinnest filaments and suspended high into the paranoic blue? And once there—breathing Nietzsche's heightened air—will we find it impossible to ever go back again and feel the same about our beliefs? As he describes in his introduction to *Ecce Homo*:

> He who knows how to breathe the air of my writings knows that it is an air of the heights, a *robust* air. One has to be made for it, otherwise there is no small danger one will catch cold. The ice is near, the solitude is terrible—but how peacefully all things lie in the light! how freely one breathes! how much one feels *beneath* one!—Philosophy, as I have hitherto understood and lived it, is a voluntary living in ice and high mountains—a seeking after everything strange and questionable in existence, all that has hitherto been excommunicated by morality. From the lengthy experience afforded by such wandering in the *forbidden* I learned to view the origins of moralizing and idealizing very differently from what might be desirable. . . . How much truth can a spirit *bear*, how much truth can a spirit *dare*? . . . Every acquisition, every step forward in knowledge, is the result of courage, of severity towards oneself. . . . *Nitimur in vetitum* [the splendid is that which is forbidden]: in this sign my philosophy will one day conquer, for fundamentally what has hitherto been forbidden has never been anything but the truth. (*Nietzsche Reader*, 52)

The German philosopher Karl Jaspers (1883–1969) believed that we should not expect a way of life from Nietzsche, or even a satisfying philosophy. For Nietzsche does not show the way, or teach, or give much to stand on. He grants no peace, but torments ceaselessly, hunts us out of our retreats, and forbids concealment.

And so unfolds the story of modern philosophy, a tale based on the notion of inexpressible inner experience. As Michel Foucault observed, the death of God in Western thought does more than simply affect the emotions: it profoundly influenced language, and the silence that replaced its source remains impenetrable. In Martin Heidegger's words, "Dread strikes us dumb."

Paranoic Dasein

Heidegger (1889–1976), who was strongly influenced by Nietzsche, had his own notion of perpetual human elusivity—Dasein, a term nearly untranslatable (being-there? or the sense of self be-ing in time?). Dasein's resistance to definition is, in fact, one of Dasein's essential qualities. For Heidegger, humans are a unique mode of being and can't be a "what," so he sees them instead as Dasein. However, Dasein's absorption in the "they" or the "world" causes "a *fleeing* of Dasein in the face of itself," or "itself as an authentic potentiality-for-Being-its-Self." Moreover, anxiety increases as Dasein watches the world withdraw into nothingness, losing all labels and definition (becoming sycphatic).

According to Heidegger, the basic state of Dasein is "Being-in-the-world," and the most fundamental mood of Dasein is anxiety arising from the precarious nature of Dasein's be-ing. And Dasein doesn't even "know what in the face of which it is anxious." For being-anxious discloses "primordially and directly, the world as world." Thus, anxiety "individualizes Dasein for its ownmost Being-in-the-world" and brings Dasein face to face with its "Being-free" for the authenticity of its Being, and "for this authenticity as a possibility which it always is" (*Being and Time*, 232). But poor Dasein is so anxious in the very depth of its being that it feels "uncanny" (unhomelike, or "not-being-at-home").

Novalis—a marvelous pseudonym for the sublime German Romantic poet Friedrich von Hardenberg (1772–1801)—stated years earlier in one of his lyrical fragments that "philosophy is really Homesickness; the wish to be everywhere at home," and urged further that "the World must be romanticized, only thus will we discover its original meaning."

This is why we want to make something of the nothing: to label and domesticate the universe, to romanticize its meaning, to "at-home" all of the objects of anxiety and dread. Dostoyevsky's Man from Underground hated the rational version of this "at-homing," which he referred to as erecting the "Crystal Palace."

With Heidegger's meditation upon "Dasein" (in his major work, *Being and Time* [1927]), a metaphysical shift does occur, perhaps the most fundamental one in Western philosophic history. The concept of "being" is redefined, away from the emphasis upon spatial existence established by Plato and followed by traditional metaphysics ever since, and toward an emphasis upon temporality. Thus, "being" is the consciousness of existing in time (Dasein) made manifest by "state-of-mind," which makes one "how one is." The world is not those entities that Dasein is not, but a characteristic of Dasein itself. Furthermore, anxiety individualizes Dasein and thus discloses it as "*solus ipse.*"

Individuation occurs after Dasein calls itself back from its fallenness in the "they-self." And why does Dasein call itself back? Because of "care." In conscience Dasein calls itself back.

> Conscience summons Dasein's Self from its lostness in the "they." . . . conscience manifests itself as the call of care: the caller is Dasein, which in its thrownness . . . is anxious about its potentiality-for-Being. The one to whom the appeal is made is the very same Dasein, summoned to its ownmost potentiality-for-Being. . . . The call of conscience [makes clear] . . . that Dasein is, in the very basis of its Being, care. . . . The caller is Dasein in its uncanniness: primordial, thrown Being-in-the-world as the "not-at-home"—the bare "that-it-is" in the "nothing" of the world. (319–23)

And Dasein, lost in the world and the theyself, doesn't always recognize the call of Care, which is also the voice of the paranoic, because Dasein, lost in the world and the they, is, therefore, lost inside the paranoidic.

Dasein's recognition of its finitude—what Heidegger terms "authentic-being-towards-death"—is the chief irony in Heidegger's thought. For even though we know that we are really nothing, we are still continually involved in the task of creating a self after anxiety brings Dasein back from the world: "In conscience Dasein calls itself."

Like Kierkegaard, for whom dread is terrible yet good, Heidegger believes anxiety to be good. Kierkegaard tells us that if we want to be free, we must suffer dread; Heidegger tells us that if we want a self, we must suffer anxiety. For Kierkegaard, "nothing begets dread"; for Heidegger, "dread reveals Nothing."

In Heideggerian terms, then, the question becomes, "What about Nothing?" And as Samuel Beckett said, "nothing is more real than nothing," which helps to explain Wallace Stevens's marvelous poem "The Snow Man," in which, only as nothing himself can the listener behold the "Nothing that is not there and the nothing that is" (l. 15).

For Stevens, the Western inability to accept nothingness is an imaginative failure. And for Heidegger, only on the basis of the manifestness of Nothing can Dasein "advance towards and enter into what-is." Dasein always proceeds from Nothing as manifest because Dasein on one level means "being projected into Nothing." In terms of transcendence, Dasein is already beyond "what-is-in-totality."

> Were Dasein not, in its essential basis, transcendent, that is to say, were it not projected from the start into Nothing, it could never relate to what-is, hence could have no self-relationship. ("What is Metaphysics?" *Existence and Being*, 344)

Of course, none of this dizzying Heideggerian thinking solves the biggest question of all: "Why is there Being at all, why not rather Nothing?"

Jean-Paul Sartre, whose existential thinking is predicated upon Heidegger's, asks this same question in his 1938 philosophic novel *Nausea*. (Indeed, Sartre's motivation to write *Nausea* came from his desire to find a more accessible way for Heidegger's philosophic ideas to reach the people.) In Sartre's novel, the narrator, Antoine Roquentin, falls into an existential crisis one day while throwing stones at the seashore. Suddenly he senses something that disgusts him, but he doesn't know if it is in the stone or in the sea.

Roquentin's crisis continues later in a cafe when he can no longer look at his beer glass, and he doesn't know why, except that he feels himself "slipping into the water's depths, towards fear" (8). And later, in a restaurant with the Self-Taught Man, a "drum-stick swims in a brown gravy. It has to be eaten" (113).

For Roquentin the nausea is brought on by his increasing awareness of objects simply existing, threatening, from underneath their assigned purpose and value. And the world, then, in Heidegger's words, seems to be "crowding around."

In the novel's existentially climactic scene in the park, the root of a chestnut tree loses its definition and becomes merely "knotty, inert, nameless." When Roquentin tries in vain to repeat "this is a root," the naming process doesn't work anymore. Language explains nothing once the nothingness behind all objects is revealed (the sycphatic condition).

As was seen in Browning and Hopkins, aesthetics also seems to fail in *Nausea* amidst the hegemony of existential awareness. This is evident when Roquentin's former lover, Anny, is unable to live anymore for the sake of "perfect moments," a sort of Keatsian attempt to fuse aesthetic meaning into "privileged situations."

"And the perfect moments? Where do they come in?"

"They come afterwards. First there are annunciatory signs. Then the privileged situation, slowly, majestically, comes into people's lives. Then the question of whether you want to make a perfect moment of it. . . . it was . . . a duty. You had to transform privileged situations into perfect moments. It was a moral question. . . . [But] there are no adventures—there are no perfect moments . . . we have lost the same illusions." (148–50)

Later, in his own philosophic tome, *Being and Nothingness* (1943)—a work not nearly as interesting and useful as his fictional works—Sartre employs two terms that polarize Roquentin's nausea: "*l'en soi,*" or "being" existing in itself; and "*le pour soi,*" or "being" existing for itself. The stone and the beer glass and the tree root are the former, and Roquentin struggling to define himself moment by moment, freely and paranoically, is the latter.

In the park, Roquentin discovers that behind the appearances of both "*l'en soi*" and "*le pour soi*" there is nothingness. Ancillary to this is the assumption that human beings have no essence or "a priori" nature, and therefore they are free to create a self, or, in Heidegger's words, Dasein. And since human beings are in a constant state of "becoming," there is no past, and, therefore, no past self about which to reminisce.

I looked around me: the present, nothing but the present. Furniture light and solid, rooted in its present, a table, a bed, a closet with a mirror—and me. The true nature of the present revealed itself: it was what exists, and all that was not present did not exist. The past did not exist. Not at all. Not in things, not even in my thoughts. . . . For me the past was only a pensioning off: it was another way of existing, a state of action and inaction; each event, when it had played its part put itself politely into a box and became an honorary event: we have so much difficulty imagining nothingness. Now I knew: things are entirely what they appear to be—and behind them . . . there is nothing. (95–96)

Memories themselves are fictions: "My memories are like coins in the devil's purse: when you open it you find only dead leaves" (32).

Roquentin had been writing a biography of the Marquis de Rollebon. But after realizing that Rollebon needed him in order to exist, and that he himself needed Rollebon so as not to feel his own existence, Roquentin abandons Rollebon, and "suddenly, noiselessly, M. de Rollebon had returned to his nothingness" (96).

Paranoic "I"

In Sartre's novel, all of Roquentin's epiphanies concerning the nothingness of self lead to his "I" becoming lost outside of self. He is without a referent, yet still existing in the text. Like Darl at the end of William Faulkner's black-comedic existential novel *As I Lay Dying* (1930), Roquentin begins to view himself in the third-person. Still, he knows he exists, that he is "here," so to speak.

> Now when I say "I," it seems hollow to me. I can't manage to feel myself very well, I am so forgotten. The only real thing left in me is existence which feels it exists. . . . Antoine Roquentin exists for no one. . . . And just what is Antoine Roquentin? An abstraction. A pale reflection of myself wavers in my consciousness . . . and suddenly the "I" pales, pales, and fades out. (170)

Moments later, when Roquentin heads for the cafe, it is because a voice has told him it is time to go there; and the "I" surges into consciousness, very much like a *you*—"it is *I,* Antoine Roquentin, I'm leaving for Paris shortly; I am going to say goodbye to the patronne" (171).

Thus, in Sartre's atheistic existentialism, the "I" elides paranoically, and dread results from recognizing contingency—the possibility that anything may or may not occur, and that existence itself is "in the way" of nothingness. This is what Roquentin realizes in the park staring at his chestnut tree. The park scene is his Jutland Heath: "No necessary being can explain existence: contingency is not a delusion, a probability which can be dissipated; it is the absolute" (131). Such dread-filled recognition is accompanied by what Sartre terms "forlornness," the recognition that there is nothing to cling to (no God or absolutes).

Yet most Westerners persist in believing that something permanent can be made out of the nothingness, that the universe can be domesticated. Sudden disclosure of the sycphatic condition, of the nothingness that exists beneath domestification, like the nondescript blackness beneath Roquentin's tree root, results in existential horror—two plus two equals zero.

In Vladimir Nabokov's novel *Despair* (1936), the self-conscious narrator, who resembles in many ways Dostoyevsky's and Sartre's narrators, feels himself sliding out of himself: "Eventually I found myself sitting in the parlor—while making love in the bedroom" (38). Just as he begins to question his sense of self, he comes across a strange man who resembles himself even more than he himself does. The book's brilliant irony lies in the narrator's act of self-discovery during the course of carrying out his own murder. Like Sartre and Nietzsche and Heidegger, Nabokov finds that, even in the death of self, the self lives.

In Samuel Beckett's prose, the constantly repeated "I" seems to confirm non-self status; Beckett's "I" implies a recently present "you," or the image one has just had of oneself. In his ultra-self-conscious novel *Malone Dies* (1953), the reader has to keep assembling the narrative selves as well the narrative world, which in Beckett's exhaustive minimalism may entail nothing more than an account of a man rolling on the ground and losing his hat.

Malone, lying in bed during his final hours in what is probably a poorhouse, decides: "I shall tell myself stories, if I can. They will not be the same kind of stories as hitherto, that is all" (2). The stories are woven out of not only created characters but also different narrative voices focusing on different realms of the past. It is not long before Malone discovers that he can't escape his own self through storytelling.

> I wonder if I am not talking yet again about myself. Shall I be incapable, to the end, of lying on any other subject? I feel the old dark gathering, the solitude preparing, by which I know myself, and the call of that ignorance which might be noble and is mere poltroonery. Already I forget what I have said. That is not how to play. . . . Perhaps I had better abandon this story and go on to the second, or even the third, the one about the stone. No, it would be the same thing. (12)

In the second half of Beckett's brief novel, Malone is gradually stripped of his possessions—maid, food, stick, speech—and his tale of a man named Macmann, who lives in an asylum, begins to resemble Malone himself. Eventually, Malone's account of his characters takes up more space than his account of the literal circumstances in his room. When his characters begin to act without his wishes, he reacts by killing them off. But before he can finish, he himself dies. In this manner, the book's last word is about Malone's last word, the fantasy of Macmann converging with the fantasy of Malone's self into one vanishing point. Death in Malone's case is Beckett's commentary on the mind's attempt to escape itself through metaphor, making his reader wonder if literary transcendence necessarily results in failure, since Malone's stories always return to himself.

Thus the conditions of self-reflexivity seem predicated upon the fact that, just when one thinks one is expanding out of the self, one is in fact ebbing into the self. Hence Beckett's idea of an inner self as nothing more than the memory of subjective anguish, which is why in Beckett it sometimes seems like there is nothing to express, nothing from which to express, and no power to express.

And which is why, sooner or later, the pursuit of the paranoic often resolves into nearly colorless variations of the Jutland Heath, where "nothing happens," and where there is no starving yourself to defeat the devil, as the Russian writer Nikolai Gogol once tried to do. Because the devil isn't there, where nothing is waiting to happen; like when I was hanging on my tree limb to feel sad, because I knew that nothing had to be, and that's why I saw the damn Russians in their smoky coats of brown and grey, all hunched together silent and pretending to take the place of what I couldn't see; and the "hoary hateful cripple" isn't there to be blamed, or the Dark Tower itself that arrives just as we begin to forget, allowing us to understand—for the first time all over again—that the Tower is round and squat because no one expects it to be, that it's an "almost-nothing-to-be" so crude that Roland's realization—"only a Last Judgment's fire will cure this place"—is his last correct thought.

But on the Jutland Heath there is no fire . . .

Yet the paranoidic journey has misled us for so long that after a while we don't know that either, which is why we are forever expecting something. So that when paranoic seeing finally envelops, we only hear a "click / As when a trap shuts—you're inside the den!"

Raising the slug-horn to our lips, then, is much more than we hitherto believed, more than a statement of endurance inside a dimension where triumph doesn't exist. The blowing of the horn is the call of the paranoic, before the grand "Nothing that is not there and the nothing that is."

6

The Paranoic
as Prayer

Petomai

When Daniel Schreber, as an eight-year-old boy, saw his father, Paul Schreber—the renowned German authority on child-rearing—come in the room once again with his instruments and apparati in hand, did he pray? . . . And was his prayer a simple Lutheran one he would have known as a child, or possibly a "made-up" prayer of deliverance? . . . And was Daniel Schreber praying to the same God he would talk to fifty years later from his darkened room in the asylum in Dresden, the God he would accuse of "unmanning" him, of violating him "through the nerves"?

And was it the same God Joan had prayed to from her turret, pleading to escape death by fire, anything to escape death by fire; and Hypatia praying Neoplatonically from her golden chariot, trapped by the doomed hands of the gleamy-eyed monks in Alexandria; and Abe in his angst on Mount Moriah; and Jesus in his sweat-blood at Gethsemane . . .

Maybe Daniel Schreber dreamed of flying, as children often do, the moment his father entered the room. Flying into the away-beyond, as the ancient Greeks used to say—Petomai (I am flying), in the paranoic sense of "on the wing of uncertain hopes" (an idea suggested in Aristophanes' *Clouds,* for instance).

Which makes me think of the expressions the martyred saints always have in their last painted moments—at the height of suffering and anguish—the look of ecstasy (Caravaggio's painting of Flavio, for instance). Beyond the runnels of faith, in their final moment of life, the martyrs are granted a flashing vision of God, a paranoic reward just as their breath expires.

Medieval and Renaissance painters captured this saintly moment and helped turn it into high Catholic kitsch. Yet they encoded "petomai" as well: you just have to view the paintings with the eyes of Vico's "fantasia" to hear the saintly cries—"I am here and not, alive and not, in flesh and not, above and below . . . suspended on uncertain hopes, beyond the no worse there is none."

But inside the culture of contentment, where the gods are hardly worth dying for, the paranoic experience of petomai is rarely apprehended. Martyrdom unconsciously equates with madness, and the saints in their full petomai, elide away . . .

E. M. Cioran, the Romanian/French intellectual, discovered this elision when he attempted to write a book about the saints. The only way to know a saint "is to become one," Cioran decided. But becoming one, he soon found out, was impossible. So he abandoned the whole saintly project and, in his 1956 work *The Temptation to Exist*, redefined the location of God as not in the innermost self, as most believe, but rather at the extreme limits of our feverish being (like the martyred saints in their final moment of pain and ecstasy). God exists, for Cioran, at the very point where "our rage confronts His, and shock results, [the] encounter is ruinous for Him and for us" (33).

The encounter with God in the asylum was ruinous for Daniel Schreber, prolonging his madness for years. Yet the encounter also delivered him from a life deprived of paranoic selfhood, ever since those earliest days when his father entered his room and tried to force-form him. Schreber-the-boy wanted to fly but couldn't; and he wouldn't until years later when madness became his prayer, madness his petomai of regeneration.

In the asylum, Schreber's paranoic conversations with God were his way of creating, in Freud's terms, a "delusional patch" to cover the fissure in his mind. And thus, Schreber's paranoic myth-making spun out into epiphanies of salvation.

And although Freud, consciously or unconsciously, misread Schreber's condition in order to support his own unfounded theory of repressed homosexuality, Freud was in the zone when he understood Schreber's delusions to be visionary texts created to heal himself from abject loneliness and despair. Cut off from his wife and job; childless, fatherless, and abandoned to an asylum, Schreber experienced a loneliness that was perhaps worse than Nietzsche's "terror of the loneliest loneliness [that] compels me to talk as if I were two." (For most of his nine years in the asylum, Schreber was allowed no visitors, and not even a wristwatch to keep track of clocked time.)

Inside the asylum, Schreber responded to his loss of the external paranoidic world with an internal catastrophe and delusionary paranoic visions that simultaneously began the reconstruction of his altar of self. The *Memoirs,* then, are the record of Schreber's madness as prayer, of his long-overdue and dangerous petomai, fifty years after being traumatized by his father's perverse discipline under the blind aegis of latent Enlightenment Germanic culture.

And, although a recent biography of Schreber by Szi Lothane (1994) argues that Schreber's madness wasn't necessarily instigated by his father's cruel treatment, the facts regarding the father are hard to ignore: it was Daniel's papa, Dr. Paul Gottlieb Moritz Schreber, who was a physician, professor, writer, and clinical instructor at the medical school at Leipzig, who was a "specialist" on physical culture for children and on the use of what he called "therapeutic gymnastics," which employed an elaborate series of strict ritualizations that were intended to break the will of the child for the sake of discipline (severe punishment was called for at the slightest infringement of the rules because the child's naturally rebellious and crude nature had to be controlled and disciplined); Paul Schreber who had published over thirty articles on the subject of child-rearing, who invented the *Geradehalter,* a contraption of boards and straps (popular until after World War II) that promised to cure any child who didn't sit up straight and practice strong German posture; Paul Schreber who fashioned paranoidic remedies and systems for nearly everything—cold-water health systems, systems to cure harmful body habits, lifelong diets, and a systematic playground called a *Schrebergarten*; Paul Schreber who had two sons—one who committed suicide and one (Daniel) who went mad and voluntarily entered the asylum (1893) after a seemingly content life as husband (despite the fact that his marriage resulted in only miscarriages and stillbirths), lawyer, and judge; Paul Schreber who suffered a head injury and became mentally ill when he was fifty-one years old, entering a dark depression and retreating onto the edges of the world to die two years later, and whose son Daniel also became mentally ill at age fifty-one, with the chief symptom he complained about being the "softening of the brain and fears of dying."

So for Daniel the asylum must have seemed quite familiar, because the asylum director, Flechsig, employed straps and railings and padded cells, contraptions not unlike the head-holding straps and chin-bands Papa Schreber had once used upon Daniel. But the asylum was also a place where a childless and fatherless man could begin again, in pure relation to God, to regenerate himself and the world, because when no one in the world is left, God himself calls on you and un-mans you, transforming you, through rays into your nerves, into a voluptuous woman so that procreation can begin. And when such a grand paranoic reality overwhelms you, you pray and soar even higher, creating other selves to enter—a Jesuit novice for instance, or an Alsatian girl obsessed with defending her honor against a French soldier.

Writing his *Memoirs* from inside the asylum, then, was Daniel Schreber's way of chronicling his years of full-blown paranoic consciousness, a way of saving himself by describing how he soared on visionary wings after the paranoidic world ceased to exist.

Thus, Daniel Paul Schreber's life seems to be the inverse of what most human beings experience: instead of building, during the course of one's life, an altar of self in context with the world, Schreber's selfhood gradually elided, beginning the moment his father first entered his childhood room and vanquished, with his contraptions, all hope for paranoic being. And Daniel's paranoic "self" really wouldn't live again until delusions set in as psychotic madness, as high petomai, as paranoic prayer.

And prayer as hallucination must be all right since it had to be that way in the beginning, when the first prayers were uttered just outside the garden, because the concept of prayer doesn't exist until the first step outside the garden (which is why "prayer" doesn't exist in Blake's world, where we are forever inside the garden of vision). Cast out as they were into the world's premier wasteland, Adam's and Eve's prayers had to be maddened ones, predicated upon a new and shockingly acquired paranoidic consciousness. And the paranoic . . . It was nothing more than a useless dream, with petomai as prayer the only relief.

And how unlike their prelapsarian state, when the primal twosome undoubtedly experienced full paranoic consciousness and, therefore, had no need for prayer, no need for the petomai of salvation, not inside the amoral Edenic, the egregious garden where anything was possible anytime.

And that is why you don't notice the use of the word "good" in the original account of creation in Genesis—that is, the "J" account, written around 1000 BCE during the reign of Solomon, the account wherein Adam and Eve are formed of the dust of the earth and given life through the intimacy of divine breath, God actually planting the garden and asking Adam to help him name things (co-creator?), and giving Adam and

Eve the garden to "tend" and to "caretake"; as opposed to the "P" account, wherein Adam is told to "subdue" and "have dominion"; hence the timeless Western duality regarding a human being's proper relationship to Nature.

In ancient Hebrew, the word "good" (*Tov*) meant pure or unalloyed. But there was no need to emphasize this notion in the "J" account because Adam and Eve were already in a paranoic state and free to think and do anything they wanted (except eat of the Tree of the Knowledge of Good and Evil). And the Jews themselves, at the time of J's composition, had no need to be reminded of their purity, of remaining "unalloyed," since, during the reign of Solomon, Jewish tribal culture was at its historical highpoint, and the Jewish people were free, powerful, and culturally paranoic.

But in the second account of creation, the "P" account (composed around 400 BCE by the Jewish priestly leaders), which actually appears first in the Bible with "In the beginning," the word "good" (*Tov*) repeats over and over, almost in incantation, as the methodical six days of creation unfold ("and God saw that it was good"). The Jewish priests undoubtedly believed that this paranoidic reminder—to remain "unalloyed"—was necessary at a time when Jewish culture was altogether threatened by an overwhelming Greek cultural hegemony. The "P" account appears, then, as a kind of coded lament for the Jews who feared for their identity inside the Hellenistic world, a lament for the lost splendor of high paranoic Hebrew consciousness, which, by 400 BC, was in decline.

And paranoic splendor was what the first couple experienced in their primeval garden (and the mystically great "J" author knew this). And an unconscious glimmer of this paranoic splendor is allowed to us in our earliest years, which we may remember if we are fortunate. And since the glimmer is imbedded into our altar of self, we always have a way back into the pureness of being, even if it takes until we're fifty-one, and we have to declare ourselves madmen, Schreber-like.

Key Romantic writers (such as Rousseau and Wordsworth) expressed great concern for the loss of childhood splendor. They believed, however, that the splendor was a chronological experience exclusive to childhood, and that it involved "natural feelings" and "instinct" and an overall "oneness with nature." The fact that these attributes are never fully regained explains why there is an overarching theme of loss in mainstream Romantic literature.

But in fact, the highest splendor of childhood is paranoic being, especially the childlike capacity to think anything at any time, and to think that anything is possible at any time; like Joan wondering, in full paranoic innocence: "Why don't we just get these English interlopers out of France? In fact, I'm going to go to the Dauphin right now and tell him he must do this," or Kierkegaard's beloved Jutland Heath where pure "possibility" is the highest education.

Paranoic being is present in the child before the desire to be happy is even a conscious mode, before securing contentment becomes a burden and obsession. As Rousseau makes clear in his great work on education, *Emile* (1762), nature wants children to be children before being men. He might as well have said that nature offers children the experience of the paranoic before the paranoidic presses in.

Perhaps Blake comes the closest to adumbrating paranoic being with his emphasis on the imagination and spontaneity, a condition he attributes to the State of Innocence, a state of being that is not chronological and not limited to childhood (setting Blake apart from his Romantic contemporaries). Indeed, Blake's poetry urges us to maintain the State of Innocence throughout our journey in the world of Generation, rather than to acquiesce to the State of Experience, which is marked by passivity and restraint.

However, recognizing that the greatest power of childhood is paranoic being (rather than natural instincts and a oneness with nature) doesn't necessarily mean that consciousness can remember it. And this is what we should lament, pressed as we are by the weight of paranoidic being the moment we step outside the garden; nudged, perhaps, by the hands of some fatherman who carries with him a *Geradehalter,* until we save ourselves through petomai as prayer, and prayer as madness.

Into the Crown Vetch

But the petomai of childhood can be perilous, *like on Kaufman's Hill one time . . . Kaufman's Hill, a bluff left standing after half of the hill, above where we used to play in the woods, was carved away in order to build one of the great new suburban department stores in the twilight year of 1962.*

Kaufman's Hill was covered with a thick honeysucklelike vine called crown vetch. Crown bitch, we used to call it when we stood at the small clearing at the top of the hill, just outside a thin patch of woods, and thought about climbing down the steep-slanted bluff of matted green which was filled with millions of spiders thriving in the warm and moist Pittsburgh summer; and beyond, at the white concrete monstrosity which had sorrowfully been imposed there, by bulldozers that we ladled with doggie shit as soon as the workmen left to go home.

Me and Taddy Keegan stealing cigarettes from the dashboards of cars in the Kaufman's parking lot and hiding them in the hollow of an old tree at the top of Kaufman's Hill; Taddy Keegan, whose arrival in the neighborhood saved me from the terrible brick street kids who had tortured me since I was six, forcing me into an early paranoidic state where I worried all the time about going outside; until I learned to survive through silence and cleverness, until the moment Taddy Keegan showed up beside our school bus one day and led me through one of the last doors of childhood—the anythingispossible door—to a paranoic place where the terrible boys couldn't exist even if they wanted to (because they were already trapped in the paranoidic); a place where you could make a canoe by folding together a sheet of corrugated aluminum, where you could ride truck-tire inner tubes down swollen creek waters after a summer storm, and where you could be brave enough to walk all the way through long dark-smelling sewer tunnels that the brick street kids were afraid to even enter.

So that when it came to flying, I trusted Taddy Keegan as well. And when he told me he could jump off Kaufman's Hill and fly, simply by squinting his body real hard in the air, I believed him. No one knows the truth about flying, he said, because they're afraid to really try.

Taddy Keegan's words made me feel giddy until he actually decided to show me one day, his body teetering on the crumbly yellow rock at the edge of the hill. But I tugged on his shirt tail and pulled him back, not because I was worried about him falling down the crown bitch hill (which I was), but because I was afraid he might really fly, and by his flying change my life forever, dooming me to become the boy who saw another boy fly. Because miracles are worse than real life.

He pushed me hard to the ground and called me a "fritzy coward," and then he went away down the path into the woods and I lost sight of him; and I just sat there in the graying light until the dark came in like curtains all around, and still I didn't care; the department store lights twinkling below in a way that maddened me, but I didn't care about that either, or about the depressing dinner hour when I was supposed to be home at seven o'clock; all the while hoping that Taddy Keegan would come back down the path to the edge of Kaufman's Hill.

Before I could feel myself get up I was already standing on the crumbly rock that looked chalky in the dim light, with the crown vetch hill slanting away unreal, gray and blurry as if it were getting ready to disappear for good into the damp smelling air.

Either way, the petomai of youth was going to leave me; whether I flew or fell; because really flying would be like God taking you someplace where you can't come back; and you are doomed if you tell anyone because you will be judged crazy, and doomed if you don't tell because you'll go mad inside yourself, which is why saints and madmen are of the same consciousness, with prayer the only way in and the only way out; and prayer dooming you, too, because if the voice of God answers back you are more doomed than flying, with the old life gone for good (that you haven't even had yet because you're too young); and if you fictionalize God's return voice then you're doomed to schizophrenia and Schreber madness, which is why most people don't really want an answer when they pray unless they need the comfort of talking to themselves, which tempts madness too. And most people really don't want a miracle to happen either, because a miracle would mean they were too weak to believe simply on faith, and that's sad too, down all the crown bitch years . . . Because if we can't indulge in the fantasy of miracle, we have to content ourselves with sending our petomaic thoughts right out into the graying void, with no reply necessary. And in this way, too, we fail at the paranoic.

Which is why I jumped down into the crown vetch hill aslant with no color, forgetting even to try the hard body squinting that Taddy Keegan talked about because I was actually jumping for the sake of failure, like Childe Roland at the end of his quest—feeling "fit to fail."

And it was like falling into water when you let your body go limp; and then to awake at the last second and arch yourself in the form that Superman takes when he flies, because that's probably what Taddy Keegan meant by "squinting your body."

But it was too late for that, even after saying out loud, "I am flying." Because Taddy Keegan was right: people don't try hard enough, and falling is easier.

Taddy Keegan wouldn't have fallen with shame into the crown vetch hill smelling of rotten honeysuckle all over with sprained wrist and nose, breathing stopped almost so you can't see; but not crying in the alone, still laying in the full darkness for God knows how long but not wanting even Him to come because that would be worse; waiting until you can't even count the insects that are all over you but not moving to scratch because you are afraid and deserve them anyway for failing to believe while falling, or for insanely jumping; thinking how Taddy Keegan would have been flying instead but I just wasn't ready to see, like the miracles of Jesus which were witnessed only by those who could handle the seeing, which is why He performed so few miracles and never on command, and why the mystery of Him isn't so mysterious after all, not after the failure on Kaufman's Hill, the failure of petomai while the soft body dreams on . . .

Petomai, which can seem like paranoia—dis-tracted thinking—to the paranoidic ones; petomai, so easy to dismiss, making everything hard to remember which is why the Greeks gave us "paramnesia"—the confusing of fact and fancy in the memory, which means I may never really know if there was madness in my jumping off Kaufman's Hill, because I can't quite make my way back to that moment. I get close, and then the moment elides; I can remember myself standing, and then . . .

But I did jump off Kaufman's Hill, because I was sorry I had stopped Taddy Keegan, or because I wanted to punish myself for not really believing in paranoic splendor, and that's why I didn't really try to fly in the gray-black air, and why I splayed myself inside the crown bitch hill, more real than I ever meant to imagine.

And I never even wondered if anyone happened to look up through the silver dusk from Kaufman's parking lot to see a boy diving into the darkness from atop some vague hill. Maybe they missed it because it made no sense, because people always miss what they believe doesn't make sense, and so doing miss the paranoic dimension lost since their petomai of youth, in a world where lessons are learned under the forever Enlightenment and placed into "making sense" dimensions where Taddy Keegan is barely a dream, just a "crazy Irish boy" who had too many brothers and sisters.

And me holding my breath for so long inside the crown vetch hill, waiting . . . like Daniel Schreber holding his breath when he knew his father was coming in.

We carry ourselves away so easily, so that when I hit the crown vetch my eyes were still open even though there was nothing to see.

And when I made up a story about the terrible brick street boys beating me up, everyone believed me because sad events are well accepted inside the paranoidic. Meanwhile, the paranoic passes away from the final childhood light, a withdrawal which I actually felt as I lay crumpled inside the wild crown vetch world, unwilling to move with the evening dampness all over me and everything crawling around.

And that is why I feel bad about Daniel Schreber, because he never had that moment inside the childhood slant of time down the green vetch hill dying; not until he was fifty-one and his Kaufman's Hill of the mind brought on nine years of madness inside an asylum where no one takes your stories for truth, not even Freud who became famous by ignoring them; stories about being unmanned and trying to fly from a God who penetrates through the nerves.

Real prayer is madness and the call of the paranoic, experienced as petomai—I am flying—inside a moment, upon an air of uncertain hopes.

The Altar of Self

In 1878, Walter Pater wrote an imaginative autobiographical essay, "The Child in the House," in which he talked about the process of brain-building, a process in which the individual assembles, moment by moment, his/her altar of the mind. In brain-building, one restructures the meanings of the past and reflects these recalculations into a new momentary sum of self, and from the consciousness of this self projects future being.

Through the childhood recollections of the dream-character Florian Deleal, Pater travels back to the house in which he spent his childhood and re-imagines the rooms of the house, their furnishings and attached sensibility. The constructive process by which the architecture, the objects, and the accompanying emotions affect the growth of his mind ("brain-building") is consonant with the Romantic tradition of the "cult of the child," especially when Pater recalls how certain childhood spaces take prominence in the expanding story of an individual's consciousness. Pater seems to suggest, then, that childhood spaces are first recollected paranoidically until, with fantasia, we remember them paranoically and aesthetically.

> the beginning of a certain design . . . of some things in the story of his spirit—in that process of brainbuilding by which we are, each one of us, what we are . . . and how his thoughts had grown up to him. In that half-spiritualized house he could watch . . . the gradual expansion of the soul which had come to be there—of which indeed, through the law which makes the material objects about him so large an element in children's lives, it had actually become a part; . . . inward and outward being woven through and through each other into one inextricable texture. . . . In the house and garden of his dream he saw a child

moving, and could divide the main streams at least of winds that had played on him, and study the first stage in that mental journey. (1–2)

Using the childhood house as a metaphor for the material texture of the mind, Pater explores how we constantly weave and re-weave our past into newly revealed consciousness. Well before Freud, Pater seems to understand not only the way in which objects and sensations fall into one's childhood being but also the extent to which "indelibly, as we afterwards discover, they affect us"; how certain capricious attractions and associations figure themselves on the "white paper, the smooth wax of our ingenuous souls" (4). These sensations are assigned rooms in the house of memory, and thus abide with us forever.

One's early inhabited spaces become an eventual shrine or sanctuary of sentiment—"a system of visible symbolism interweaves itself through all our thoughts and passions; and irresistibly, little shapes, voices, accidents—the angle at which the sun in the morning fell on the pillow—become parts of the great chain wherewith we are bound" (4).

Although Pater's trust in the authenticity of the childhood mind's "indelible" images would later become the target of suspicion by postmodern thinkers—as in Nabokov's autobiography, *Speak, Memory* (1947), for instance, where he claims to have traveled back to Russia as a biographer in order to investigate his purported memories—the personal process of brain-building would not. Pater seemed to understand, before Heidegger's notion of "Dasein," the sense of the self "being" in time; how consciousness moment by moment fires into the future and the past, all the while balancing on the thinnest membrane of presenticity; how we suspend ourselves on a sort of Nietzschean rope that vanishes and reappears, and that stretches between a constantly disappearing self in the momentary past and a constantly reassembled image of our self in the future. Thus, in a paranoic sense, the story of the self isn't even told by the self, since the self is reborn during every second of the telling (making one wonder just who is telling the story).

In modern literature, aesthetics and memory are favorite ways of suspending the elision of self, and Pater understood this as well, his essays imaginatively mixing memory and aesthetics in a meditative hybrid of paramnesia. Apropos of Pater, we can be "into" the music (like Roquentin's obsession with a certain jazz song in *Nausea*), or "into" a painting or landscape (like Pater's own famous meditation upon the *Mona Lisa* in his essay on the Renaissance—"all the thoughts and experience of the world have etched and molded there"), or "into" a mode from the past where, with the help of Vico's "fantasia," the past lives and the present self drop away (in Pater's work *Imaginary Portraits*, for instance).

The ability of the self to drop away implies that the "self" may not be a being at all, but a mode of being (in a Heideggerian sense), a necessary construct to allow us to function in time, allowing us to create, for example, the iconography of Western culture.

And maybe something happened to this "mode" along its way into the story of self and civilization, and by some paranoidic glitch it got tricked into thinking selfhood itself is the thing, thus turning a mode into a projected end (which is the problem with happiness as a goal); all the while not knowing (how could it?) that too much selfhood as *being-fixed* makes one anxious in a paranoidic way (rather than in a paranoic way—being as the essence of possibility). Unable to bear up under all the paranoidic pressure, the self's paranoic soul elides . . .

We can feel this elision of soul any time we wish, if we are courageous enough to let the self slip away; try and forget who we are for a moment, let go of the everyday "I am," let being go . . .

In Jorge Luis Borges's parable "Borges and I" (1962), the speaker (presumably the "I") complains because Borges "is the one things happen to." The I, which remains in Borges yet separate, seems to be a rather shiftless character lost in the creation of the man known as Borges; every time the I tries to free itself—by moving, for instance, from the "mythologies of the suburbs to the games with time and infinity"— Borges takes over. Little by little, the I gives up everything, and "everything belongs to oblivion, or to him [Borges]" (*Labyrinths*, 247).

Frustrated by this synthetic relationship, the I yearns to speak independently of Borges. However, at the end of the parable, in a typically Borgesian twist, the I admits that it does not "know which of us has written this page." Thus, the author suggests that it may be impossible for the I to ever free itself from Borges, raising the question of whether the I really exists at all as a separate identity.

The Quixotic Paranoic

The tragic separation of soul from self, the collapse of petomai in the face of the bourgeois paranoidic world, was perhaps never more brilliantly depicted than in Cervantes's *Don Quixote* (1615), where defeat doesn't come to the archetypally idealistic hero until at the end, when

Quixote sees his paranoic visions as absurd illusions. As the critic Mark Van Doren pointed out, Don Quixote becomes deluded only when he tries to assess the progress of his enterprise. Don Quixote's failure, then, is his inability to realize that paranoic vision cannot be assessed, since it is basically a qualitative experience and therefore not accountable from the quantitative realm of paranoidic experience.

Cervantes originally intended *Don Quixote* as a burlesque of the exaggerated deeds of chivalric heroes. But Quixote's self-consciousness regarding his illusions is, in the end, the novel's most remarkable attribute; self-consciousness is what keeps the erstwhile hero from becoming mad. Unlike Schreber, Quixote was always free to pursue or resist his illusions, and it is his conscious decision to become a knight errant that is most paranoically beautiful. Moreover, that we still find ourselves talking about Quixote (nearly four hundred years later) proves that he did, in fact, become a knight.

Don Quixote paranoically imagined a picture of himself and through petomai heroically reshaped his life in the true spirit of his mind's picture. And if, to some, Quixote seems to lose, it is only because his desire was too great, which in itself is a paranoic victory; which makes me think of Bernard Shaw saying something about how the reasonable man adapts himself to the world, and the unreasonable one persists in trying to adapt the world to himself; therefore, all progress depends on the unreasonable man.

Blake believed that those who adapt to the world restrain imaginative desire because "theirs is weak enough to be restrained . . . until by degrees [they] become passive and are only a shadow of desire" (*Heaven and Hell*, pl. 5). Fittingly, Blake is one of the unreasonable ones, since he repudiated the sanctioned world of commercial publishing to work inside his own house, engraving and water-coloring by hand his paranoic and ingenious prophesies while many in the outside world labeled him a madman. Blake and Joan and Schreber and Hypatia . . . all "unreasonable" and all paranoic heroes by the immensity of their desire.

And even Plato, who institutionalized the pejorative concept of paranoia as off-track thinking leading to madness, maintained, as Nietzsche said, that it was "through madness that the greatest things came to Greece" (*Daybreak*, Hollingdale, 14). And yet, who among us has the courage, in Nietzsche's words, "to look into the wilderness of bitterest and most superfluous agonies of the soul in which probably the most fruitful men of all times have languished?" (*Daybreak*, 14–15)

Nietzsche did.

Ah, give me madness, you heavenly powers! Madness that I may at last believe in myself! Give deliriums and convulsions, sudden lights and darkness, terrify me with frost and fire such as no mortal has ever felt, with deafening din and prowling figures, make me howl and whine and crawl like a beast: so that I may only come to believe in myself! (*Daybreak,* 15)

Nietzsche believed that even the "weakened" age of early Christianity proved to be a most fruitful time for saints and desert solitaries, and that there existed "in Jerusalem vast madhouses for abortive saints, for those who had surrendered to it their last grain of salt" (*Daybreak,* 15).

And Cervantes's Don Quixote, the most paranoic loser of all because he never accomplished anything inside the substantive world. In fact, his paranoic quest doesn't even begin until he is willing to repudiate his life of paranoidic contentment on his estate, risking all in order to live in a way that defies reason and sense. This, of course, is Quixote's exquisite petomai, because he never truly believes he is a knight errant, but only that he is trying to *become one,* flying on the wings of uncertain hopes.

At the end of his series of misadventures in part 1 (wherein he continually confuses illusion with fact), Don Quixote becomes convinced that he himself is enchanted and allows himself to be placed in a cage (the end of petomai) and carried back home. In part 2, after a more serious search for the "real" behind appearances, Cervantes's knight errant finally decides that the world is nothing but schemes and plots, all working at cross-purposes.

In his elision from the paranoic to the paranoidic (his only *real* failure), Quixote decides that he has been mad all along, and as his soul elides he takes to his bed and dies of a broken spirit.

The book's final sycphatic irony, however, is that the reader ends up admiring the man who suffered from illusions more than the triumphant materialists he confronts. Moreover, it is Quixote the idealist who actually gets things done and his "sidekick," Sancho Panza, the touchstone of corporeal reality, who is all talk.

Yet Sancho Panza achieves his own paranoic journey. He first follows Quixote out of greed, then out of love, and finally because he believes in the idea that Quixote represents. And when Quixote dies because he has "cured" himself of his splendid illusions, Sancho inherits his old master's faith. And Sancho Panza's paranoic conversion affects the reader as well with the desire to believe in paranoic seeing over paranoidic fact. In this sense, Quixote's desire never dies out, even though the world he battled dies over and over again.

Cervantes, like Blake and Nietzsche and Kierkegaard, grasped the most dangerous paranoic truths about human beingness by standing alone and transcending the sad paranoidic world that is predicated on the promise of contentment. Cervantes haunts our souls from the lost world where petomai never ceases.

The American Theatre of Contentment

Some cultural mythologies seem to resist this separation between the paranoidic and the paranoic. The American myth, for instance, has traditionally been about ordaining both: the hero is great because of his grand vision, yet the vision is worthy only if greatness pans out in a material and measurable manner. Otherwise the visionary is a loser.

Some postmodern American writers have used their fiction to indict the hegemonic unison of vision and happiness (Vonnegut and DeLillo, for instance). And there is Thomas Pynchon, who, in his ingenious and slim novel *The Crying of Lot 49* (1965), offers an ineluctable bifurcation of "ones and zeroes"; who offers an America where one must choose between paranoia or complacency, an America with "no middles." At the end, the novel's reluctant hero, Oedipa Maas, chooses "the orbiting ecstasy of a true paranoia . . . it seemed the only way she could continue, and manage to be at all relevant . . . as an alien, unfurrowed, assumed full circle into some paranoia" (182).

The life of the committed "paranoic," however, is not only lonely but exhausting, unless you have the strength of Jesus or Joan. This is precisely what Franz Kafka realized when he wrote his strangely fantastic (and rarely read) novel *Amerika* (1913), Kafka's singularly optimistic major work and presumably the least significant of his three fragmentary novels (the other two being *The Trial* and *The Castle*, all three forming what Max Brod calls the "trilogy of human solitude").

Amerika was a dream fantasy for Kafka, a release from his dreary existence in Prague, the only place he ever really knew (although he did travel as far as France and northern Italy). The novel projects an America of the mind, a place where, after many dark and sordid experiences, a young German could find a brighter life in a glorious landscape.

Working on *Amerika* gave Kafka unending delight, especially the final incomplete chapter about the Nature Theatre of Oklahoma; a sort of "limitless" land where the hero, Karl Rossmann, was to find freedom, human connection, and happiness. Such an ending is quite the opposite from the doom that befalls the tragic heroes of Kafka's other two novels. Unlike Joseph K. in *The Trial*, for instance, Karl is happy despite the torture of his experience.

Kafka spoke no English and knew no Americans at the time he began writing *Amerika* in 1913. His impression of America had been shaped by the autobiography of Ben Franklin and the poetry of Walt Whitman. Yet there *are* uncanny truths to *Amerika*, truths that have nothing to do with the many false details and descriptions Kafka offers of American life. And although Kafka's narrative is not mimetically true, its symbolic and moral statement is consistent with the vision of writers who knew America intimately—Sherwood Anderson, Nathanael West, Vladimir Nabokov, and Thomas Pynchon. Their fictions of America include images and themes present to some degree in Kafka's *Amerika*: images of the grotesque, of the emptiness behind dreams, of nightmares blossoming unpredictably, of the sinisterness behind seeming innocence, and of a civilization declining amidst its ascendancy.

Sherwood Anderson was one of the first American writers to paranoically portray the paranoidic life behind the walls of American contentment, to refute the notion that small-town America produced a loving people filled with beauty and goodness. Reading *Winesburg, Ohio* (1919) is like entering a cluttered attic where the forgotten junk of America is stored. Grotesque characters such as Hands Biddlebaum and Alice Hindman loom everywhere, their grotesqueness expressed by mental traits rather than physical attributes. The American cultural establishment of the early 1920s became infuriated with Anderson for implying that all Americans might be similarly alienated and paranoid and defeated by the inability to communicate.

Likewise, Karl Rossmann in *Amerika* seems unable to enter into the American world of communication. Whenever he tries to make himself heard—such as in his speech defending the stoker, or in his argument before Mr. Pollunder—Karl's stilted and formalized expression is either ignored or misunderstood. And although the American grotesques with whom Karl has trouble communicating differ from Anderson's (Kafka borrows his grotesques from Dickens, and they are, therefore, more outwardly aggressive and scoundrel-like, while Anderson's grotesques in *Winesburg* are relatively passive and suffer from an inner turmoil), the conclusion of both books is the same: many people in America are neither fulfilled nor happy.

Thus, although Kafka may have wanted to consciously believe Americans were humorous and optimistic, he paranoically (and presciently) chose to portray them as grotesques capable of nightmarelike transformations (such as the sudden and inexplicable change that comes over Uncle Jacob when he cruelly casts Karl out). Kafka's grotesques cause Karl continuing bewilderment and despair until he finally escapes into the Nature Theatre of Oklahoma (at once a satire of the American utopia and a dream fantasy of contentment desperately projected by the increasingly despairing and morose Kafka) where "everyone is welcome":

> Everyone, that meant Karl too. All that he had done till now was ignored; it was not going to be made a reproach to him. He was entitled to apply for a job of which he need not be ashamed, which on the contrary, was a matter of public advertisement. And just as public was the promise that he too would find acceptance. He asked for nothing better; he wanted to find some way of at least beginning a decent life, and perhaps this was his chance. (273)

The protagonists in both *Amerika* and *Winesburg* seem to be one step removed from the innocence of traditional American heroes such as Huck Finn. Karl Rossmann, who is honest and filled with good intentions, harbors guilt for an event that caused him to leave Germany: he blames himself for the seduction of the family maid, yet when the story is actually told it is Karl who seems the innocent party, not the middle-aged woman.

Nathanael West's *The Day of the Locust* (1939) includes many "vividly drawn grotesques," as F. Scott Fitzgerald called them, and the plot revolves around characters like Faye Greener, sinful yet innocent, and thus embodying a new version of the American Dream. Even when Tod Hackett realizes that everything about Faye is fake, he still desires her because she is such an "accomplished fake." Unlike Anderson's grotesques, who are refugees of failed dreams, West's grotesques are products of the dream itself, making *The Day of the Locust* that much more disheartening. As Tod realizes soon after his arrival in Hollywood, "few things are sadder than the truly monstrous" (24).

In a way, *The Day of the Locust* is about the co-opting of Kafka's Nature Theatre of Oklahoma. In West's brief novel, America dreams its last paranoidic dream, a dream about manufacturing dreams of itself. Existence in Hollywood, at the western edge of America, leaves no escape from the grotesqueness of a deteriorating civilization. Characters either fit into the dream-life, accepting the fact that such a life is a paranoidic illusion, as Claude and Faye do, or they go crazy, as Tod does. The only other alternative is death—the fate of Homer, a character who, much like Anderson's Hands Biddlebaum, has experienced a life of frustration. "Scattered among these masquerades were people of a different type. . . . Tod knew very little about them except that they had come to California to die" (23).

The fact that Homer is attending a crowded premier showing at Kahn's Persian Palace Theatre is strikingly similar to Karl Rossmann entering the Nature Theatre of Oklahoma. Both Karl and Homer are confronted by high-powered advertising and promise. Homer, however, will not be allotted any surreal transportation.

Sharing many similarities with West's Faye Greener is the "nymphet" in Nabokov's *Lolita* (1955). Kafka and West can both be found in this ingenious novel written by the foreign-born Nabokov after he had carefully studied and come to know America. As his first work in English, *Lolita* is simultaneously an act of conquest and a great literary achievement. Lolita is America, both figuratively and literally, as Humbert Humbert journeys across the country with her. Yet she is also the embodiment of a dream that began forty years earlier in Europe with a girl named Annabel. The failure of that dream results in the writing of a book about a girl whose childhood Humbert steals away.

Led on by the promise of erotic fulfillment, Humbert discovers soon enough that Lolita and the country are both quite vulgar, despite their innocence. He tries to aestheticize his experience as much as possible and ignore the continuous lure of roadside advertisements:

> there would be a slow suffusion of inutile loveliness, a low sun in a
> platinum haze with a warm, peeled peach tinge pervading the upper
> edge of a two-dimensional, dove-gray cloud fusing with the distant
> amorous mist . . . Claude Lorrain clouds inscribed remotely into
> misty azure with only their cumulus part conspicuous against the
> neutral swoon of the background. (140)

Inevitably, though, the erotic and the aesthetic turn into a profane reality in which "Kumfy Kabins" allow even the most corrupt to hide their lusts. Humbert realizes that, after traveling everywhere in the vast country, they had actually seen "nothing":

And I catch myself thinking today that our long journey had only de-
filed with a sinuous trail of slime that lovely, trustful, dreamy enormous
country that by then, in retrospect, was no more to us than a collection
of dog-eared maps, ruined tour books, old tires, and her sobs in the
night—every night, every night—the moment I feigned sleep. (160)

Like her country, Lolita's corruption occurred before Humbert knew
her (she had already lost her virginity). This befouled but beautiful
being, Humbert realizes, is the real America, an America flawed but en-
dearingly naïve, innocent yet vulgar.

As in Kafka's *Amerika,* Nabokov's *Lolita* offers the possibility of a
happy and just life beyond Kumfy Kabins and the neon; it will simply
not be the same as the dream-life. But when Lolita goes off as Mrs.
Richard F. Schiller to live in Alaska, comedy and satire turn into pathos.
Out on the frontier, Lolita and her child die, leaving Humbert's book as
testimonial to the dream and enabling Lolita to live in the minds of later
generations—"I am thinking of aurochs and angels, the secret of
durable pigments, prophetic sonnets, the refuge of art. And this is the
only immortality you and I may share, my Lolita" (281).

Pynchon's *The Crying of Lot 49,* published a decade after *Lolita,* has
characters who call to mind John Ruskin's definition of the grotesque—
that which is "ludicrous" and "terrible." And the proliferation of modern technology in Pynchon's work exaggerates grotesqueness until the
world itself seems poised on the brink of chaos. The nightmarish blossoming of the Tristero and the paranoia that it causes in Oedipa Maas
were already present, albeit to a lesser degree, in *Amerika.* Like Oedipa,
Karl faces the realization that something about which he knows nothing is going on; the story of his destiny seems to have been scripted out
to everyone but himself. His choice is either to comply with a fate he
cannot scrutinize or to rebel against his persecutors and trust no one.

But unlike Oedipa, Karl refuses to give in to paranoia; he fails to acknowledge any Tristero-like situation behind the America he encoun-
ters. For this reason, the endings of the two books are antithetical. By
marching off into the Nature Theatre of Oklahoma, where all are welcome, Karl enters a realm of cultural entropy. Considered in a derisive
way, the Nature Theatre becomes a disdainful place based on the purported American principle that all are equal. This notion may lead to a
state of bliss, but it is an entropic bliss—all things leveling out into
sameness until, to use Pynchon's metaphor, the ball stops bouncing.

The Tristero in *Lot 49* offers escape from the very condition that Karl so eagerly accepts. The Tristero inhibits civilization's slide into entropy wherein all towns will be like San Narciso—indistinguishable, like circuits on a transistor board:

> San Narciso lay farther south, near L.A. Like named places in California it was less an identifiable city than a grouping of concepts—census tracts, special purpose bond-issue districts, shopping nuclei, all overlaid with access roads to its own freeway. (24)

As Oedipa's revelations move her from narcissism to paranoia, she rejects the very life that Karl welcomes. Ironically, she is searching for a final revelation by following the signs of the muted horn of the Tristero, while Karl walks into a Nature Theatre welcomed by angels blowing large apocalyptic trumpets. Oedipa ends up at the brink alone, and Karl ends up enfolded inside the many; she moves toward alienation, he away from it. And there are no middles . . .

The Crying of Lot 49 presents the reader with a greater problem, however. Do we want an America of San Narcisos or an America of the lonely disinherited? Do we want solipsism or alienation?

Such a divisional problem would not have existed for Kafka, who would have simply chosen the way of the disinherited. He made such a choice in his personal life, sacrificing love and domestic happiness for his art. The message in his writings supports this kind of choice, except in *Amerika,* which embodies a dream of escape from the misery that was Kafka's self. Kafka chose to remain in the gloomy streets of Prague, where, in his friend Max Brod's words, "The city, numb and solemn, welcomes her prodigal son." Oedipa finds out the same thing about the Tristero. Its truth seems to be beyond history and culture.

In the novel *In Country* (1985), by Bobbie Ann Mason, the nineteen-year-old female protagonist, Sam Hughs, embarks on a quest to find out who she is and what America is by first finding out who her father was and what the Vietnam War was all about. (Her father died in the war before she was born.) Sam succeeds in finding out about her father and a little bit about the war, but the problem of herself and America remains elusive. The author implies that one can't get lost in America long enough to find oneself. The entropic culture of malls and music and videos and fast-food chains is all-encompassing. The anywhere is everywhere, and as Sam notes early in the novel—"You can't get lost in the United States. I wish I could, though. I wish I'd wake up and not know where I was" (6).

As the nineteenth-century image of America as brutal, pure, and ever-moving diminishes entropically, the notion of America as ever more mechanical and mediagenic becomes less consoling.

The problem with the rapid effects of cultural dislocation is that Americans end up not knowing themselves, nor do they know how to maintain any sense of cultural integrity. Yet how is one to transcend the San Narciso world? Instead of well-understood communally comprehended rituals to measure growth and insight, one is left with illusive private symbols, such as Oedipa's Tristero and Sam's new Beatles song that she isn't sure exists.

Near the end of *In Country*, Sam goes to the woods and tries to re-live her father's experience in Vietnam. Like Thoreau at Walden, she tries to "front the essential facts" about herself. She does succeed in finding out a bit more about real life, yet her information does not arrive through the process of culturalization or by examining history. As her uncle Emmett tells her: "You can't learn from the past. The main thing you learn from history is that you can't learn from history. . . . There are some things you can never figure out" (226).

In *Amerika*, Karl succeeds at his quest only on a collective level by entering into a socialized utopia. On a personal level, he fails to achieve selfhood. He finds the promise of purported happiness but not of truth, and that is the way Kafka wanted it in his "comic" novel. The personal quest continued inside Kafka himself, alone in the dark streets of his Central European city.

Indians and Barbarians

The problem with Nature Theatres is that the Indians are always coming. The Indians are coming, the Indians are coming . . . even after there are hardly any Indians left in America—because there is always some other people to take the Indians' place, barbarians who want to invade the wholesome furrows of the National Being and destroy the American Theatre of Contentment.

Since our Puritan beginnings and the early colonists' paranoidic fears of Indians all around, the enemies inside the gates have been deemed much more dangerous than the enemies outside the gates, which is why the Puritans greatly feared the "praying" Indians whom they had "Christianized." The paradox of dread, American-style, is that "the enemies within" are feared for being different, and feared for assimilating (taking part in the drama of the American dream).

The most important contemporary novel to focus on this pathology wasn't written by an American but rather by the South African J. M. Coetzee, recent winner of the Nobel Prize in literature. His sublimely mythical *Waiting for the Barbarians* (1980) is beyond time and place; the setting could be South Africa or elsewhere in the world; the year could be 1960 or 1920 or 1880. The only necessary constructs are the outpost of "civilization" on the fringes of the empire amidst a severe climate, and the surrounding wilderness peopled by the purportedly dangerous and nearly "inhuman" Barbarians.

Such a construct was certainly familiar in classical Greece, and even though a few paranoically enlightened ones such as Solon or Herodotus argued otherwise—that barbarian culture was interesting and an integral source in making Athens wise and strong—the Athenians didn't want to listen. Their paranoidic mindset had already been set, their sense of "being" permanently predicated upon the nearly nonbeing status of barbarians. And for most Americans, as well, the same predication: an "I am" based upon the barbarian who is "I am not."

In Coetzee's novel, the mantra of paranoidic fear is "the barbarians are coming." And when Colonel Joll, the Gestapo-like torture-inquisitor, shows up in the provincial capital, it is because he is certain, based upon no evidence (except his own paranoidic projections) that the barbarians are preparing for an uprising. And so he tortures some random fisher-people—an old man and a boy—for answers they cannot give. "How do you know when a man has told you the truth?" the local magistrate asks Colonel Joll. "There is a certain tone," Joll says. "A certain tone enters the voice of a man who is telling the truth. Training and experience teach us to recognize that tone" (5).

Before Colonel Joll arrived, the magistrate (the novel's protagonist) was in charge of the outpost; and, although the magistrate is against Joll's torture practices, he can do nothing to stop them. The magistrate does not believe that the barbarians are coming, for no barbarian army has ever been sighted; yet he knows that, in the paranoidic mind, the notion of barbarian aggression against the empire's outposts is forever present. In language that archetypally represents the universal paranoidic fear of all Indians and Barbarians, the magistrate imagines the timeless nightmare that feeds inside the minds of the citizens of empire:

> once in every generation, without fail, there is an episode of hysteria
> about the barbarians. There is no woman living along the frontier

who has not dreamed of a dark barbarian hand coming from under the bed to grip her ankle, no man who has not frightened himself with visions of the barbarians carousing in his home, breaking the plates, setting fire to the curtains, raping his daughters. These dreams are the consequence of too much ease. Show me a barbarian army and I will believe. (8)

The magistrate inexplicably finds himself taking in a barbarian girl who has been blinded by Joll's torture methods. With paranoic sympathy, the magistrate struggles to know the barbarian girl as human and suffering. Strangely, he finds himself caught up in a nightly ritual of bathing her feet and body, trying to know her "being" through the flesh. But she remains quiet and sublimely beyond him. He can't get inside her on any level. (Sexually he is "unable to get inside her" [the magistrate's words], until they are away from the empire's settlement and out in the wilderness.)

The magistrate makes his wilderness journey, traveling across harsh winter terrain, in order to return the barbarian girl to her people. And for this trespass into barbarian territory, Colonel Joll imprisons and tortures the magistrate as if he were a barbarian, until he is "no more than a pile of blood, bone and meat." The magistrate's torture climaxes with being hanged upside-down by his feet wearing a woman's frock (a disturbing moment that startlingly serves to unite the novel's sexual and political themes).

Attempts at summary will, of course, not do justice to Coetzee's colossal achievement in *Waiting for the Barbarians*, his ingenious dissection of paranoidic reality inside the empire of contentment. But the point I emphatically wish to make is how difficult the journey is—humanizing oneself through the paranoic. The magistrate's quest for forgiveness and regeneration, by struggling to undo the codes and ontological constructs of the paranoidic world, has only just begun by the novel's end—"This is not the scene I dreamed of. Like much else nowadays I leave it feeling stupid, like a man who lost his way long ago but presses on along a road that may lead nowhere" (156).

Once again we see how paranoic consciousness is predicated upon petomai—the soaring upon uncertain hopes, a journey that may indeed "lead nowhere"—which is why I admire, even though I can only partially understand, the heroes of the paranoic, and why we need to salvage them from the sad-long trails of paranoidic history, and herald them with paranoic seeing.

Champion the paranoic ones, I say, the purported losers who gave up on adapting to the paranoidic world, and who insisted, instead, upon paranoically drawing the world inside themselves. As Heidegger said, "Dasein does not take place in the world, the world takes place in Dasein." However, Heidegger failed to realize how this occurs inside a dimension as thin as prayer, and nearly as unreal.

And the journey looks like madness, from the perspective of those who are standing clear. Because their consciousness elides from the magistrate's questing to know the barbarian, from the paranoic questings of Joan and Jesus, and Kierkegaard and his Abraham, and Hypatia, and Schreber, and William Blake, who, in his early poem "Mad Song," proclaimed his paranoic renunciation of the culture of contentment:

> I turn my back to the east,
> From whence comforts have increas'd;
> For light doth seize my brain
> With frantic pain.
>
> (ll. 21–24)

And perhaps Samuel Beckett, when he lay dying in a second-rate hospital on the outskirts of Paris in 1989—like his fictional character Malone, who, during his final hours in a poorhouse, tells himself stories—concocted fictions during his last hours to try to impede the closing of death's curtain. Like Malone, perhaps Beckett held onto only a diminishing nub of a pencil when he scratched onto a bedside notepad his final words, with nobody there to witness this quintessentially Beckettian moment except maybe some of Beckett's own shadowy characters.

Beckett's final words are hauntingly similar to those of Coetzee's magistrate when he talked of pressing "along on a road that may lead nowhere." Yet Coetzee, who wrote his Ph.D. dissertation on Beckett, could not have known, at the time of his writing *Waiting for the Barbarians* (1979), that Beckett's final death-bed words would actually be: "I have never in my life been on my way anywhere, but simply on my way."

Which harkens us back to the "process" notion of human beingness; most archetypally, to the Bible's Ecclesiastes (300 BC), one of the most honest works in the history of wisdom literature, and to the preacher's existential lament that, since nothing in the world is worth living for, because "all is vanity," we must learn to find fulfillment in our toil during all of our days.

Which was, for Camus, the fate of Sisyphus, the timeless hero of the absurd who is "superior to his fate" and "stronger than his rock," a rock that he must ceaselessly roll to the top of a mountain, "whence the stone would fall back of its own weight."

And our toil is a "dangerous going-across, a dangerous wayfaring, a dangerous looking-back," as Nietzsche would say, adding that what "is great in man is that he is a bridge and not a goal; what can be loved in man is that he is a *going-across*" (*Zarathustra, Nietzsche Reader*, 239).

And "going-across" brings us back to the Indians, because who, besides the Indians, knows more about life as a dangerous and beautiful wayfaring that has nothing to do with Western goal-consciousness and the idea of "progress"; who but the Indians—an enigmatic people we still know little about because they left no written records, and our attempts to speculate so feeble because Indian moments are about expanding into the infinite blue, while our moments are about things to be landed, collected, recorded, and sold.

Indians are, in the fullest sense, the paranoic ones; Indians know the sweet illimitable experience of paranoic being, an ability that the paranoidic masses of the world view with resentment. Indians know of the grand petomai suspended by the paranoic as prayer, for they are the experts of petomai.

And at the outpost of Western civilization, where the paranoia/contentment signpost remains, the Indians still beckon, calling us into the illimitable direction of the high paranoic, where off-track thinking is still a virtue because Indian priests always revered the sublime visions of the off-track mind, a cultural reality quite antithetical to the paranoidic notion of off-track thinking Plato and his followers handed down to us, causing us to feed on the fears of ourselves and of the barbarians until we gathered around our smoky fires and built our castles and holy spires so our kings and priests of the paranoidic could dwell within, until down all the West-fall years the paranoidic was all we had to take cover under, all we ever had in the eversince . . .

If you don't believe me, just go to one of the ancient Indian mesas out in the American West, like New Mexico's Acoma, for instance, which was first settled by Pueblo Indians more than a thousand years ago. Scientific minds are still wondering why the Indians would want to live on an exposed and elemental mesa when the source of water and the best soil was below in the canyon valleys. The paranoidic reply is that the Acoma Indians chose to live on the mesa for military reasons; they wanted the high ground to protect themselves from their enemies; thinking not unlike the assumptions Colonel Joll makes as he appropriates and projects the barbarian mind.

The paranoic truth is, however, that the visionary-endowed Acoma Indians built on the mesa because they simply liked the view, with its welcoming availability into nature's transcendent; a mesa probably believed to be a sacred promontory into the center of the universe, as the ancient Greeks considered Delphi to be. And though no one misunderstands the Greeks' intent at Delphi, most find it hard to believe that the Acoma thought in a similarly paranoic way . . . up on the mesa where the wind and sky expand from the same source, where the paranoic resuscitates itself every moment, where the sublime blue crosses over from eternity.

Go on and find yourself a fissure among the Acoma rocks where you can hide for a while; peer out from your tunnel while the wind whips your mind into believing, and the passages of time speak without words.

And if nothing happens, just keep trying, learn to "fail better," as Beckett would say; learn how to allow yourself to be educated by "possibility," like standing amidst Kierkegaard's Jutland Heath until you can feel time itself passing from on high, like ribbons of silk across vanishing flesh, until, almost nothing yourself, you are suspended.

As with all visionary moments, you must convince yourself to believe until you feel the paranoic reality all around, and then still fight off the relentless voices of the paranoidic, whispering for you to reaffirm what you thought you already knew.

In the Altamira caves in southern France, the oldest human paintings of any kind have been found, paintings so natural and masterful that they get in the way of scientific logic with most scholars reluctant to believe in the correct carbon-dating (which would make the Altamira cave paintings approximately thirty thousand years old), because such a fact messes up the "accepted" timetable of history and evolution. Instead, they deductively argue the impossibility of pre–Ice Age art (which would limit the age of the paintings to about eleven thousand years), because the idea of pre–Ice Age humans mimetically portraying characters of their environment is deemed incongruous with the notion that art had to evolve slowly over the millennia, just like everything else; that the mimetic drawing-capability could only be the result of a long-aged artistic development. Such a defensive and paranoidic argument is predicated upon the notion that, since young children can barely paint, it follows then that the ancient children of humankind could barely paint. (This "presumption" of evolutionary theory is formally known as the "Law of Recapitulation.")

"Magnum miraculum est homo" (humankind is a great miracle). And the painted works by the native beings who lived thirty thousand years ago miraculously still exist in the caves of Altamira; paranoically brilliant pictures of bison fighting, and rhinoceroses and lions . . .

More absurd than the evolutionary miscalculations about Altamira is the notion first put forth by the leader of German expressionist painting, Wilhelm Worringer (in *Abstraction and Empathy* [1908]), claiming that imitation of nature in art is rooted in empathy, a feeling alien to primitive human beings whose (paranoidic) dread of reality would result in an art of abstraction. And if pre–Ice Age art (such as Altamira) contradicts this principle, then pre–Ice Age art is simply not art!

But the falling bison and horses on the Altamira cave walls are like sketches from the drawing books of a young Leonardo. Most important, the Altamira cave paintings prove that the earliest human beings were indeed paranoic, not paranoidic; that they *were* capable of getting beyond their defensive fears of the truly dark world in order to paint in the cave darkness; and to paint with vision, and for no reason other than to express "being" in moments when fear ceased to be; barely suspended by petomai and inside the ancient earth's sublime, uncanny and beyond seeing, except maybe by their kin—the champions of the above-earth sublime—the Acoma Indians of the mesa.

Maybe Schreber could have understood them, since Schreber was, in his way, an Indian and barbarian too; he just didn't know it. And Jesus and Joan and Blake and Hypatia—all barbarians of the highest degree because they all partook of a paranoic consciousness inherent, since the beginning, inside the barbarian mind.

And Jeremiah, as well—like an Indian of the wind and sands, the hot Egyptian waste—watching and listening, thinking into the ancient world blue, hoisted by the sheerest strands of Hebraic petomai; and with probably some scrappy little dog barking at his swollen heels.

Jeremiah, that good man, whose mouth the Lord actually touched in order to give the gift of prophecy, but who could have barely imagined the great Alexander journeying and conquering a few centuries later across the same Egyptian sands. Instead of paranoically lamenting the fate of his people before the face of a disappointed God, as Jeremiah did, Alexander would turn the man/God construct around in a Hegelian way and envision the history of empire ending with himself, Alexander III of Macedon; experiencing his paranoidic fantasy—that he was the son of God, near the remote desert city of Siwa; his paranoidic delusion somehow instilling in him the confidence and genius to conquer most of the Mediterranean and Persian world, which in turn led him to realize his most presageful paranoic notion of all: that despite their obvious differences, people everywhere were really equal, which was why he freely adopted the practice of wearing "Oriental" clothing (to the dismay of his soldiers) and even required that his men marry into the opposing cultures in support of his grand paranoic vision of all of his "people" together under his one law and aegis.

185

"*Latrare, latrare,*" I would like to say to the god Alexander; we bark nonsense, therefore we are. But *latrare* is sometimes the only path we have into the paranoic, like Jeremiah with his lamentations. But Jeremiah's *latrare* was paranoic and prophetic, while Alexander's *latrare* was mostly paranoidic and delusional; and our job, whether we have the care to acknowledge it or not, is to figure the difference.

Which means, of course, that we have a double burden: we have to love life and love life's meanings. Dostoyevsky, with his dark St. Petersburg mind, saw this situation causally: we must love life before we can love its meaning; and Albert Camus, in his notebooks, countering Dostoyevsky with his own tragic humanism—when love of life disappears, no meaning can console us.

And thus the ongoing struggle to love what is imperfect in humanity, even when there is no immediate meaning to console us, a condition that Coetzee's magistrate humbly acknowledges at the end of *Waiting for the Barbarians*. The magistrate learns, by necessity, to love the frail soul of paranoic being, composed at first of only eros and dust.

Which makes me think that maybe Karl Jaspers was right when he maintained that paranoia is a meaning disorder; and since all thinking is about meaning, directly or indirectly, then "being" actually involves the self trying to understand how to use the disorder courageously and creatively rather than fearfully and defensively; which is no less than the triumph of the paranoic over the paranoidic, a soaring into the infinite blue, upon the sheerest of wings.

Which is why Indians and Barbarians are our paranoic heroes, because they know how to love life and love its meaning inside the same expanding moment; being and time in one essence of paranoic freeness that we can only conceive through prayer.

Indians know, from atop their mesas and inside their caves, that paranoic being is not a meaning disorder but rather a meaning *reorder,* causing one to evaluate experience moment by moment and thus to live inside the paranoic sublime all the while avoiding elision into the para-noidic near-self.

And sometimes paranoic being chooses to sing, like in Wallace Stevens's visionary poem "The Idea of Order at Key West" (1934). Out of the paranoic blue a human song brings new order every moment, an order that is fluid and beyond nature yet of nature; in a Nietzschean way, the painful transcendence of self without metaphysics, until one hears the singer's song more than the sea—"Whose spirit is this? we said, be-cause we knew / It was the spirit that we sought and knew / That we should ask this often as she sang" (ll. 18–20).

Perhaps Stevens knew of the "spirit" and didn't tell, or else he did tell if we could only listen.

And the spirit we hear is ourselves, paranoic and free; a voice that makes the "sky acutest at its vanishing":

She was the single artificer of the world
In which she sang. And when she sang, the sea,
Whatever self it had, became the self
That was her song, for she was the maker.

(ll. 37–40)

Until there "never was a world for her / Except the one she sang and, singing, made." Like the world of Daniel Schreber, where he sang in his madness . . .

But one has to be careful with song and prayer, because if we are just pretending and don't really believe, we can elide into the delusional and perhaps the psychotic; which is why Joan's words at her trial, regarding how she knew the voices were really Saint Michael's, are so crucial—"I believed it immediately, and desired to believe it," a statement that may have seemed to her inquisitors to be a final barking.

And the final barking for Jeremiah, that good man? There are no final words for those inside the sublime paranoic, like Blake's vision of Los from his garden in Felpham: Los, the tireless craftsman forever at his furnace, rebuilding the world, moment by moment, into the eternal city of Jerusalem.

And Jeremiah, at his visionary best with his words about the potter and the broken vessel (18:3), a vessel we needn't really care about, unless our love is with the paranoic: "And the vessel he was making of clay was spoiled in the potter's hand, and he reworked it into another vessel, as it seemed good to the potter to do so."

Paranoic heroes remake the self out of broken clay in every moment of being, even though the desire to do so may seem like madness; because the prayer for "remaking" is the call of the paranoic; it is Jeremiah's call, experienced as petomai, and suddenly we are flying . . . inside a moment, upon an air of uncertain hopes.

Coda

The Paranoic and the
Productions of Time

"Eternity is in love with the productions of time," William Blake said, which is why the call of the paranoic must do more than just "call," it must result in a reformulation of the terra firma—Jeremiah remaking his vessel of clay. The journey into contingency must weigh into the "on-track" world, which is precisely what the paranoic call is trying to tell us. We cannot live in the paranoic, which would equate with Schreber-madness, but we can recognize the call and visit there, in order to *live*.

Richard Rorty, the most important contemporary American philosopher, argues in a similar fashion when he maintains that abstract philosophy is nearly useless amidst the complicated modern world unless it manages to connect intrinsically to our sociopolitical concerns. In the case of America, Rorty has repeatedly called for a new sense of moral and social self-sufficiency, for a new American "everyday self." Drawing on Nietzsche as well as the American tradition of national self-consciousness, Rorty argues that the greatest accomplishment of American liberal democracy is the sense of irony; that is, Americans' unique ability to understand the gap between public commitments and private interests.

Thus we return to the dilemma central in the history of Western ethics, the one which Václav Havel attempted to settle with the "Gaia principle" and Rousseau with "general will." For Rorty, the public versus private dilemma isn't a philosophic problem but rather a question of understanding the contingency of history through the interpretation of literature. The question for America, then, seems to be whether we can avoid believing the kitsch, which means interpreting American culture and history from an "individual" and moral perspective, and, of course, dealing with all the requisite dread that follows.

This is the journey, then, for translating paranoic vision into an everyday self inside the terra firma, a journey that becomes more complicated by the fact that the everyday self must also, paradoxically, fashion a narrative outside itself for its ownmost regeneration. And the key to this paradox is attaining an individual sense of beauty, which allows Dasein to fire in both directions: imagining the beauty of Dasein's ownmost self, beauty that separates it from the world and the "they" allowing it to Be for itself; and imagining the beauty in the selves outside the self, which are, then, worth sacrificing for.

However, the individual's quest for the beautiful, both inside and outside the self, is daunting amidst the leveling effects of the postindustrial commercialized world. But if one can continuously re-accomplish a sense of the beautiful, then the "call of care" has something intrinsic to call Dasein back to, away from the banal being-in-the-world they-self.

This task is especially difficult for Americans who, living in such a mediagenic world, find it almost impossible to dream an individual dream separate from the kitschy American myths proffered through advertising, religion, politics, and the media.

In this sense, the recent award-winning film *American Beauty* (1999) offers a brilliant cautionary tale. The film—which most believe to be about an empty man's mid-life crisis wherein he rebels by quitting his job, smoking pot, lifting weights, buying a sports car, and lusting after a sixteen-year-old girl—is actually about the failure of Americans to fashion an essential self through an individual apprehension of the beautiful. Hence, the real American Beauty in the film is demonstrated by the voyeur-neighbor boy, who, with this video camera, captures an image of a seemingly insignificant plastic bag floating in the dirty air of some urban alley. This mesmeric-aesthetic image, the soul of the film, allows him to exist separate from the hegemonic sameness of American culture.

William Blake anticipated this condition two hundred years earlier in his poem "Chimney Sweeper" (*Songs of Innocence*), which features a little boy, Tom Dacre, who has been condemned to chimney-sweeper slavery where "your chimneys I sweep & in soot I sleep." At night Tom dreams about an Angel with a "bright key" who opens the coffins of black and sets the boys "all free." The Angel tells Tom "if he'd be a good boy, / H'ed have God for his father, & and never want joy" (ll. 19–20).

The poem is troubling enough with its portrayal of religious dogma cajoling the poor to accept their misery because they will eventually be in heaven with God. But what's more troubling is that the reader knows poor Tom's dream through the poem's narrator, a veteran chimney sweeper. And this is the subversive meaning of the poem: the narrator knows Tom's dream because he has had the same dream, because the church and state have fed them all the same cajoling dreams.

Thus, as is often the case in Blake, the larger tragedy in the poem is imaginative failure. The chimney sweepers are incapable of dreaming their own dreams and are enslaved both mentally and physically, until they cannot "live."

This condition is many times worse in the contemporary American world where a child's imagination and sense of beauty, from day one, is manipulated by a multitude of media influences until the child can barely dream his/her own dream; which is why the female protagonist of *In Country* laments, "I wish I'd wake up and not know where I was." And if you can't get lost, you can't find the beauty of the self, or the beauty beyond the self. In this way, a personal aesthetic becomes crucial. Even Childe Roland achieves a new self-aestheticized image of his doom; and Sartre's Roquentin, at the end of *Nausea*, leaves for Paris to write a novel because personal art is the only way he can transcend his existential anguish; and Schreber with his artistically maddening dream visions; and Joan's beatific dream of France's salvation; and the aesthetics of Hypatia's Neoplatonism; and Jesus' torturous twilight vision in Gethsemane . . .

In *The Awakening* (1899), Kate Chopin's prophetic tale of a woman struggling to achieve selfhood in Creole New Orleans at the turn of the century, Edna Pontellier (the protagonist) experiences a growing distaste for "that colorless existence which never uplifted its possessor beyond the region of blind contentment, in which no moment of anguish ever visited her soul" (268).

Edna's paranoic ascent into individuation occurs simultaneously with an increasing consciousness of the beautiful, especially in context with the paranoic sea, which is "seductive, never ceasing, whispering . . . inviting the soul to wander for a spell in abysses of solitude" (214). At the end, Edna achieves her vision but fails at reshaping her life in the terra firma, at remaking her "vessel of clay." Paranoic exhilaration overwhelms her, and unlike Joan and Hypatia, Edna isn't strong enough for the consequences in the paranoidic world, a world in which she no longer seems to fit.

In Virginia Woolf's magnificently lyrical novel *To the Lighthouse*

(1927), Mrs. Ramsay achieves inner self-expression by orchestrating her family and friends and summer seaside house into unities of beauty, such as her perfect "Boeuf en Daube" dinner. But the burden is sometimes onerous: "The room was . . . shabby. There was no beauty anywhere. . . . Nothing seemed to have merged. They all sat separate. And the whole of the effort of merging and flowing and creating rested on her" (83).

When Mrs. Ramsay's daughter, Rose, disturbs the beautiful whole-ness of the fruit bowl by taking a pear, Mrs. Ramsay can only think she has "spoilt the whole thing."

But in keeping with the book's exquisite wistfulness, Mrs. Ramsay is wise enough to recognize the transience inherent in the unities of beauty that we create or apprehend:

> It was necessary now to carry everything a step further. With her foot on the threshold she waited a moment longer in a scene which was vanishing even as she looked, and then, as she moved . . . and left the room, it changed, it shaped itself differently; it had become, she knew, giving one last look at it over her shoulder, already the past. (111)

In the final part of the novel, Lily, an artist and spiritual daughter to Mrs. Ramsay, can move toward individuation, and independence as a woman, only after she completes her painting of Mrs. Ramsay, which she had started ten years earlier. In the process, Lily realizes—as Mrs. Ramsay herself had probably sensed—that the power to re-unify beauty results from paranoic intuition.

> The whole mass of the picture was poised upon that weight. Beautiful and bright it should be on the surface, feathery and evanescent, one colour melting into another like the colours on a butterfly's wing; but beneath the fabric must be clamped together with bolts of iron. It was a thing you could ruffle with your breath; and a thing you could not dislodge with a team of horses. And she began to lay on a red and a grey, and she began to model her way into the hollow there. (171)

In contemporary America, the need for personal aesthetic achieve-ment is even more pressing because—despite our wealth and power and history—America lacks a mythology for taking the individual be-yond the self. And the occasional sacrifice will not do, even though the politicians and media love to capitalize on some hero who throws him-self into the freezing Potomac to save a drowning airline passenger. Because there is no accompanying mythology in this. Moreover, how many Americans will actually find themselves in such a position?

Thus we are still a myth-needy country; we still await a narrative that, in an unkitschlike manner, will take us beyond the contentment goal.

The other problem with Potomac-divers is the resulting hero-worship that, turned into patriotic kitsch, can actually inhibit the creation of self, rather than forwarding it. This, of course, is a difficult case to make for a country so dependent on its heroes and flags, a country so dependent on its own sense of virtue that it is capable of believing, over and over again, that it has lost its innocence (the Civil War, Hiroshima, Vietnam, Watergate, the Iraq War . . .) and yet somehow still remains pure. And it is more than a little ironic that America's "enemies" also identify through metaheroic dreams. In fact, in the last fifty years, our most formidable collective enemies—the communists and the Islamic radicals—come from intensely heroic cultures. Moreover, the common enemy of both communists and Islamic radicals is Western materialism. For in both cases, the image of Americans living capitalistic, contented, and fattened lives inside their high towers is precisely the image they want to destroy. Meanwhile, it is the followers of both communism and radical Islam who purportedly give up "worldly" interests.

In the American culture of contentment, self-interest has almost always had priority over self-realization, in contrast to our current "enemies," who choose self-sacrifice over self-realization. They create more angry suicide warriors, we create more contented desk-trained executives.

Yet what is most startling about our enemies is their life-affirming energy in the midst of their acceptance of death, whereas most Americans and Westerners, pursuing happiness and security above all things, often feel their life-affirming gusto eliding away.

And this is why the paranoic call to individuation is so difficult for most Americans, because their myth of "self" never recognizes the Kierkegaardian truth that "to be an individual is the hardest of things." The American emphasis has always been on the right to safety and happiness, which is pursued until we experience what Freud termed the "psychological poverty of groups." Even classic American myths such as "rugged individualism" are embraced in a herdlike manner.

One cannot transcend the self by simply shifting into a "we" consciousness, because the "we" is most often a collection of other egos brought together for common gain. In fact, the real "we" is not even composed of "I's"; it begins in a place where the "I" has never been;

which is why it is so hard to hear the regenerative call of the paranoic in America.

And our enemies fail at heeding the call as well, the very moment they trade off expansive thinking for psychotically driven fears and hatreds. Radical Islam, in fact, goes paranoidic the minute it fixates on the blood of its enemies, whenever it is driven by absolute principles of God and salvation.

... and I want to live in that mud hut in the palm grove near the banks of the Tigris River; I want to live that simple meditative life, a nearly Thoreau-like life, except for the occasional stealing of an egg, or perhaps the wringing of the neck of some chicken, or eating damaged fish from the swollen brown river ...

I want to live in that mud hut with the high-thatch fence all around, with the nearest house over a quarter mile away, and with an optional spider hole to hide in when the going gets tough, which demands a nastier descent than even Dostoyevsky imagined of his mouse hole Underground, and so different from the catacombs of old with their tunnels twenty to sixty feet deep ...

I want to live in that mud hut, and from the dusty palm yard, and even from inside the underground, try to be a prophet and a painter, and make up for what has been missed, especially the "peripeteia," as Aristotle called it, the final tragic insight when even madmen understand the nature of their transgressions ...

I want to live in that mud hut, where the red evenings hang suspended, so that the old prophets of days can pass right through, and we can maybe talk to them, reaching with feet first ...

I want to live in that mud hut, when the night is somehow still a glitter, while I sweep the courtyard and rearrange the cooking pots above the humble stove.

For America, and for America's purported enemies, the greatest Nietzschean truth has been ignored: human beingness is a "dangerous wayfaring," and what is great in human beings is that they are a "bridge and not a goal," and, most important, "I love him who lives for knowledge ... and who thus wills his own downfall" (*Nietzsche Reader*, 239).

Like Christianity, the Islamic faith was born inside the paranoic. All visionary religions are (as Blake makes clear in his hybrid poem "All Religions Are One"). And the call to Allah was originally a call to be free and expansive, a call to pursue a higher good. But the call turned paranoidic, as it did for the Christians centuries earlier with Paul's obsessive system-building and with the monks' murder of Hypatia, and with the nonchalant killing of village Jews by the Christian Crusaders as they made their way across Europe to vanquish the Muslim intruders in the Holy Land.

There is no paranoic blue in any of this, but only paranoidic elision. And it makes one wonder, especially in the current American culture of self-interest, just where the paranoic call might come from.

Whether an American bourgeoisie or a follower of Islam, the quest is the same: can we inhabit the brilliant "paranoic" long enough to gain a vision, and can we remake the terra firma without eliding into the strangling paranoidic?

And the paranoic vision need not always be grand. In fact, it can be a regular part of a new everyday self (like Rorty called for), allowing us to cross-check our thinking about sociopolitical issues for instance, so that we may wonder, in an off-track way, about an administration's unfounded claims of weapons of mass destruction in some distant country that it simply wishes to preemptively invade. From inside the paranoic, we can see through paranoidic manipulation based on fears and delusions.

And only by virtue of the paranoic can we journey into a self, and only by virtue of the paranoic can we journey out of the self. For only the paranoic calls for both an expansion of being, and an expansion into Being, with no elisions either way.

And the paranoic even supplies an answer to Dostoyevsky's cry for "realism" at the end of *Notes from Underground* (after his critique of Enlightenment and Romantic culture). Because the problem with a call for "realism" is defining the kind of realism we want.

The realism I urge is the most potent of all—the realism of the paranoic. You just need to find yourself a Jutland Heath somewhere. It could be in your own living room, where nothing much seems to happen, except maybe a shifting in light, a seemingly imperceptible shudder of a curtain; where you can feel the sublime thrill of possibility that the Acoma Indians used to know . . . You only need to think paranoically for a while, about trying to enter the paranoic.

Bibliography

Abrams, M. H. *Natural Supernaturalism.* New York: Norton, 1971.

Adams, Henry. *The Education of Henry Adams.* Boston: Houghton Mifflin, 1961.

Aeschylus. *Prometheus Bound.* Translated by David Grene. In *Aeschyulus,* vol. 2, edited by David Grene and Richard Lattimore. Chicago: University of Chicago Press, 1959.

———. "Seven Against Thebes." In *Aeschylus,* vol. 2, edited by David Grene and Richard Lattimore. Chicago: University of Chicago Press, 1959.

Ambrose, Stephen E. *Undaunted Courage: Meriwether Lewis, Thomas Jefferson, and the Opening of the American West.* New York: Simon and Schuster, 1996.

American Beauty. A feature film. Directed by Sam Mendes. California. Dreamworks, 1999.

Anderson, Sherwood. *Winesburg Ohio.* New York: Viking, 1964.

Aquinas, Thomas. *Summa Theologica.* Translated by Fathers of English Dominican Province. Chicago: Encyclopedia Britannica, 1952.

Aristophanes. *Clouds, Wasps, Birds.* Translated by Peter Meineck. Vol. 1, *Aristophanes.* Indianapolis: Hackett, 1998.

Arnold, Matthew. *Poems.* New York: Penguin, 1985.

Augustine, Bishop of Hippo. *City of God.* Translated by Marcus Dodds. New York: Modern Library, 2000.

Beckett, Samuel. *Malone Dies.* New York: Grove, 1957.

———. *Waiting for Godot.* New York: Grove Weidenfeld, 1982.

Bettelheim, Bruno. *Surviving and Other Essays.* New York: Vintage, 1980.

Beowulf. Translated by Kevin Crossley-Holland. New York: Farrar, Straus, and Giroux, 1968.

Blake, William. *Blake: Complete Writings.* Edited by Geoffrey Keynes. London: Oxford Press, 1974.

Borges, Jorge Luis. *Labyrinths.* Edited by Donald A. Yates. New York: New Directions, 1964.

Brontë, Emily. *Wuthering Heights.* Oxford: Oxford University Press, 1976.

Brooks, Polly. *Beyond the Myth: The Story of Joan of Arc.* New York: Lippincott, 1990.

Bibliography

Browning, Robert. *Selected Poetry*. Edited by George M. Ridenour. New York: New American Library, 1966.

Byrne, David. *Fear of Music*. Talking Heads. Sound recording made by Sire Records, 1979.

Camus, Albert. *The Myth of Sisyphus and Other Essays*. Translated by Justin O'Brien. New York: Random House, 1955.

Cervantes, Miguel de Saavedra. *Don Quixote*. Translated by Charles Jervas. 2 vols. Oxford: Oxford University Press, 1929.

Chamfort, Sebastien. *Maxims, Anecdotes, Letters, Historical Writings*. Translated by C. G. Pearson. Glastonbury: Walton Press, 1973.

Chopin, Kate. *The Awakening and Other Stories*. Edited by Lewis Leary. New York: Holt, 1970.

Cioran, E. M. *The Temptation to Exist*. Translated by Richard Howard. Chicago: Quadrangle Books, 1968.

Coetzee, J. M. *Waiting for the Barbarians*. New York: Penguin, 1980.

Coleridge, Samuel Taylor. *Coleridge's Poetry and Prose*. Edited by Nicholas Halmi, Paul Magnuson, and Raimonda Modiano. New York: Norton, 2003.

Conrad, Joseph. *The Portable Conrad*. Edited by Morton Zabel. New York: Penguin, 1983.

DeLillo, Don. *White Noise*. New York: Viking, 1985.

Democritus. *The Presocratics*. Edited by Philiip Wheelwright. New York: Odyssey Press, 1966.

Diderot, Denis. *Interpreter of Nature: Selected Writings*. Edited and translated by Jean Stewart and Jonathan Kemp. New York: International Publishers, 1963.

Donne, John. *The Complete Poetry of John Donne*. Edited by John T. Shawcross. New York: Doubleday, 1967.

Donoghue, Denis. *Walter Pater—Lover of Strange Souls*. New York: Knopf, 1995.

Dostoyevsky, Fyodor. *Notes from Underground*. Translated by Andrew R. MacAndrew. New York: New American Library, 1961.

Dzielska, Maria. *Hypatia of Alexandria*. Cambridge: Harvard University Press, 1995.

Eliot, T. S. *Complete Poems and Plays*. New York: Harcourt, 1971.

Euripides. *The Bacchae*. Translated by William Arrowsmith. In *Euripides,* vol. 5, edited by David Grene and Richard Lattimore. Chicago: University of Chicago Press, 1959.

———. *Electra*. Translated by Emily Townsend Vermeule. In *Euripides,* vol. 5, edited by David Grene and Richard Lattimore. Chicago: University of Chicago Press, 1959.

———. *Hecuba*. Translated by William Arrowsmith. In *Euripides,* vol. 3, edited by David Grene and Richard Lattimore. Chicago: University of Chicago Press, 1958.

———. *Iphegenia in Aulis*. Translated by Charles R. Walker. In *Euripides,* vol. 4, edited by David Grene and Richard Lattimore. Chicago: University of Chicago Press, 1958.

———. *Orestes.* Translated by William Arrowsmith. In *Euripides,* vol. 4, edited by David Grene and Richard Lattimore. Chicago: University of Chicago Press, 1958.

Faulkner, William. *As I Lay Dying.* New York: Vintage, 1985.

———. *The Sound and the Fury.* New York: Vintage, 1990.

Flaubert, Gustave. *Madame Bovary.* Translated by by Francis Steegmuller. New York: Random House, 1957.

Forster, E. M. *Alexandria: A History and a Guide.* Garden City, N.Y.: Anchor, 1961.

Foucault, Michel. *Madness and Civilization.* Translated by Richard Howard. New York: Vintage, 1988.

Freud, Sigmund. *The Freud/Jung Letters.* Translated by Ralph Manheim and R.C.F. Hull. Princeton: Princeton University Press, 1974.

———. *Group Psychology and the Analysis of the Ego.* Edited and translated by James Strachey. New York: Norton, 1959.

———. "Psycho-analytic Notes on an Autobiographical Account of a Case of Paranoia." In *Three Case Histories,* edited by Philip Rieff. New York: Simon and Schuster, 1996.

———. *The Standard Edition of the Complete Psychological Works of Sigmund Freud.* Translated by James Strachey in collaboration with Anna Freud. 24 vols. London: Hogarth Press, 1953–74.

Fromm, Erich. *The Dogma of Christ and Other Essays on Religion, Psychology, and Culture.* New York: Holt, 1963.

Frye, Northrop. *Fearful Symmetry.* Princeton: Princeton University Press, 1969.

Furbank, P. N. *Diderot: A Critical Biography.* New York: Knopf, 1992.

Gardner, John. *Grendel.* New York: Vintage, 1989.

Gibbon, Edward. *The Decline and Fall of the Roman Empire.* New York: Modern Library, 1954.

Gilchrist, Alexander. *Life of William Blake.* London: J. M. Dent and Sons, 1945.

Goethe, Johann Wolfgang von. *The Sorrows of Young Werther.* Translated by William Rose. London: Scholartis Press, 1929.

Gogol, Nikolai. *The Diary of a Madman and Other Stories.* New York: New American Library, 1960.

Guillaume de Lorris, *The Romance of the Rose.* Translated by Frances Horgan. Oxford: Oxford University Press, 1994.

Havel, Václav. Speech at Independence Hall in Philadelphia when President Havel received the Philadelphia Liberty Medal. July 4, 1994.

Hegel, Georg Wilhelm Friedrich. *Phenomenology of Spirit.* Translated by A. V. Miller. Oxford: Oxford University Press, 1977.

Heidegger, Martin. *Being and Time.* Translated by John Macquarrie and Edward Robinson. New York: Harper and Row, 1962.

———. *Existence and Being.* Translated by R.F.C. Hull and Alan Crick. Chicago: Henry Regnery Gateway Editions, 1960.

Heraclitus. *The Presocratics.* Edited by Phillip Wheelwright. New York: Odyssey Press, 1966.

Bibliography

Herodotus. *The Histories*. Translated by Aubrey de Selincourt. London: Penguin, 1972.

Hesiod. *Works and Days, and Theogony*. Translated by Stanley Lombardo. Indianapolis: Hackett Publishing, 1993.

Hillman, James. *On Paranoia*. Dallas: Spring Publications, 1988.

Hobbes, Thomas. *The Elements of Law*. Edited by Ferdinand Tonnies. London: Cass, 1969.

Hofstadter, Richard. *The Paranoid Style in American Politics*. New York: Knopf, 1965.

Homer. *The Iliad*. Translated by Robert Fitzgerald. Garden City, N.Y.: Doubleday, 1974.

———. *The Odyssey*. Translated by Robert Fitzgerald. Garden City, N.Y.: Doubleday, 1961.

Hopkins, Gerard Manley. *Poems*. Edited by W. H. Gardner. Oxford: Oxford University Press, 1970.

James, William. *The Varieties of Religious Experience*. Cambridge: Harvard University Press, 1985.

Jaspers, Karl. *The Future of Mankind*. Translated by E. B. Ashton. Chicago: University of Chicago Press, 1961.

———. *Nietzsche: An Introduction to the Understanding of His Philosophical Activity*. Translated by Charles F. Wallraff and Frederich J. Schmitz. Tucson: University of Arizona Press, 1965.

Joyce, James. *A Portrait of the Artist as a Young Man*. New York: Dover, 1994.

Kafka, Franz. *Amerika*. New York: New Directions, 1962.

———. *The Trial*. New York: Schocken Books, 1984.

Kaplan, J. D., ed. *Dialogues of Plato*. Translated by Benjamin Jowett. New York: Washington Square Press, 1950.

Keats, John. *The Complete Works*. New York: AMS Press, 1970.

Kierkegaard, Søren. *The Concept of Dread*. Translated by Walter Lowrie. Princeton: Princeton University Press, 1957.

———. *Either/Or*. Translated by David Swenson. Princeton: Princeton University Press, 1971.

———. *Fear and Trembling*. Translated by Howard Hong. Princeton: Princeton University Press, 1983.

Langbaum, Robert. *The Poetry of Experience*. New York: Norton, 1957.

Lilla, Mark. *G. B. Vico: The Making of an Anti-modern*. Cambridge: Harvard University Press, 1993.

Locke, John. *An Essay Concerning Human Understanding*. Oxford: Clarendon Press, 1987.

Lothane, Zvi. *In Defense of Schreber: Soul Murder and Psychiatry*. Hillsdale, N.J.: Analytic Press, 2000.

Lovejoy, A. O. *The Great Chain of Being*. New York: Harper and Row, 1960.

Machon. *Fragments*. Edited by A.S.F. Gow. Cambridge: Cambridge University Press, 1965.

Mason, Bobbie Ann. *In Country.* New York: Harper and Row, 1985.

Meissner, W. W. *The Paranoid Process.* New York: Jason Aronson, 1978.

Mill, John Stuart. *Three Essays.* London: Oxford University Press, 1975.

Milton, John. *Complete Poems and Major Prose.* Edited by Merritt Y. Hughes. Indianapolis: Odyssey Press, 1957.

Montaigne, Michel de. *Essays.* Translated by Donald M. Frame. Arlington Heights, Ill.: Harlan Davidson, 1973.

Nabokov, Vladimir. *Despair.* New York: G. P. Putnam's Sons, 1966.

———. *Lolita.* New York: Berkley Books, 1983.

———. *Speak, Memory: An Autobiography Revisited.* New York: Putnam, 1979.

The New Oxford Annotated Bible. Revised Standard Edition. Edited by Herbert G. May. New York: Oxford Press, 1973.

Niederland, W. *The Schreber Case: Psychoanalytical Profile of a Paranoid Personality.* New York: Quadrangle, 1974.

Nietzsche, Friedrich. *Daybreak.* Translated by R. J. Hollingdale. Cambridge: Cambridge University Press, 1982.

———. *A Nietzsche Reader.* Translated by R. J. Hollindale. London: Penguin, 1977.

———. *The Portable Nietzsche.* Translated by Walter Kaufman. New York: Penguin, 1976.

———. *Nietzsche: A Self-Portrait of His Letters.* Translated and edited by Peter Fuss and Henry Shapiro. Cambridge: Harvard University Press, 1971.

Novalis. *Hymns to the Night and Other Selected Writings.* Translated by Charles E. Passage. New York: Liberal Arts Press, 1960.

Paine, Albert. *The Girl in White Armor.* New York: Macmillan, 1927.

Patchen, Kenneth. *Memoirs of a Shy Pornographer.* New York: New Directions, 1945.

Pater, Walter. *Selected Writings.* Edited by Harold Bloom. New York: New American Library, 1974.

Perceval, John. *A Narrative of the Treatment Experienced by a Gentleman during a State of Mental Derangement: Designed to Explain the Causes and the Nature of Insanity.* Stanford: Stanford University Press, 1961.

Pick, John. *Gerard Manley Hopkins: Priest and Poet.* New York: Oxford University Press, 1942.

Plato. *The Dialogues of Plato.* Edited by J. D. Kaplan. New York: Washington Square Press, 1951.

Plotinus. *The Essence of Plotinus.* Translated by Stephen Mackenna. Oxford: Oxford University Press, 1934.

Plutarch. *The Rise and Fall of Athens.* Translated by Ian Scott-Kilvert. London: Penguin, 1960.

Pope, Alexander. *The Poems of Alexander Pope.* Edited by John Butt. New Haven: Yale University Press, 1972.

Pynchon, Thomas. *The Crying of Lot 49.* New York: Harper and Row, 1966.

Retterstol, Nils. *Paranoid and Paranoiac Psychoses.* Springfield, Ill.: C. C. Thomas, 1966.

Bibliography

Rilke, Rainer Maria. *The Selected Poetry of Rainer Maria Rilke.* Translated by Stephen Mitchell. New York: Random House, 1982.

Rorty, Richard. *Contingency, Irony, and Solidarity.* Cambridge: Cambridge University Press, 1989.

Rousseau, Jean-Jacques. *The Confessions of Jean-Jacques Rousseau.* Anonymous translator. New York: Random House, 1945.

———. *Emile: Or On Education.* Translated by Allan Bloom. New York: Basic Books, 1979.

———. *The Social Contract and Discourses.* Translated by G.D.H. Cole. London: Dent, 1973.

Ruskin, John. *The Complete Works.* London: Chesterfield Society, 1900.

———. *The Works of Ruskin.* Edited by Cook and Wedderburn. London: Library Edition, 1905.

Sagan, Eli. *The Honey and The Hemlock: Democracy and Paranoia in Ancient Athens and Modern America.* New York: Basic Books, 1991.

Sappho. *Greek Lyrics.* Translated by Richard Lattimore. Chicago: University of Chicago Press, 1960.

Sartre, Jean-Paul. *Being and Nothingness.* Translated by H. E. Barnes. New York: Philosophical Library, 1956.

———. *Existentialism and Human Emotions.* Translated by Bernard Frechman. New York: Philosophical Library, 1957.

———. *Nausea.* Translated by Lloyd Alexander. New York: New Directions, 1964.

Schreber, Daniel Paul. *Memoirs of My Nervous Illness.* Translated by Ida Macalpine and Richard A. Hunter. New York: New York Review of Books, 2000.

Schweitzer, Albert. *The Psychiatric Study of Jesus.* Translated by Charles Joy. Boston: Beacon Press, 1960.

Shakespeare, William. *The Riverside Shakespeare.* Boston: Houghton Mifflin, 1974.

Shelley, Mary. *Frankenstein.* Oxford: Oxford University Press, 1969.

Shelley, Percy. *The Selected Poetry and Prose of Shelley.* Edited by Harold Bloom. New York: New American Library, 1966.

———. *Shelley on Love.* Edited by Richard Holmes. Berkeley and Los Angeles: University of California Press, 1980.

Smith, Charlotte. *Romantic Women Poets.* Edited by Duncan Wu. Oxford: Blackwell, 1997.

Sterne, Laurence. *The Life and Opinions of Tristram Shandy.* Boston: Houghton Mifflin, 1965.

Stevens, Wallace. *Collected Poems.* New York: Knopf, 1975.

Swanson, David. *The Paranoid.* Boston: Little Brown, 1970.

Symons, Arthur. *William Blake.* New York: E. P. Dutton, 1907.

Synesius. *Letters, Essays, and Hymns.* Translated by A. Fitzgerald. Oxford: Oxford University Press, 1930.

————. *The Letters of Synesius of Cyrene.* Translated by A. Fitzgerald. London: Oxford University Press, 1926.

Thoreau, Henry David. *Walden.* Columbus, Ohio: C. E. Merrill, 1969.

Thucydides. *The Portable Greek Historians.* Edited by M. I. Finley. New York: Penguin, 1977.

Tolstoy, Leo. *Anna Karenina.* Translated by Constance Garnett. New York: Modern Library, 1950.

The Trial of Joan of Arc: Being the Verbatum Report of the Proceedings from the Orleans Manuscript. Translated by W. S. Scott. London: Folio Society, 1956.

Van Doren, Mark. *Don Quixote's Profession.* New York: Columbia University Press, 1958.

Vico, Giambattista. *The New Science.* Translated by Thomas Bergin. Garden City, N.Y.: Doubleday, 1961.

West, Nathanael. *The Day of The Locust.* New York: Penguin, 1983.

Wheelwright, Phillip, ed. and trans. *Aristotle.* New York: Odyssey Press, 1951.

————. *The Presocratics.* New York: Odyssey Press, 1966.

Wills, Garry. *Lincoln at Gettysburg: The Words That Remade America.* New York: Touchstone, 1992.

Wilde, Oscar. *Essays.* Edited by Hesketh Pearson. London: Methuen, 1950.

Wollstonecraft, Mary. *The Vindications.* Ontario: Broadview Press, 1997.

————. *A Wollstonecraft Anthology.* Edited by Janet M. Todd. Bloomington: Indiana University Press, 1977.

Woolf, Virginia. *To the Lighthouse.* New York: Harcourt, 1981.

Wordsworth, William. *The Complete Poetical Works.* Edited by Andrew J. George. Cambridge: Houghton Mifflin, 1932.

Worringer, Wilhelm. *Abstraction and Empathy.* Translated by Michael Bullock. Cleveland: Meridian Books, 1967.

Zenos, A.C. *The Ecclesiastical Histories of Sozomen and Socrates Scholasticus.* Oxford: Parker, 1891.

Index

Index

Index

Index